D1650889

Hierarchomachia

or

The Anti-Bishop

Hierarchomachia or *The Anti-Bishop*

Edited, with an introduction and notes,
by SUZANNE GOSSETT

Bucknell University Press
London and Toronto: Associated University Presses

Associated University Presses, Inc.
4 Cornwall Drive
East Brunswick, New Jersey 08816

Associated University Presses Ltd
69 Fleet Street
London EC4Y 1EU, England

Associated University Presses
Toronto M5E 1A7, Canada

Library of Congress Cataloging in Publication Data
Main entry under title:

Hierarchomachia.

Bibliography: p.
1. Catholic Church in England—History—Drama.
2. Great Britain—Church history—17th century—Drama.
3. Smith, Richard, Bp. of Chalcedon, 1566–1655—Drama.
I. Gossett, Suzanne.
PR2411.H62 1980 822'.4 78-75201
ISBN 0-8387-2151-6

Printed in the United States of America

CONTENTS

PREFACE

The Venerable English College in Rome was officially founded in 1579 to train English Roman Catholic priests. The students had Jesuit masters, whose educational theory encouraged amateur acting to prepare the students for public speaking and to strengthen their memories. By the early seventeenth century there was an active theatrical life in the College, about which modern scholars have known little more than the names of a few plays produced. In 1971 I visited the College, seeking information about its early theatrical history. How were plays presented in this unusual English-Continental theater during the period when the Elizabethan and Jacobean drama flourished in the students' native land? And what were the plays like?

The investigation was rewarding. Account books and other documents yielded a picture of the annual dramatic events, the rehearsals, costume preparation, stage building, and audience.[1] Most of the plays were in Latin, influenced by the Continental Jesuit drama, but there were three exceptions. A brief academic morality, called *Blame Not Our Author*, was apparently a private College entertainment, recalling undergraduate plays performed by the students' contemporaries at Oxford and Cambridge.[2] A more elaborate English play, *The New Moone*, called for music and properties, and was probably performed for invited guests in 1633.

The third English play manuscript was entitled *Hierarchomachia*. This complex allegory does not seem to be part of the College's theatrical history: the manuscript bears no sign of having been used for production, and there are no references in the *spese* (account books) or the *giornaletti* (diaries) to the play. Furthermore, *Hierarchomachia* is much longer than any play presented in the College theater. Approximately the length of *Hamlet*, it would have severely strained amateur actors. Fr. Cyril Murtagh, who found the manuscript among other College papers while he was the student archivist in the 1950s, hypothesized that it had been sent for inspection to one of the College fathers, and then had made its way into the Archives (missing one quire, which probably concerned the College).[3]

Hierarchomachia, however, is noteworthy in itself. Because it is a contemporary account of the seventeenth-century Chalcedon controversy written by a staunch partisan of the second bishop of Chalcedon, it gives an immediate sense of the personalities and issues involved. Both the archivist and the rector of the English College urged me to edit the play. As a scholar of English literature I was hesitant to undertake the necessary research on the historical background to the allegory, but a summer spent in the Archives of the archbishop of Westminster was decisive. Letters there referred to the play and the characters in it; it became apparent that an edition incorporating this background would serve recusant historians and literary scholars alike.

Editing *Hierarchomachia* presents one unusual difficulty. Recusant historians have frequently written about the Chalcedon controversy, but their descriptions differ widely. The bishop who came to England in 1623 was not welcomed by all factions among the Catholics there, and by 1631 Richard Smith, the second bishop and subject of our play, had departed for France, never to return. Bishop Smith believed and said that his enemies were the regulars, primarily the Jesuits. His opponents denounced him as a tactless man who came into a country where Catholicism was proscribed and behaved exactly as if Catholicism were a religion freely and openly practiced. Pamphleteering on both sides often bordered on the libelous. Where does the truth lie? The contemporary documents emerge from one faction or the other, and unfortunately some scholarship has implicitly taken sides. The account of the controversy in Pastor's monumental *History of the Popes* is strongly anti-bishop, and ignores the bishop's defense of his actions. Thomas Hughes's *History of the Jesuits in North America*, which prints many relevant sources because Lord Baltimore, the colonizer, was one of the bishop's opponents, strives for objectivity but perhaps inevitably emphasizes the Jesuit viewpoint. Philip Hughes sought to redress the balance by presenting the bishop's side in *Rome and the Counter-Reformation in England*, but he was prevented from consulting primary sources by the outbreak of the Second World War and the book must be used with caution.

Recent studies, particularly by A. F. Allison, Maurus Lunn, and John Bossy, are more dispassionate. Allison and Rogers plead for objectivity in a comment summing up ten years of editing the journal *Recusant History*: "in writing of centuries during which the Catholic Church itself was torn by internal conflicts, the historian must not allow any partisan loyalties to warp his faculty of judgment. The task, however distasteful, of describing these internal conflicts, is not one that he can shirk...."[4] While unfortunately none of the newer studies has given a detailed history of the Chalcedon controversy, there is an important account of the strengths and weaknesses of Bishop Smith's character in an article by Allison which is primarily concerned with the political implications of the appointment, and John Bossy brilliantly explores the social context of the gentry's rejection of the bishop as the church evolved toward what Bossy calls sectarian status.[5]

Hierarchomachia has a strongly pro-bishop bias. The contemporary documents relating to it at the Archives in Westminster come largely from the personal files of the bishop's agents in Rome or England, and they share this bias. In the introduction and notes to this edition I have tried to explain the historical allusions, the allegory, and enough of the background to make the play intelligible. This has frequently meant explaining from the author's, and hence the bishop's, viewpoint, but I cannot strongly enough disclaim any intention of taking sides in the controversy. The historical information in the following edition is presented in all diffidence. I make no claim to an original interpretation of the Chalcedon controversy; indeed, I attempt to avoid interpretation. The notes are held to a minimum; the interested reader must look elsewhere for a full description of such things as Lateran Councils, papal decrees, and the early or later life of incidental characters. (A selected bibliography is included for the convenience of those desiring to pursue the complexities of the controversy.) The play is offered as part of the human attempt to recapture the past, which means recapturing significant misconceptions as well as facts. In *Hierarchomachia* historians will find the passionate views of one side; perhaps this will help them reconstruct the feelings and attitudes that led English Catholics into divisive internal squabbling. As the specific embodiment of an argument based on philosophy and theology, *Hierarchomachia* cannot enlighten us about the rights and wrongs in the Chalcedon controversy. It can only tell us how that controversy felt to one faction; in its very partiality it may tell us why the controversy was never satisfactorily resolved.

I would like to thank the many people who made this edition possible. Two rectors of the English College, the Right Reverend Leo Alston and Monsignor Cormac Murphy-O'Connor, granted me access to their precious Archives. Monsignor Murphy-O'Connor gave permission for the publication of this edition. Mr. Kevin McGinnell, former archivist of the College, was an invaluable guide and friend; a recent archivist, Mr. Paul Chavasse, was most cooperative, as was Monsignor Charles Burns of the Vatican Archives.

Several recusant scholars have been helpful with the background material, especially Mr. A. F. Allison and Mr. Maurus Lunn. Miss Poyser, archivist of the Archives of the archbishop of Westminster, welcomed me to Archbishop's House and put all her knowledge of the Archives at my disposal. I also wish to thank Professor David Bevington of the University of Chicago and Mr. Richard Proudfoot of King's College, London, for discussions about fine points of editing, and Mr. Alan Keiler of Brandeis University for suggestions about the Latin in the seventeenth-century letters.

Research for this edition was supported by a much-appreciated Summer Stipend from the National Endowment for the Humanities.

My deepest gratitude goes to my husband, who believed it could be done.

NOTES

1. Cf. Suzanne Gossett, "Drama in the English College, Rome, 1591-1660," *English Literary Renaissance* 3 (1973): 60-93.
2. My edition of this play will appear in a Malone Society *Collection*.

3. Murtagh announced his discovery in ''Hierarchomachia or the Anti-Bishop,'' in the English College magazine, *The Venerabile* 17 (1955): 164–68. John P. Feil tried to identify the female characters in ''Sir Tobie Matthew and his *Collection of Letters*,'' Ph.D. diss., University of Chicago, 1962. No other research has been done on the play.

4. A. F. Allison and D. M. Rogers, "Ten Years of *Recusant History*," *Recusant History* 6 (1961): 10–11.

5. A. F. Allison, ''Richard Smith, Richelieu and the French Marriage. The political context of Smith's appointment as bishop for England in 1624,'' *Recusant History* 7 (1964): 148–49; John Bossy, *The English Catholic Community 1570–1850* (London, 1975), pp. 49–59.

INTRODUCTION

Hierarchomachia is a unique dramatic document, the only known private English Catholic allegorical play of the seventeenth century. A single defective manuscript exists in the Archives of the Venerable English College in Rome; no other copies have been found. Once there were more, for at the time of its composition the play was disturbing enough to be mentioned in correspondence from England, Paris, and Rome, and copies circulated among those concerned. Dealing with the so-called Chalcedon controversy, *Hierarchomachia* elucidates the disastrous quarrel between regular and secular clergy that left England without a Roman Catholic bishop for fifty years after the first attempt at reestablishment of the hierarchy failed. Personalities and events are faithfully recalled, and several previously unknown details of the controversy emerge.

In addition to its historical interest, the play exemplifies the widespread literary culture of the Stuart period in England. The unknown author was probably a priest, living in hiding or abroad. Though he must have been relatively isolated from the stage, he knew the works of Shakespeare and Jonson, and wrote competent blank verse. His plot is coherent, his characters clear, and despite his inevitably argumentative tone, he is often amusing. In accordance with classical literary theory, the author of *Hierarchomachia* attempts simultaneously to teach and to delight.

1. *Historical Background*

Hierarchomachia records a tense moment in the Chalcedon controversy, the dispute that followed the appointment of Dr. Richard Smith as bishop of Chalcedon for England. From the opening of Elizabeth's reign in 1559 episcopal Catholic jurisdiction could not be legitimately exercised; English Roman Catholics had no bishops to lead them, though the last of the Marian bishops lived until 1585. Meanwhile, despite persecutions, imprisonments, and martyrdoms, the number of priests in England grew.[1] All were obliged to live in hiding and under aliases, for they were constantly at the mercy of the pursuivants, who were messengers of the courts employed particularly in their apprehension. The secular priests, in addition to being persecuted, suffered from a lack of organization without the customary bishop as their superior. On the other hand, the regulars, those belonging to orders like the Benedictines, Dominicans, and, most important, the Jesuits, gained strength in this period; for direction they looked to the heads of their orders, not to a bishop. Consequently agitation for a bishop came from among the secular clergy.

From 1598 to 1621 there was an unsatisfactory ad hoc solution in the appointment of a series of three "archpriests," who were heads of the secular clergy but did not have the powers of bishops. This novel system did not work; in fact, it divided the clergy into factions, especially since it was alleged by his opponents that the archpriest was to carry on the government of the clergy "by the advice of the Fathers of the [Jesuit] Society."[2] One faction, the Appellants or those who appealed to the pope against the archpriest, was, roughly speaking, pro-bishop, anti-Jesuit, and, as has recently been shown, slightly more supported by the French than the Spanish. The other group was more friendly to the Jesuits.[3] Though the Archpriest controversy cannot be described here, it partially anticipates the Chalcedon controversy, especially in the factional divisions, and it certainly exacerbated Catholic difficulties. Finally, in 1623 the new pope, Gregory XV, "yielding to insistent demands by the leaders of the English secular clergy," appointed a bishop.[4]

The first bishop, coincidentally William Bishop by name, was given the titular see of Chalcedon in Asia Minor. He was an old and experienced priest, and he attempted to deal at once with the two major problems he anticipated: the government of a vast territory in which, ostensibly, no Catholic priest could operate, and relations between the regulars and the seculars. Before he slipped into England he created a system of administration, appointing archdeacons, rural deans, and a chapter of canons. This system was not authorized by Rome, which regarded it as a "grave breach of ecclesiastical discipline,"[5] and, according to Pastor, it "roused the King, Parliament, and the Protestant Bishops against him."[6] Once in the country he succeeded in making a treaty with the Benedictines, hoping thus to avoid any problems that might arise from conflicts between the bishop and the regulars who were answerable not to him but to their superiors.[7] The Jesuits did not ratify this pact, saying that they needed time to consult their superiors in Rome. Then William Bishop died of natural causes, in April 1624, eight months after he had arrived in England.

The appointment of Richard Smith to succeed William Bishop was a catalyst to the opposition. Smith, a scholar, had been a tutor to Cardinal Richelieu, living in his household for many years. The Jesuits distrusted Smith before he ever arrived in England; they correctly suspected that his appointment was connected to the negotiations for a marriage between Prince Charles and the French princess Henrietta Maria. Furthermore, Smith had an ancient grudge against the Jesuits, and "since Jesuits and seculars had to work side by side on the mission in the face of common dangers and difficulties, it was essential that there should be mutual understanding and co-operation at all levels; a bishop who was hostile to the Jesuits could easily bring disaster to the mission."[8] Finally, Smith was not a man well suited in personality to handle the extremely delicate situation he was in as the bishop of a proscribed Catholic flock in a Protestant country. Allison concludes that both ideological conflict and a breakdown in personal relations caused the crisis that led to Smith's resignation; Smith, "though a man of many gifts, lacked precisely the qualities that were most needed. He was devout and learned, a good theologian and a redoubtable controversialist, but he was doctrinaire, tactless and overbearing."[9]

Smith was appointed at the end of 1624 and came to England in April 1625. In the interim James I had died and Charles had become king. Henrietta Maria arrived in England shortly after Smith, in May 1625. The situation looked promising for the English Catholics, who had a new bishop and a staunchly Catholic queen. Furthermore, Charles had secretly promised to protect the Catholics as part of the marriage agreement. But Charles needed money, and he could only get it from Parliament. Once Parliament was summoned, it reaffirmed its opposition to leniency by confirming the penal statutes against the recusants. Neither Louis XIII nor his sister had understood that Charles's promises were worthless without parliamentary consent.

The Catholics themselves, like their clergy, continued to be divided into pro-bishop and anti-bishop factions, though it is impossible to be certain of the respective numbers. (When signatures of the nobility were collected later on, charges of forgery abounded.) Argument centered on two issues: the nature of Smith's powers, and "approbation." A bishop is commonly an "ordinary," that is, he derives his powers from his office as defined by canon law. It is also possible for a bishop to function with delegated powers, that is, powers given or delegated to him by the pope for a definite time and purpose. According to the latest research, both William Bishop and Richard Smith acted as ordinaries, and Smith stoutly claimed to be ordinary, when in fact "the brief [of his appointment] made his powers dependant on the Pope's *beneplacitum* and subordinate to those of the Paris Nuncio."[10] Smith's claim of ordinary powers increased the fears of his flock, with the ultimate effect of limiting, rather than extending, his authority; this is a prime example of his tactless insensitivity.

The opposition crystallized around the question of approbation. One decree of the Council of Trent was that, in order for a regular or secular priest resident in a certain area to give absolution, his approbation by the bishop of that diocese was needed. Though the decrees of the Council of Trent could not be published in English parish churches, and therefore their force in England was debatable, Anthony Browne, Viscount Montague, a leading Catholic nobleman in whose family Smith had once lived, inquired whether his confessor did not need approbation, now that there was a bishop in England.[11] The confessor, a Benedictine, went to Smith, and Smith admitted that he had "been worried by this matter ever since his arrival in England."[12] In April 1627, Richard Blount, the Jesuit provincial, and Mark Crowder, the Benedictine provincial for the south, met with Smith at his request. At first they agreed to ask for approbation, but in a few days they backed off into a state of firm noncompliance, and would not even see him again.[13]

No doubt word of this quarrel got about among the more important of the lay Catholics, and the bishop became uneasy. He appealed to Rome to settle the question of approbation, and he wrote a letter to the lay Catholics of England on October 16, 1627, in which he set forth his position and attempted to reassure his flock. This was rapidly answered in a letter signed "your Lordships obedient Lay Catholics of England," but always referred to, more correctly, as the letter of the three lay Catholics.[14] The letter was actually written by Sir Basil Brooke, Sir Thomas Brudenell, and Sir Tobie Matthew, who was widely known to be a secret priest.

The letter reveals that the three gentlemen were preoccupied with the bishop's claim to be ordinary, that is, to have the full powers of a bishop. They "crave[d] leve" to remind the bishop of the "extent of this assumed authoritye." An ordinary, they wrote, "hath power of questioninge and provinge of wills, 2° of grantinge of administrations, 3° of decidinge of controversies of Tythes, 4° of contracts marriages divorses alimonie bastardye And fiftlye of slaunders and many other."[15] They were afraid that if the bishop set up a tribunal in competition with the civil courts, the Catholics would be forced to choose between committing high treason in using the ecclesiastical court, and spiritual disobedience in using the civil courts. The gentlemen were trying to maintain both their religion and their estates, which were subject to ruinous fines for recusancy, and they feared that the bishop might destroy them by attempting to exercise authority as was done in Catholic times in Catholic countries. The letter concludes with the gentlemen's urging the bishop not to insist, and begging that "these differences may be carryed with such charitie sweetness candor and without noise as may advance . . .union. . . ."[16]

The bishop replied in a letter of December 2, 1627, assuring the Catholics that "nether intend I hereafter to doe anything that may increase their temporal troubles" and asking them to urge their confessors to seek approbation "as a charitie done to their penitents."[17] He repeatedly denied that he had any intention of setting up a court.[18]

The matter was supposed to be resolved by a decree issued by the Holy Office in December 1627. As we now know, in it "Smith was told not to call himself Ordinary nor to concern himself with the approbation of regulars. On the other hand the regulars were told to seek approbation for the administration of the three 'parochial sacraments', baptism, matrimony and extreme unction. Unfortunately this decree was lost somewhere in transit between Rome, the Nunciature in Paris and England." Predictably, "each side claimed a victory.''[19] Tensions between the bishop's supporters and his opponents were exacerbated, and pamphlets began to appear on both sides.

Meanwhile the bishop lived sometimes with Lord Montague at his mansion at Cowdray, but chiefly in the house of the French ambassador in London. Apparently he managed to meet regularly with other seculars living in London. Then, in the fall of 1628, some of his opponents seem to have decided that the most efficacious means of hindering the bishop's power was to arouse the wrath of the state. John Southcot (or Southcote) who seems to have served as the bishop's secretary, described their tactics in a letter to Blacklo, the clergy agent in Rome, dated December 19, 1628:

> I ame credibly informed that some of the hoatest among the laity (Ployden being thought to be the chiefest of them) haue putt vp a kind of petition to the king in the name of all Catholickes, wherin they do disclaime from the Bishop's power....They haue also vsed meanes...to informe secretary Cook of no lesse then nine probats of wills made by this Bishop or by his authority (which is altogeather false) and hereupon the saied secretary at the councell table very lately produced this information the king him self being present, and both he and the Lord Keeper spake very vehemently against this proceeding of the Bishop.[20]

Accounts of this affair vary in detail. Philip Hughes, though expressing skepticism at the entire story, quotes a letter in which it appears that the gentry were urged on by the Jesuits, and Bossy, who accepts the tale, suggests that the nobleman who presented the statement to the Privy Council was probably Brudenell.[21] It is certain, however, that the state was stimulated to intervene, and on December 11, 1628, and March 24, 1629, two proclamations were issued for the bishop's arrest.[22] Considering the reward offered, these were surprisingly ineffective, unless one knew that, as Southcot's letter continues, ''when these matters were in hoatest treaty, the state was certainly informed where the Bishop was, and could haue then apprehended him, if they had meant it really, and besides the Lord that was knowen ordinarily to harbour him, had expresse warning sent him by order from the king to look to him self....''[23] Thereafter the bishop remained in the French embassy in an oddly anomalous status: at the very time that he was a proscribed traitor, the king was sending to him for a dispensation so that the pregnant queen could eat meat on fast days.

It was not the proclamations or fear of the state that drove Smith from England; it was the papal brief *Britannia* of May 9, 1631. In it the pope, Urban VIII, suppressed the controversy, forbade the reading or writing of controversial literature on the subject, announced that confessions made to regulars were valid without approbation, and rebuked Smith as a troublemaker.[24] In August 1631, probably shortly after he received the brief, the bishop left England for France, never to return. He was not replaced.

2. *Characters in the Play*

It is necessary to recall the historical background because *Hierarchomachia* is a specific, though allegorical, treatment of the early stages of the controversy. Many important people involved in the dispute appear in the play, only thinly disguised under anagrammatized names.[25] As an excuse for bringing together on stage the most prominent personalities among the anti-bishop forces, the author invents a synod at which both lay and clergy meet to discuss the attitude to be taken toward the bishop. Several waverers are included—the leading Dominican, and Sir Thomas Brudenell, for example—to provide an opportunity for presenting the arguments on both sides. None of the bishop's supporters is present except one woman, so the author adds imaginary eavesdroppers who criticize the bishop's enemies and reveal the flaws in their arguments.

The three important orders opposing the bishop are represented as three groups of knights. The Jesuits are the Knights of the Golden Fleece, the Benedictines are Knights of Malta, and the Dominicans are Knights of St. James. Among the Jesuits Bolnutus is Richard Blount, who was appointed the first provincial when England was declared a Jesuit province in 1623. Onoplutus, the procurator, is Thomas Poulton, and Jargus, an important figure in the plot, is Lawrence Anderton, who used the aliases of Grey and Scrupe or Scroop. A letter from the bishop's secretary to the agent in Rome in 1628 warns, "Haue an eye to Mr. Gray the Jesuit who came thither a fortnight before you, and do what you can to discredit his informations, for he is thought to be . . . a great politick. . . . "[26]

There are four Benedictine opposers, more than from any other order, which is in accord with Maurus Lunn's conclusion that "the Benedictines, not the Jesuits, had the dusty glory of assuming the lion's share of opposition to the Bishop for the first five years of this dispute."[27] The Benedictines are also given more individualizing traits. Coredorus is the southern provincial, Mark Crowder, who had met with Smith in 1627. Ambitious Spirius is Dom William Benedict Price (alias Jones), who led the monks in their opposition to Smith. Davus is Dom David Codner, who was open to attack for irregularities in his own life, and Saperton, called in the list of speakers "a Ghibelline writer of that order" is Dom Thomas Preston. Preston was commonly assumed to be the author of works written under the name Roger Widdrington. The books defended the Oath of Allegiance, the provisions of which were abhorrent to most Catholics; among other things the oath denied the pope's power to depose the king. As a result Preston was protected by the government and the archbishop of Canterbury.[28]

The two Knights of St. James, or Dominicans, are Thomas Middleton as Nicodimus (an anagram on Dominican) and George Popham as Pamoppus. Middleton was appointed vicar-general of the Dominicans in England in 1622. Popham, it seems, was more active in opposition to the bishop, and the play shows him persuading an uncertain Middleton.[29]

Besides the knights there are the lay gentlemen, and two men of anomalous status. One of these, Bitomattus, Sir Tobie Matthew, receives the fullest characterization in the play. He was a well-known figure in the period. Son of the Protestant archbishop of York, he was widely and correctly suspected of being a secret Jesuit despite his gaudy clothes and extravagant courtliness. As a young man he was exiled for his conversion. He managed to join Prince Charles and Buckingham on their abortive trip to woo the Spanish Infanta in 1623, and was knighted upon his return. A writer and a friend of the great, he was always known for bizarre behavior.

His friend, Aggeus, is George Gage. Nivetta thinks he is a "knight . . . of the holy court." Celia corrects her with, "He is a gentleman but not a knight" (11. 2053-55). In the system of the play this may mean that he is a priest but not a regular, or it may mean that Gage is a gentleman but not a priest. Gage is now believed to have been a secular priest.[30] He had served King James in the negotiations to obtain a papal dispensation for Prince Charles to marry the Infanta—a letter asserts that he presumptuously styled himself an ambassador—and he remained friendly with Sir Tobie all his life.[31]

The three "lay champions for the Ghibellines" are Rudelbinus, Sir Thomas Brudenell; Corbus, Sir Basil Brooke; and Polinodus, Mr. Francis Plowden. These three were all engaged against the bishop, but it is noteworthy that the author makes a mistake: in lines 891-980 the bishop's letter to the lay Catholics is analyzed and the reply written by Corbus-Brooke, Rudelbinus-Brudenell, and Polinodus-Plowden, while in fact Brooke, Brudenell, and Matthew wrote it.[32] The mistake was natural, because Plowden was one of the bishop's staunchest opponents. A descriptive list of prominent Catholics drawn up in 1635 (probably for the papal envoy Panzani) notes that "franciscus ployden vel ploydon . . . . à Tobia Matheo ac Jesuitis . . . actus est ad oppugnandum Episcopum eoque in negotio intemperantissimè se gessisse deprehensus, desijt à plerisque. Sapiens haberi, quin potius pro temerario et ridiculo passim denotatur à Catholicis, qualis ad viuum depingitur in comoedia, qua dicitur Antiepiscopus. . . . "[33]

The pursuivants are also all historical. Rocs is Humphrey Cross, a famous priest hunter; Finger is John Griffin; Amoy, Thomas Mayo; and Milston, Richard Tomlins. All were familiar figures in this period, and their names are frequently found in the State Papers. One note in 1636 charges all four together, as "messengers employed in the apprehension of priests" with doing just what is enacted in *Hierarchomachia*:

> They have abused the warrants committed to them for apprehension of particular persons by using them to search all recusants' houses . . . and in their searches . . . as they have taken sundry priests, so it appears for bribes they have discharged them; and there is no recusant's house into which they enter, but they will have some composition or gratuity before they depart.[34]

The three women are the only important characters not definitely identified. They are Nivetta, a follower of the bishop; Celia, a follower of the Jesuits; and Valeria, a follower of the Benedictines. Part of the difficulty arises from woman's position in the period: unless a woman caused a scandal by lewd behavior, conversion, or abandoning her husband, she seldom even merits a first name in documents and history books. On the other hand, though Polinodus and Corbus question the propriety of women's speaking in a synod (11.3158-60), recusant women were highly significant members of the church. ''The integration of religion into the household accounts for a fact which has been universally observed as characteristic of English Catholicism, the importance of the position occupied in it by women.''[35] Bossy cites a number of cases of wives who engaged in an ''active and proselytising'' Catholicism despite the objections or indifference of their husbands, especially before 1620.[36] Many aristocratic converts were women, and after 1625 they were encouraged by Queen Henrietta Maria.

A few tentative identifications of the ladies have been proposed. Murtagh suggested that Valeria might be Elizabeth Carey, Viscountess Falkland.[37] John P. Feil, in a knowledgeable dissertation on Sir Tobie Matthew, thought it likely that Nivetta, Valeria, and Celia ''stand for the Duchess of Buckingham, Olive Porter, and one of the Ladies Arundel,'' but admitted his uncertainty.[38] None of these identifications can be proved, and some are impossible. It is also peculiar that the names of the ladies proposed are not adequate originals of the anagrams. (Throughout the play the anagrams refer to surnames.)

The suggested identifications of Valeria are the most interesting. She cannot be Olive Porter, because Olive Porter was ''one of the first of the Court ladies whom the Pope's legate, Con...had converted to Catholicism...,'' and he had arrived only in the summer of 1636, well after the composition of *Hierarchomachia*.[39] Furthermore, Mrs. Porter kept a Jesuit to serve her private chapel, whereas Valeria follows the Benedictines.[40]

Elizabeth Carey, Lady Falkland, on the other hand, was a notorious Catholic and devoted to the Benedictines, but no attempt has been made to depict her well-known idiosyncrasies in Valeria. She was the daughter of Lawrence Tanfield, Lord Chief Baron of the Exchequer, and was described by Clarendon as a woman ''of most masculine understanding, allyed with the passions and infirmities of her sex.''[41] Books were dedicated to her, and her knowledge and wit respected. A passionate intellectual, she translated Seneca's *Epistles*, probably wrote a closet drama, and early in life began to read religious works. Bossy comments that she was ''one of the very few among the sixteenth-century crop of learned women, if not the only one, to convince herself by reading of the truth of the Catholic faith.''[42]

It is unclear when her formal conversion occurred. One account comes from a manuscript biography in the Imperial Archives at Lille, probably written by one of her children. In this version, ''she never questioning . . . but that to be in the Roman Church were infinitely better and securer; thus (from the first) she remained about two-and-twenty years, flattering herself with good intentions.''[43] In another version she converted three years after her marriage but hid this from her husband for twenty years.[44] In either case her Catholicism became known in 1625, when she returned from Ireland where her husband was Lord Chief Deputy. There ensued a tragicomedy: the king banished her from court for going to mass with the queen; he attempted to send her home to her mother, who refused to receive her; her six youngest children were placed with their eldest brother, Lucius Carey, from whom she kidnapped them to send them for Catholic education abroad; finally she subsisted in London on allowances, notable for her neglected dress and abstracted demeanor. All four of the young daughters became nuns in the English Benedictine Abbey at Cambrai, and one of the younger sons became a Benedictine. Her private confessor was William Benedict Price, the Spirius of our play.

I think that Lady Falkland is referred to in *Hierarchomachia* but does not appear. Mention is twice made of learned ladies who may have inspired Nivetta's powerful argumentative style. Bitomattus says,

> It seems my mistress lately is inspired
> With Odoena and Falconia's style,
> And like another Sappho can enchant
> The hearer's sense with raptures of her wit.
>
> (11. 2010-13)

and Valeria asks her, ''hath not Odoena's head/A finger in this plot?'' (11. 2125-26). Odoena is unidentified, but Falconia would be a sufficient anagram for Falkland in the playwright's system. Valeria, who displays no particular wit or learning, nor any of Lady Falkland's eccentricities, remains unidentified.

The models for Celia and Nivetta are also uncertain. The Duchess of Buckingham, whom Feil proposes for Nivetta, was Katherine Manners, daughter of the Earl of Rutland. She was originally a Catholic, converted to marry the Duke of Buckingham, and converted back after the assassination of the favorite in 1628. But Albion says she was a penitent of the Jesuits, while Nivetta is the bishop's supporter.[45] Nor can I find anything definite enough to associate Celia with one of the Arundel ladies. It may be that these ladies are typical rather than specific portraits; they serve the author as convenient mouthpieces.

The remaining characters of the play are, I believe, invented. Therulus and Lucianus, who appear in the introduction and then after each act, are Protestant and Puritan ministers respectively. Their ''personalities'' are merely expressions of their theological positions. The other commentators are Erudius, identified as a ''Guelf, or follower of the bishop,'' and Candle, a ''neutralist, or time critic.'' In these cases the name is not an anagram but a signal of the author's attitude: Erudius comes from the Latin *erudire*, to instruct, and Candle gives most of the light in the play. A servant and a constable complete the cast.

3. Date

I have ruled out Olive Porter as a character on the basis of the date of the play. *Hierarchomachia* cannot have been written before March 1629, when the second of the two proclamations against Bishop Smith was issued: "Two several proclamations from the king/ Were by the lords procured to apprehend him" (11. 253-54). The question, then, is how soon after the proclamations? I believe that it was written before December 1630, that is, in the midst of the controversy.

First of all, the later stages of the controversy are not considered in the play. For instance, George Calvert, Lord Baltimore, does not appear, yet by 1630, when he returned from America, he had become one of the most prominent of the bishop's opponents. No mention is made of a dispute raging 1630-32 about the true opinion of the noble lay Catholics of England, in which the Spanish ambassador was brought to testify to their opposition to the bishop and the French ambassador to testify to the contrary. The main document against the bishop was the "Protestatio declaratoria," which stated that the noblemen who signed it did not believe the bishop to be an ordinary. Accusations of false signatures were rife, and it is hard to believe that the satirist would have dwelt exclusively on the letter of the lay Catholics of 1627 once the later pamphlets were circulating.[46]

More important, the controversy is not yet decided. In lines 244-45 we hear that "the bishop's part/ Inclines again" and in lines 261-62 "The pope, to whom this cause/ Is now referred, stands doubtful what to do." The play occurs while "matters are suspended" (1.273). This virtually guarantees that it dates before the brief *Britannia* of May 9, 1631. There would be little point to writing such a play once the bishop had fled and the issue was decided: besides, the brief expressly forbade reading or writing about the controversy, and *Hierarchomachia* is a large project to undertake in defiance of such an order.

Perhaps we can be more precise. In line 1476 we hear of Onoplutus (Thomas Poulton, S.J.) as "general procurator for the knights," that is, the Jesuits. On December 12, 1630, Poulton, then procurator, was dismissed from the Society of Jesus by Richard Blount (Bolnutus) for making "certain reflections" upon Cardinal Richelieu.[47] Poulton, who here "with cringes courts Bolnutus so" (1. 1474) and whose "zeal/ Against the bishop puts him in esteem/ And favor with the master Ghibelline" (11. 1483-85) is not yet in disgrace.

Poulton's remarks about Richelieu were connected to his opposition to bishops in England; he wrote to a friend that "Richelieu is going back to Paris with *asini di ritorno* and a longe nose. Our busseling Chalcedon is now dead in the neast. . .his rurall Deanes must now goe seeke a new Ordinary, and new places att Chalcedon, for there is none to be had as yet in England."[48] These words referred to the death of William Bishop in 1624; Basset, a recent historian of the Jesuits, says that Smith dragged them up six years later to discredit Poulton. Blount's superiors in Rome insisted that Poulton be dismissed to appease Cardinal Richelieu; much against his will, Blount obeyed. In this way Smith revenged himself temporarily, but Poulton was readmitted to the society after Smith left England. Since the reinstatement occurred after the brief *Britannia, Hierarchomachia* must show Poulton before the dismissal.[49] Thus the internal evidence dates the play between March 1629, when the second proclamation appeared, and December 1630, when Poulton was dismissed.

Letters mentioning the play support this approximate date.[50] A letter from George Leybourne, in London, to Peter Fitton, the clergy agent in Rome, dated March 1, 1632 (1633), tells him how to answer complaints about the comedy: "signifie the tyme wherin it was composed,—the very heat of the controversie and by an vnknowne Author. . . ."[51] A second letter to Fitton, this time from John Southcot, dated January 18, 1633 (modern 1633 by its reference to Walter Montagu's *The Shepherd's Paradise*), says, "it was penned and finished aboue two yeares agoe."[52] A third, undated, but placed by Allison in early 1633, says "ante triennium composita fuit."[53] Finally, a letter from W. East to the bishop, dated only 6 February but noted in the archives as 1633, says, "it was written in the heat of theire bookes, and when the Spongia called the RRPP [Reverend Fathers] of france assembled crocitantes ranunculas. . . ."[54] The *Spongia* was written by the English Jesuit John Floyd as part of the pamphlet war of the controversy. Floyd (under the name Daniel à Jesu) had written "An Apology of the Holy See Apostolicks Proceedings for the Government of the Catholicks of England. . . " in 1630. Translated into Latin, it was condemned by the Sorbonne in February 1631. Floyd's reply to their condemnation, the *Spongia*, which attacked the Sorbonnists as croaking frogs, appeared in the same year.[55] East's comment, that the play was written "in the heat of theire bookes" places the play in 1630 or 1631, and illuminates the controversial atmosphere in which *Hierarchomachia* was but one more paper bullet.

4. *Author*

Who wrote *Hierarchomachia?* The bishop claimed not to know "either the work or the Author for certaine,"[56] and the surviving correspondence contains only a series of denials; in fact, much of our information about the play comes from letters refuting various allegations of authorship. One person accused was Father William Drury. This had a certain plausibility, since Drury was a playwright. There are several editions of the three Latin plays he wrote for students at Douai, but no English works are known. On January 18, 1633, John Southcot wrote about the play to Peter Fitton in Rome, saying:

> you may answer [any complaint] that the clergy in generall doth not auow any such worke, nor hath any knowledg of it, nor that Mr. Drury is the author, but

> rather are persuaded that he could not be the author by reason of his sore arme (his right arme) which hath held him these 6 or 7 yeares, wherby he is altogeather unable to write with that hand.[57]

A similar statement is found in a Latin memo made by Fitton from letters written by Southcot to the bishop, adding, besides the sore arm, that "uana est eorum suspicio, nam sacerdos iste . . . Authorem se pernegit. . . ."[58]

There is corroboration of Drury's illness, though not of its duration. It was traditional for Catholic ambassadors leaving England to request, among their farewell perquisites, the right to be accompanied by priests released from the English prisons. The government thus achieved an informal banishment. When the Venetian ambassador received the usual permission in 1635, Drury wrote explaining that he had had a septic arm for four years and begged to be released but to remain in England. He was, indeed, discharged from London's Clink Prison on March 24, 1635.[59]

I have found some reason to suspect Peter Fitton, the agent of the secular clergy in Rome from 1631 to 1638, of the composition. The Archives of the archbishop of Westminster preserve three letters (two undated) written by one Valentine Lane to an unnamed "loving cousin," who, he hears, has written a play that sounds like *Hierarchomachia*. Valentine Lane was a student at the English College in Rome from October 1629 until March 1634, and fortunately the *Liber Ruber*, the College register, and the *Responsa Scholarum*, the answers to questions put to new students, are preserved. From these we learn that Valentine Lane was really a Harcourt from Staffordshire. His father was Humphrey Harcourt, his mother Bridget Biddulph. The *Liber Ruber* also tells us that Fitton's real name was Biddulph, of county Stafford; other genealogical evidence reinforces the presumption that they were Biddulph cousins.[60]

Lane's movements, like those of all the students at the English College, were carefully controlled; he was probably allowed out only to schools (i.e., classes) and sometimes on a walk with another student. This explains the oddity that he is writing from Rome to a cousin in Rome to whom he does not have free access. He mentions "last night when I met you," explains why he has been unable to visit "oftner then I haue," and begs "let me meet your man vppon Tuesday next againe at the Scholles."[61]

That the correspondent in Rome must have been Fitton becomes more evident as we attempt to date the letters. Lane writes to his cousin of "the mission that came with you . . . John Coniers one of your mission, and my onely trustie frend in the howse. . . ." Conyers, *vere* Poulton, arrived at the College October 22, 1631; Fitton was appointed agent in July 1631 and arrived in Rome a few months later, probably having journeyed with prospective students of the English College. This letter, catalogued A, 27: 127, seems to be from late 1633, for there is a reference to Conyers's desire to "be admitted [as an alumnus, a sort of student in the College] this May Day," and Conyers took the oath March 25, 1634.[62] The second letter, A,

25: 70, is from 1633 or 1634, for there is a reference to "our new oawth . . . first taken it is 7. yeares." The first time this oath (to be explained shortly) was taken was in 1627.[63] The third letter, A, 27: 126, is dated 2 December, with a postscript dated 9 Januarie 1634.

Most significantly for the history of our play, Valentine Lane was unhappy at the English College under the rectorship of the Jesuit Thomas Fitzherbert. Though the College was founded in 1579 to train English secular priests, a variety of early difficulties led to the installation of Jesuit masters. This was a constant source of irritation to those students who desired to become secular priests. They felt that the Jesuits tried to attract students to their own order. Lane's letters are riddled with complaints that the Jesuits in the College are unfair to students who wish to become seculars. He conveys thanks to his cousin from other members of the College who "acknowledge themselfes greatly obliged vnto you for the great curtesies you haue shewed them in the face of the fathers. . . ."[64] and protests that he is "willinger to prosecute any designements, and to certifie you the better, because I hope that therin I shall manifest my selfe a poore seruaunt vnto the whole [secular] Clergie. . . . I see herein manie abuses to be committed, and iniurie done vnto our Clergie I deeme it my part to acquaint you with it, who haue better meanes to see it remedied that [*sic*] I haue anie."[65]

In defending the secular clergy, Lane was acting in the family tradition. His cousin Peter Fitton had led one of the most famous of all the "stirs" against the College Jesuits, and Lane was not allowed to forget it:

> Soe one day . . . discoursing of matters of the Collidge [a fellow student] tould me that you had carried your selfe verie shamfullie towardes father Rector [Thomas Fitzherbert, S.J., Rector 1618-39], and that you had disgraced our nation and manie more circumstances, and I asked him how he knew that you had done soe, he saide that father Rector had both tould him, and alsoe shewed him a booke of the proceedings you vsed then. . . . This booke father Rector sheweth priuatly vnto most of the schollers.[66]

The book no doubt gave the Jesuit interpretation of the so-called Fitton rebellion of 1623-24.[67] Peter Fitton and four others were expelled from the English College because of insubordination toward the Jesuit masters. The expulsion became a cause célèbre; the students went to the pope, there were visitations and testimonials. The Office of Propaganda, which did not consider the students' behavior serious, ordered them sent to Douai College at the English College's expense. One result of the rebellion was the new oath, referred to above. This was to be taken by students at pontifical colleges, promising that for three years after ordination they would not join an order of regulars without special permission of the holy see. The intent was that the students become the secular priests that the colleges ostensibly existed to train.[68]

Fitton's history in the College suggests an explanation for the missing quire of *Hierarchomachia*. Lane twice mentions a play in his letters:

> father Rector telleth the schollers that the seculars haue had a comodie of the Regulars but I beleeue it not,[69]

and, more precisely:

> father Rector telleth my cosen Dracot, that you are out of fauour with the Pope, and that Cardinall Barbarino hath checed you for making an action [a play], wherein you brought father Blunt, and father Scrupe [another alias of Anderton, i.e., Jargus] in the forme of a diuel a benedictant, and a dominican of ech side of him whipping him [cf. 11. 2556-68]. I pray you let me know if you euer made anie such thinge, and whether you haue beene checed by Cardinall Barberino euer for this matter.[70]

These sufficiently identify the play as *Hierarchomachia*. Lane, only a student, had evidently not seen it, but our manuscript was obviously sent to the English College, and probably dismantled there. The missing seventh quire comes after the following lines:

Bitomattus. They [Ghibellines or regulars] were nursed,
I'm sure, as well or better than the Guelfs [seculars],
And came to be their masters in the end
And rule their colleges.
Rudelbinus. There lies a tale
That made them proud; pride drew ambition on,
Ambition envy, envy causèd strife;
Strife partiality; and that self-love;
Then covetousness the devil came at last
And set some plots afoot against the state,
All fathered on these masters of the Guelfs,
The scholars resting innocent and free.
(11. 3128-38)

Presumably what followed was a pro-Guelf, that is, pro-secular, account of the troubles in the College, especially the most recent one, the Fitton rebellion of 1623-24. Perhaps Fitzherbert burned the offending quire, perhaps he merely extracted it for easier handling while he and other Jesuits pondered a reply.

It is tempting to say that Fitton wrote the play. Lane's letters are found among Fitton's papers; Fitton's answers, if they existed, are naturally not there. Fitton had all the prejudices of the author: he was in Rome to defend the bishop's interests, he was anti-Jesuit, and most particularly, he was angry about Jesuit rule of the English College, which is somewhat irrelevantly introduced into the play. Lane's note that Fitton has been "checed" by Cardinal "Barbarino" has a ring of plausibility, because Barberini was "protector" of the English and kept an eye on their affairs.

On the other hand, Lane's knowledge seems to depend on Fitzherbert. Fitzherbert detested Fitton and cannot be a reliable witness to his authorship. Also, in Southcot's letter to Fitton of January 18, 1633 he gives a circumstantial description of the play and makes this offer: "If you desire a coppy of it, lett me know your mind, and I will gett Mr Duckett to carry vp one with him." This makes it seem unlikely that Fitton was the author unless the secret was very well kept.[71] Fitton had been in Paris at the Arras College from November 1627 until he left for Rome in 1631. Arras was a college of English priests engaged in controversial writing; one of its senior members for many years was Richard Smith. No doubt information and gossip circulated there, but could Fitton have known the personalities so well after only brief visits to England? It seems implausible that he could write the play in Paris, especially without his colleagues' knowledge. Fitton is an attractive candidate for author, but the only certainty is that the play was written by a follower of the bishop, most probably one of the many priests in hiding in London.

5. Reputation and Diffusion

Hierarchomachia enjoyed a certain notoriety among those Catholics actively engaged in the controversy surrounding Richard Smith. Probably the author never expected to have a wider audience. The play is prefaced by an address to the reader, presumably of a manuscript; there are no references to printing, which would have been extraordinarily difficult under recusant circumstances. Furthermore, the text is not prepared for acting, although the play is a complete drama (see §§ 6 and 7). Production in England was unthinkable, and the audiences at English colleges abroad, where acting of Catholic plays did take place, were remote from the satirized personalities. Realistically, the author must have been aware that he was writing closet drama.

Manuscripts of the play did circulate somewhat in London; a series of letters to Fitton in Rome and to the bishop in Paris tried to explain why and how. These letters also illuminate the play's context, so I quote them extensively.

1. *A letter from Southcot to Fitton, January 18, 1633*
I imagin there will be great complaint made there of a certaine English Comedy supposed to be made by Mr Drury, called the Antibishop, wherin some Benedictins, Dominicans, and Jesuitts, as also the 3 first opposers, and Sir Toby Mathew & Mr G. Gage are broght in vppon the stage, being full of scoffs and taunts against them. I was tould lately that Mr Ployden hath gotten a coppy of it, and that he and his complices that are toucht in it, haue had much consultation about it this Christmasse. If any such complaint be made there you may answer that the clergy in generall doth not auow any such worke, nor hath any knowledg of it, nor that Mr Drury is the author....neither doth my Lord Bishop know either the work or the Author for certaine, but only by hearsay. nor is it in his power as things stand with

him to take any order for the hindering or suppressing of any such writing by reason of the opposition made against him. nor in fine did any of those who are touched their, euer yet complaine to him to that purpose. so that my Lord and the clergy must needs be blamelesse herein, whosoeuer the author were. Besides it was penned and finished aboue two yeares agoe, and few coppies are to be found, so little common or publick it is. Finally the plaintifs (if any shew them selues) haue little cause to except against this, considering their own shamfull actions, which were fitter to be derided vppn [*sic*] a stage, then answered with reasons, and so they may thank their own folly by which they haue made them selues so ridiculous to the world.[72]

2. *A letter from W. East [the alias of another secular] to the bishop, February 6, 1633*
Lett Mr Fitton know that a Comedy called the Antibishop is now much in the mouth of your aduersaryes, hee must know that [the] Auctor who soe euer it was is but gessed at by them, that it nameth noe man, that it was written in the heat of theire bookes....besides the coppyes which they now disperse are very much corrupted and made to speake many absurdityes which the first manuscrip hath not; and they haue done this of purpose to procur a Censure agaynst it at Rome, which they say they will doe, which will sound heer very ridiculous.[73]
3. *A letter from Southcot to Fitton, February 8, 1633*
The Jesuits followers invaigh much against two writings that goe about here vnder hand, the one is a certaine comedy wherin the opposers of the Bishop are made ridiculous.[74]
4. *A letter from Southcot to Fitton, March 1, 1633*
The Jesuits do giue out here that one Anthony Smith a fallen Priest diuulgeth coppies of the Comedy callled the Antibishop, but the truth is he was no secular Priest but a Jesuitt and, while he was Jesuit, as I heare he had children for which cause they putt him out.[75]
5. *A letter from George Leybourne to Fitton, March 1, 1633*
The Jesuists keep a great doe about the comedy and I hear that they haue translated it into Italyen but very vntruely as many doe imagine, my Maister formerly haith instructed you how you are to make your answere and therfore it is not needfull that I saye any more. onely signifie the tyme wherin it was composed,—the very heat of the controversie and by an vnknowne Author, how my lord did suppresse it vntill now that the Jesuists gott a copie of it and did diuulge it, and you may iustly accept against the translation. Here is one Smith a falne Jesuist besyds the scandale is like to doe much hurt.[76]

Small contradictions between these letters raise questions. Leybourne states that the Jesuits are divulging the play; East says that "they," presumably referring back to the bishop's adversaries, are dispersing copies; and Southcot says that Anthony Smith divulges copies. Plowden and "his complices" might well have wanted to see how they were depicted, as Southcot says, but it is implausible that the Jesuits would disperse copies of an anti-Jesuit play except to Rome for a censure. The play is too convincing to be used to ridicule its author or to boomerang against the bishop.

The history of Anthony Smith is a separate and complex issue. He was a fallen Jesuit who might indeed have been employed against his former associates. Furthermore, Allison has traced a connection between Richard Smith and Anthony Smith; the "fallen Jesuist" was the priest on whose testimony the bishop based an ill-founded accusation against the famous priest John Gerard. More important, Allison shows that Southcot, "close supporter of the Bishop though he was," was unaware of this connection.[77] Thus it is possible that Anthony Smith was circulating the copies, and even conceivable that he had orders directly from the bishop at the same time that the bishop's assistants were "in hand with Mr Anthony Smith a fallen Priest and Jesuitt... to go ouer to do pennance, & reconcile him self againe...."[78] On the other hand, a letter from the papal envoy Panzani in London to Barberini in Rome, written March 9, 1635, says that "Il Smitheo," not definitely the same Anthony, has been in prison, has come to see Panzani, and "non può confessare, perche è stato sospeso dal Vescovo Calcedonense essendo tenuto per alquanto scemo."[79] If the bishop suspended Anthony Smith's faculties, how long did he employ him?

By whatever means the copies were being divulged, in 1633 it was easy for Southcot to offer to obtain one, Plowden had one, and there were enough in circulation so that some could be labeled corrupt. (The tale of translation into Italian I am inclined to discount as fabrication—the play is nearly 4,000 lines long—though a summary in Italian sent to Rome for examination is possible.) The satire seems to have been widely known among the inner circle of English Catholics. The same letter of East's quoted above has another paragraph beginning "Bitomattus is euen cried downe by his owne side...," and another letter, written two years later by Father Nicholas Day to Mr. French (the bishop?), begins, "M. Perkins wrotte to my Lord...." Next to "Lord" is a signal to the margin, in which is written "Rudelbin."[80] These two names from the play, then, had gained a certain currency among Catholic correspondents of the bishop. Also the conclusion of the Latin description of Plowden: "pro temerario et ridiculo passim denotatur à Catholicis, qualis ad viuum depingitur in comoedia, quae dicitur Antiepiscopus...,[81] implies that the reader may recall this lifelike depiction. Apparently the play had achieved the notoriety the author aimed at; without affecting the outcome of the controversy he had given it its most vivid description.

6. Hierarchomachia *and Contemporary Drama*

Whoever wrote *Hierarchomachia* "was a man whose style presumes a familiarity with Shakespeare and Ben Jonson, a man whose control of language was not merely indifferent."[82] Indeed, the literary culture of this unknown dramatist is surprising and suggestive. The play, despite its partisan subject, is considerably indebted to contemporary popular drama. *Hierarchomachia* copies one character from Shakespeare, recalls a scandalous play by Thomas Middleton in its use of allegory, and, most important, takes as its literary model Ben Jonson's *Every Man Out of His Humour*.

Hierarchomachia is subtitled "A Comic Satire," pointing at its forebears, the early seventeenth-century "comical satires" of Jonson and Marston. On June 1, 1599, the Anglican bishops banned and burned satires, decreeing that "noe *Satyres* or *Epigrams* be printed hereafter."[83] The bishops had in mind the conventional literary forms, in prose and verse, that denounced folly and abuse. These were extremely popular in London in the 1590s, and the bishops failed to foresee that the same critical spirit could be expressed in plays. John Marston, for instance, whose formal satires were specifically prohibited, immediately turned to the stage, and Ben Jonson's next play, *Every Man Out of His Humour*, bore the descriptive subtitle "*A Comicall Satyre.*"

A comic satire, as exemplified in Jonson and our author's work, was a play conceived to "strip the ragged follies of the time,/ Naked, as at their birth."[84] In *Hierarchomachia* the follies are the quarrels between the regular and the secular priests. The method was to draw satiric portraits of the characters, "to pursue them with hostile comment, and either to dramatize their reformation or. . .to eject them from the play, still cherishing their folly—futile and defiant."[85] The author had to establish a standard from which to satirize excess and deviance, which he usually did by creating normative characters to deride and censure the others. The form was also well adapted for ridicule of one's opponents, whose beliefs could be made to seem obsessions, or "humors," while the comic elements lightened the attack and emphasized the sanity and balance of the author.

The structural similarities between *Every Man Out of His Humour* and *Hierarchomachia* are immediately evident. Jonson's play contains two sets of commenting characters. The first, Cordatus and Mitis, remain on stage throughout as critical spectators. Asper says, "I leaue you two, as censors, to sit here:/ Obserue what I present, and liberally/ Speake your opinions, vpon euery *Scene*" (*Jonson*, 3:434). Each time they speak the folio marks the interruption GREX. This term is carefully explained during the long introductory exchange concerning the nature of comedy and satire, when Mitis defines what he means by "lawes of *Comedie*":

> Why, the equall diuision of it into *Acts*, and *Scenes*, according to the *Terentian* manner, his true number of Actors; the furnishing of the *Scene* with GREX, or CHORVS; and that the whole Argument fall within compasse of a dayes businesse.
>
> (*Jonson,* 3:436)

Cordatus has seen the play about to be performed and proceeds to inform Mitis about it, discussing both the style and certain details:

> Mitis: what's his *Scene?*
> Cordatus: Marry, *Insula Fortunata*, Sir.
> Mitis: O, the fortunate Iland?
>
> (*Jonson*, 3:438)

In a similar manner, *Hierarchomachia* opens with a scene between Therulus, a Protestant minister, and Lucianus, a Puritan one. Therulus announces that despite former disagreements they now "are friends" because "The Papists have obtained/ A bishop for their head." Still, their common enemy is weakened by dissension:

the Papists now divided are
Into two factions much like thine and mine:
One for the bishop stands, the other strives
Him to suppress, and his authority;
(11. 161-64)

When not distracted by Lucianus's hostility, Therulus manages to give a detailed summary of the recusants' situation, the opposition to the bishop, the proclamations against him, the pope's uncertainty, "The strange invented plots of anarchists" (1.274). Finally he invites Lucianus:

The sum of this expressed in lively scenes
Shall in a comedy today be shown
Within this place. Say, wilt thou sit by me
And see it acted?
(11. 281-84)

Though protesting against the profanities of common plays, Lucianus admits "My spirit moves me to sit down." and Therulus explains to him, "For I have read the play," that the story is told in "feignèd names":

Those of the bishop's side are callèd Guelfs,
The other Ghibellines. . . .
. . . .
But now the music sounds, the prologue comes.
(11. 286-98)

The Prologue gives the scene:

Gentle spectators, first he bids you frame
This climate under the Antarctic pole,
Where our antipodes, a famous isle
Called Bintriana, lies, and there our scene.
(11. 303-6)

As in Jonson, Therulus and Lucianus are regularly identified in the manuscript as Grex. The introductory explanation of the play by one character who has read or seen it, the "lawes of *Comedie*," which are carefully observed in *Hierarchomachia*, and even the trivial disguising of the

British island are copied from *Every Man Out of His Humour*. The opening exchange, which in Jonson's play concerns the nature of comedy and "humor," here is transformed into a functionally similar explanation of the allegory; both conversations prepare the audience for what will follow. The most important difference in the use of these sets of characters is that Mitis and Cordatus occasionally comment in the course of a scene; Lucianus and Therulus speak only at the beginning and end of each act, although they remain onstage throughout.

Jonson's play has a second set of censuring figures, Asper-Macilente and Carlo Buffone. These two become involved in the plot. Again our author takes over the construction from Jonson. The play proper opens on Erudius and Candle disputing hotly. Erudius, a Catholic layman of good sense and moderation horrified by the excesses of the controversy, replaces Jonson's Carlo Buffone, a fool, but Candle is closely modeled on Asper. Each is a severe critic of those around him; each disguises himself, Asper as Macilente, Candle as a scrivener; each invents a plot that causes the other humorous figures to exhibit their follies; each voices his author's attitudes; and each is criticized for excessive fervor. The opening lines echo Jonson:

> *Erudius*: Pray, gentle Candle, hold, forbear extremes,
> Be not so passionate.
> *Candle*: Erudius,
> Pray stand aside and give my fury vent,
> Or else my heart will break. Shall I endure
> To see religion by these apes abused,
> And yet stand mute and patient like an ass?
> *Erudius*: I prithee what religion dost thou mean?
> For thou hast none.
> *Candle*: I tell thee to have none
> Is better than have any in these days.
> . . . .
> *Erudius*: Thou art more mad,
> That think'st thou art alive when thou art dead.
> *Candle*: Dead?
> *Erudius*: Yes. Thou only hast a walking tongue,
> That like a ghost doth haunt the world and rail,
> That tires upon the vices of each man.
> (11. 329-50)

In these lines we hear Asper, in the Introduction to *Every Man Out of His Humour*, asking, "Who is so patient of this impious world,/ That he can checke his spirit, or reine his tongue?" (*Jonson*, 3: 428), and Mitis begging Asper, "Containe your spirit in more stricter bounds" (*Jonson*, 3: 429). The general notion of "tiring upon" the vices of each man not only describes Asper, but explains the function of these characters in both plays. Both sets of exterior figures help to hold the audience at a distance from the satirized characters, but the second pair particularly serves to create a hostile spirit of mockery. Like Carlo and Macilente, Candle and Erudius are onstage through almost all of the play, anatomizing the errors of the other characters and ultimately contributing to the denouement.

The rest of the play is not so closely modeled on Jonson's, for the author has a specific argument to conduct and Jonson does not. Yet both the handling of the characters and the structure show Jonson's influence.

The general method of introducing the characters is borrowed from Jonson and emerges gradually throughout the play. First we meet a group of Jesuits, then of Benedictines, then of Dominicans, nobles, ladies. Each time the natures—or humors—of the individuals must emerge from the conversation between them. In *Every Man Out of His Humour* this method is defended by Cordatus against Mitis's objections:

> Mitis: hee might haue altered the shape of his argument,
> and explicated 'hem [individual humours] better
> in single *Scenes*.
> Cordatus: That had beene single indeed: why? be they not
> the same persons in this, as they would haue beene
> in those? and is it not an obiect of more state, to
> behold the *Scene* full, and relieu'd with varietie
> of speakers to the end, then to see a vast emptie
> stage, and the actors come in (one by one) as if
> they were dropt downe with a feather, into the
> eye of the spectators?
>
> (*Jonson*, 3: 479)

Individually, *Hierarchomachia* also copies the psychological system of characterization through humors that Jonson made popular. Jonson satirized the uxorious husband, fantastical gallant, and absurd traveler; our author likewise gave his characters—or copied from real life—identifying quirks. Corbus is always triggered to speak by mention of the "wits," among whom he counts himself; Davus peppers his conversation with Italian tags and references to his spectacles; Spirius, who hoped to become head of his order, is ambitious and always ready to pick a fight; Pamoppus is equally choleric but absurdly small. The author creates the individual humors by the predictable repetition of the characters' reactions. Only in the case of Sir Tobie Matthew, whose excessive courtliness was especially foolish since his identity as a priest and a Jesuit was widely known, does the author attempt a full-length portrait. As is usual in the many contemporary descriptions of Matthew, he is here particularly satirized for fulsome flattery and inappropriate attachment to women. His first entrance with one of the ladies, Nivetta, is typical:

Nivetta: Then, servant, you can court as well as pray.
Bitomattus: Yes, madam; courtship is a prayer to saints.
Nivetta: What saints?
Bitomattus: To women, images of God.
Nivetta: You teach idolatry.
Bitomattus: Mistake it not,
Nivetta. Thus I make my saying good:
From outward beauty that in women shines,
I take a scantling of their molded souls
Into God's liking; thence I find a way
To court the Deity, so make my prayer.
(11. 1828-36)

Of course, all of these characters were based on real individuals and so could not be reformed by the playwright. Jonson was able to cure his humors figures because they were not still active in the world outside the play. *Hierarchomachia* can only "deride them upon the stage" and leave them cherishing their follies.

Neither *Hierarchomachia* nor *Every Man Out of His Humour* has much action; the attention focuses on verbal description and exposure, just as it would in verse satire. Thus the first act of *Hierarchomachia* is primarily revealing talk: Candle and Erudius eavesdrop on Bolnutus and Jargus as the two Jesuits plot to involve the Benedictines against the bishop, then Bolnutus and Jargus eavesdrop on the Benedictines Coredurus and Spirius, and the act ends with the successive comments of the critical characters. First Erudius expresses his horror at the intrigue, while Candle delights to tell him that the church "your rock; /'Tis now become a rock of scandal" (11. 663-64), and then Lucianus threatens to leave because Candle has sworn "by heaven." Lucianus is only persuaded to stay because he is so pleased by the plot against the bishop, "and could wish my brain/Against our bishops were so well employed" (11.685-86).

In both plays commentators are used to manipulate the sketchy plots. In *Every Man Out of His Humour* Asper-Macilente invents the tricks that put the other characters out of their humors. Candle, too, can say, "this plot/ Was first begun by me" (11. 1083-84). In the second act the Jesuit Jargus, disguised as a Guelf or secular priest, is talking with recusant nobles but is abruptly deserted by them when servants announce that pursuivants have been sighted approaching the tavern. Candle, amused, dresses Jargus as a devil and hides him in a chimney. Most of the remaining activity hinges on this disguise. For instance, in the fourth act, which seems from Valentine Lane's letter to have been a contemporary high point (at least for the bishop's supporters), Jargus, asleep behind an arras, is spotted by Onoplutus (the Jesuit Thomas Poulton). Onoplutus alerts the other knights, and Pamoppus (George Popham, the Dominican) decides to attack this devil: "I am resolved to strike and try him" (1. 2564). He is accompanied by Davus (Dom David Codner, a Benedictine), thus giving Lane's "father Scrupe in the forme of a diuel a benedictant, and a dominican of ech side of him whipping him." When Jargus, roused, calls them by name, they flee in terror. Later they return to conduct a full exorcism with bell, book, and candle, but Jargus has again taken refuge in the chimney.

Candle's plan also creates the climax of the play. In the fifth act the long-expected pursuivants, assisted by Constable Pumpkin, finally arrive at the tavern where the synod is meeting. Once again the author takes a cue from Jonson. Toward the end of *Every Man Out of His Humour* several characters are having a party in a tavern. They are rudely interrupted by a constable, who threatens to break down the door if he is not admitted. He arrests one gallant "to answere till the rest can be found out" (*Jonson*, 3:586), and promises to pursue the others. In *Hierarchomachia* the pursuivants likewise interrupt the meeting at the tavern. After they have extracted bribes from all the other characters they prepare to arrest Erudius, that voice of reason, who has no money; "he goes to prison for the rest/ That can come fairly off; we keep withal/ Our reputation current with the state" (11.3497-99), that is, by producing Erudius they will show that they have actually been hunting priests and recusants; he will answer till the rest can be found out. Then, at the critical instant, Candle, disguised as a scrivener called in to write up the bonds that some of the recusants have given the pursuivants, produces his devil, Jargus, and scares away the superstitious pursuivants. This saves the day; it is also dramatically subtle, for the act of disguising the Jesuit vice-provincial as a devil, used to scare away that other devil, Rocs, although an indication of the author's attitude toward him, yet seems appropriately necessitated by the exigencies of the action.

Oddly enough, it is in this last scene that the author's acquaintance with a Shakespearean character emerges briefly. His Constable Pumpkin speaks only a few lines, but instead of being businesslike, in the manner of Jonson's constable ("Lay hold vpon this gallant, and pursue the rest," *Jonson,* 3:585), he is apparently an imitation of *Much Ado About Nothing*'s Dogberry. Pumpkin is "The simplest card. . .in all the bunch" (1.3367), and his line, "I reprehend the king's own person here" (1.3369) recalls, "This is your charge: you shall comprehend all vagrom men....you, constable, are to present the Prince's own person."[86] Rocs and Milston treat Pumpkin with disrespect, much as Conrade and Boracchio treat Dogberry, but Pamoppus notes that Pumpkin is the "honestest"man among them.

Despite the minor nod to Shakespeare, the literary example behind the structure of *Hierarchomachia* is *Every Man Out of His Humour*. The two sets of framing and censuring characters, the tone of derision, the procession of satirized characters first presented in groups, the observation of the traditional and Jonsonian laws of comedy, the conclusion, and above all the genre—all demonstrate that the author found a distinguished model in Jonson's play.

Yet there is nothing allegorical about *Every Man Out of His Humour*; it was not from Jonson that our author learned to write controversy in dramatic form. He had, in fact, a hard time finding a model play dealing with similar material. *Hierarchomachia* only slightly resembles contemporary controversial or allegorical religious plays, but this is not surprising, for virtually all of them were anti-Catholic.

There were three places in which a religious or controversial allegory might appear on the stage: in schools, universities, and professional theaters. Only in the Catholic schools on the Continent was there pro-Catholic drama. Yet most of this was not allegorical or controversial, but either recounted the stories of martyrdoms or dramatized important moments in the history of the Church. (The plays of Joseph Simons, most important of the English Catholic dramatists, exemplify both genres.) The one *school* historical-religious allegory I have found mention of is Thomas Carleton's *Fatum Vortigerni*, performed in 1619 at the College at Douai. This is said to be Catholic commentary on Henry VIII and Anne Boleyn; I have not been able to see it.[87]

Fatum Vortigerni was in Latin; so were the notable (non-Catholic) university plays that touch on questions of religion. A glance at three of these, Robert Burton's *Philosophaster* (written 1606, altered 1615, produced 1617), *Risus Anglicanus* (1614-25), and John Hacket's *Loyola* (1623) will show how different *Hierarchomachia* is. *Philosophaster* is basically a gulling play. The chief "philosophaster" is Polupragmaticus, a Jesuit, who is accompanied by Equivocus, his servant. The Jesuit accuses himself of the usual evils: in Paul Jordan-Smith's translation he says, "*Jesuit* is the word that describeth me best....What will a man of this class not dare? Into what King's palace, or woman's chamber will he not rush? What dastard deed doth he leave untried?"[88] When Equivocus is seeking his master he comments, "At what hour doth he not go? Hither, thither, everywhere, through all quarters of the city, a night-prowler, he creepeth forth at all hours, now clad as a man, now mincing along like a woman, assuming all shapes: bawd, midwife, sometimes e'en as a soldier. Methinks Proteus himself is not more changeable than that man, nor fox more sly & crafty."[89] This was the usual English attack on Jesuits for craftiness and disguise, although in the plot the Jesuit is merely a clever imposter. In general, the drama is neither allegorical nor basically concerned with religion.

John Hacket's *Loyola*, a play from Trinity College, Cambridge, acted before King James in 1623, has a typical Roman comedy plot: there are two girls, virgins, although one resides in a bawdy house and the other is disguised as a mute boy; three suitors including a father and son; various tricks including disguise as an Aethiop; and a final sorting out of lost sisters, fathers, and lovers that leaves everyone happy. Added to the usual cast are Ignatius

Loyola and Iodacus, a Franciscan. They are trying to persuade one of the young men, Philander, to become a Jesuit, and they are persistently satirized for their methods. For instance, they promise to obtain his beloved for him, although as a potential Jesuit he may sleep with her only as a man with his mistress, not as a husband with his wife. At another point Loyola lies and says in an aside, ''Non est igitur pejeratio, sed quaedam mentalis reservatio.''[90] The English were horrified by what they believed was the Jesuit doctrine of equivocation, and the choplogic here is meant to expose that technique. Loyola is also satirized by means of a little show he presents, which includes a chorus of historical Jesuits (Xaverius, Aquaviva, Personius, Campianus) along with a ''*Chorus virtutum Jesuiticarum*'': Caeca obedientia, Pseudo-miraculum, Regicidium, Index expurgatorius, Æquivocatio, Arrogantia. At the end, the other characters are ready to hang Loyola, who confesses to a variety of sins including sexual transgressions, poisonings, and drunkenness, but he is finally released as part of the wedding festivity. Once again we have satire of Jesuits (and incidentally, of Puritans), but neither controversy nor consistent allegory.

Closer to *Hierarchomachia* is *Risus Anglicanus*. This Latin play survives only in a Folger Library manuscript of miscellaneous seventeenth-century plays, poems, and tracts, which were bound together in the eighteenth century. Among other pieces the manuscript includes *Periander*, which was acted at St. John's College, Oxford, in 1607. Because the manuscript is a compilation, no conclusion about the provenance of *Risus Anglicanus* can be drawn from the other plays, but staging and subject suggest a connection with one of the universities.[91] The play was intended for acting on a stage with five fixed locations with the following inscriptions above them: Ignatianum, Forum Romanum, Vaticanum, Forum exoticum, and Ianua Ditis. Numerous stage directions send characters back and forth among these houses. This old-fashioned method was long gone from the public stage.

The central resemblance between *Hierarchomachia* and *Risus Anglicanus* is that each concerns a religious controversy. *Risus Anglicanus* ''relates the alleged tribulations and failures at Rome of the leading Jesuit publicists to counteract the, to them, dangerous implications of the Oath of Allegiance of 1606...and the important theoretical justifications thereof put forth by James I.''[92] Well-known Catholic controversialists appear as characters under their real names, except for Bellarmine, who is called Matthaeus Tortus from one of his own pseudonyms. Certain incidents resemble those in *Hierarchomachia*: the brief of the pope against taking the Oath of Allegiance is planned on stage, as was the letter of lay Catholics. There are little devils, daemunculi, in the Latin play, who become involved in considerable horseplay, somewhat as Jargus's disguise as a devil is the occasion of laughter, especially when he is first spotted. The connection implied between Ignatius Loyola, Pope Paul V, and Lucifer, who together open *Risus Anglicanus*, makes the same point as disguising Jargus as a devil. In general, both plays, while alluding to specific books and incidents of their respective controversies, reduce to *ad hominem* attacks on the opposition, primarily the Jesuits. The most amusing satire in *Risus Anglicanus* ridicules Thomas Fitzherbert, the same rector of the English College who may be responsible for the missing quire in the manuscript of *Hierarchomachia*. Fitzherbert, who appears in the fifth Act of *Risus Anglicanus*, speaks only English, which the devils think is Hebrew. He further reveals his ignorance by insisting that Latin is only for scholars, a statement given ironic application to him because he has come to defend his English book, *An Adioynder to the Supplement of Father R. Persons his Discussion of M. Doctor Barlowes Answere* (1613). Finally the ghost of Robert Persons appears, arguing that Fitzherbert's book is useful because there are many illiterate women in England who will like it, though it nauseates the erudite.

In a summation R. H. Bowers writes: "The play lacks a secure sense of dramatic structure, and the dialogue is often wooden, but it [has] ...great historical interest. Despite 'poetic license' and a somewhat fantastic introduction of devils, the text shows the author to be well versed in the great European logomachia of his day as he tries valiantly to produce satire of importance. A contemporary English audience would have relished the play's content...."[93] With only minor adjustments, this comment is equally appropriate to *Hierarchomachia*. Yet the extraordinary characteristic of our play, which links it more to public than to university drama, is that its obviously learned author chose to write in English.

Drama in English, from the Reformation onward, had a decidedly anti-Catholic bias. There are frequent depictions of a corrupt Catholic clergy in Protestant moralities and patriotic histories, but these plays were not usually allegorical nor concerned with theological questions.[94] It was, after all, forbidden from 1559 on to play anything "wherin either matters of religion or of the gouernaunce of the estate of the common weale shalbe handled or treated," and thirty years later, when the Privy Council felt that "players take upon themselves to handle in their plaies certen matters of Divinytie and of State unfitt to be suffred," they appointed a person "well learned in Divinity" to assist the Master of the Revels in allowing, or forbidding, plays.[95]

The few plays allowed that managed indirectly to touch on matters of religion tended to cater to popular prejudices. For instance, Barnabe Barnes's *The Devil's Charter*, acted by the King's Men in 1607, is allegorical only insofar as it shows Pope Alexander VI making a league with the devil. Basically historical, it attacks Catholicism by dwelling on a bad pope. Caesar Borgia upbraids his father:

> Haue you not sold your selfe vnto the Diuill,
> To be promoted to the Papacie:
> Haue you not sould the liuings of the Church?
> . . . .
> Haue yee not (since your inauguration)
> Poysoned and done to death six Cardinals?[96]

The play also adapts to the purposes of religious satire the tradition of Machiavellian villains on the English stage. Alexander states: "things are as they seeme,/Not what they be themselues; all is opinion."[97] While the bias is secure, nothing else in the play is coherently handled; artistically it is a disaster.

About the same time, Dekker's chauvinistic *The Whore of Babylon* was acted by the Prince's Men. This play is overtly allegorical; an advertisement to the readers says:

> *The Generall scope of this Drammaticall Poem, is to set forth (in Tropicall and shadowed collours) the Greatnes . . . and other the incomparable Heroical vertues of our late Queene. And (on the contrary part) the inueterate malice, Treasons, Machinations, Vnderminings, and continual blody stratagems, of that Purple whore of* Roome.

Among the dramatis personae are "TITANIA the Fairie Queene: vnder whom is figured our late Queene Elizabeth" and "TH'EMPRESSE OF BABYLON: vnder whom is figured *Rome*."[98] The play recounts several of the plots against Elizabeth, and shows the empress uncomfortable because the fairy queen has banished her "soothsayers." Dekker combined allegorical portraits of real people, like Elizabeth and Lopez, the physician executed for an alleged attempt to poison the queen, with embodiments of abstract ideas: Time, Truth, Plaine-dealing. Allegory based on historical events (e.g., the Armada) is mixed with religious and moral allegory, and there are also some simple personifications, like the seventeen states of the low countries portrayed as the seventeen daughters of the fairy queen's neighbor. The whole is a hodge-podge, very nationalistic but quite inconsistent as a dramatic form. Once again the Jesuits are singled out for criticism: the author of *Hierarchomachia* was close to English Protestant dramatic tradition when he cast the Jesuit as the devil.

These early anti-Catholic plays were rather remote to have influenced *Hierarchomachia*, but there was a more recent example. The regulations against putting questions of religion on stage had never been so spectacularly infringed as they were by Thomas Middleton's violently anti-Catholic *A Game at Chesse* (1624), which openly flaunted all restrictions on handling matters of divinity or depicting a living Christian king. As an expression of the vast public rejoicing when Prince Charles returned from Spain in 1623 without a Spanish bride, Middleton's allegorical chess game between black Spanish pieces and white English ones is a celebration of triumph, probably written under the protection of a powerful patron.[99] The plot, put simply, is one in which the black house attempts to subvert and conquer the white house, but is defeated when the White Knight (Prince Charles) checkmates them "by discovery," that is, in the words of the latest editor, "a discovery of the perfidious design behind the Spanish negotiations, the intention of converting the future King of England to Roman Catholicism."[100]

Most of London seems to have seen the play. In a contemporary letter the irate Spanish ambassador complains that "during these last four days more than 12,000 persons have all heard the play of *A Game at Chess*...including all the nobility still in London. All these people come out of the theatre so inflamed against Spain that, as a few Catholics have told me who went secretly to see the play, my person would not be safe in the streets...."[101] A less biased observer, John Chamberlain, also notes that the play was "frequented by all sorts of people old and young, rich and poor, masters and servants, papists and puritans, wise men etc., churchmen and statesmen...."[102] If the author of *Hierarchomachia* was not one of these papists, of these clandestine Catholic spectators, he had probably read one of the three quartos that immediately circulated. While he would not have sympathized with Middleton's attitudes, he understood his method. In this period no other play could have served him so well as an example of a consistent dramatic allegory on a controversial subject involving religion, and its popular success may have suggested to our author that he should write his allegorical play in English.

In its conception *Hierarchomachia* is closer to *A Game at Chesse* than to any of the haphazard or incomplete allegories present in the other plays mentioned above. First of all, each playwright has a consistent system for satirizing his contemporaries: Middleton divides his figures into white and black chess pieces; our author divides the pro- and anti-bishop forces into Guelfs and Ghibellines, then divides the various regulars into the sets of knights. In each case, beneath the disguises there is precise historical realism, whether of Prince Charles's trip or of the opposition to Bishop Smith. Both plays work to a climax where one side is, at least temporarily, defeated: the black pieces end in Hell Mouth; the knights are ignominiously freed from the pursuivants and forced to flee. In each case the author emphasizes the internal division of the side he does not favor: in *A Game at Chesse* the black house plays against itself, while the white house illustrates cooperation; in *Hierarchomachia* the Dominicans join the Jesuits only from a desire to share their wealth; Jargus hides in the chimney as a devil while his fellow Jesuits try to exorcise him as an evil spirit; and the synod concludes with the regulars and their supporters expressing sharp disagreement about lay participation.

There may originally have been a link between the contents of the two plays. In *A Game at Chesse* the only player about whose identity there is modern critical doubt is the White King's Pawn. In 3.i this white character is revealed to be black underneath. The White King upbraids him for his treachery, making mention of the favors he has done for this pawn: "raysed thee/ From a Condition next to popular labour....And grafted thee into a Branch of honor...," and charges him with falling "from the Top-bough by the rottennes,/ Of thy alone Corruption...."[103] Bald shows that in thus falling the Pawn resembled Lionel Cranfield, Earl of Middlesex, who began life as a city apprentice, rose to be lord treasurer, and was impeached and found guilty of peculation in 1624, the year of *A Game at Chesse*.[104]

After publishing his edition Bald found an earlier version of the play, a manuscript dated August 13, 1624, in other words, completed by the scribe during the nine days' run of the play. In this version certain lines are omitted that refer to the Pawn's humble birth and place in council; instead, ecclesiastical rewards from the black side are promised: the "strong Crosier-staff/ And the red Hat," which could hardly attract Cranfield.[105] In the nineteenth century Bullen had proposed that the White King's Pawn might be Sir Tobie Matthew. The opening description of him, where the Black Knight (Gondomar, the Spanish ambassador) says to the Black Bishop's Pawn, a Jesuit:

> Hee's made our owne (man) halfe in Voto youres,
> His hearts in the black house, leaue him to mee,
> Most of all frends endeerde, pretiouslie spetiall[106]

seems better adapted to Matthew's Jesuit vows than to Cranfield's economically based opposition to war with Spain. The trial of Cranfield occurred while the play was being written, so Middleton must have decided to change Matthew to the more currently notorious figure after he had finished the play and had it copied. Though it is unclear to what extent this earlier version circulated in manuscript, the Catholic author may have seen or heard of it. Tobie Matthew was an obvious butt for our playwright, but considering the attention I believe he gave to the general method of *A Game at Chesse*, he may also have found suggested there the beginnings of his satirical depiction.

Matthew's secret identity was well known to Catholics and Protestants alike. All the personalities veiled in *Hierarchomachia* had considerable current interest. By writing in English rather than Latin the author was bidding for a wider reading audience, including women, who were interested in the controversy and who may also have known about the scandalous anti-Catholic play that *Hierarchomachia* recalled. If they frequented the theater or read plays, they would have recognized that formally the playwright was guided by Jonson. Yet, despite these recollections of contemporary drama, *Hierarchomachia* follows no one model; it is an original creation.

7. *The Play*

Hierarchomachia is not merely a treatise or a satire turned into dialogue; it is conceived as drama, though its didactic purpose remains paramount. Whether he expected production or not, the author envisioned the play on an Elizabethan stage with a balcony: in 3.iv-vii Candle and Erudius stand "above," commenting on the action below. In general, a fairly large stage, like the thrust stages of the public theaters, seems presupposed by the author's most persistent dramatic device, that of having one group of actors overhear and comment aside upon another group. This technique is exemplified in Act 1, when Erudius and Candle, apparently on the main stage, eavesdrop on Bolnutus and Jargus, who then eavesdrop on Coredurus and Spirius, while all three groups are observed by Therulus and Lucianus, who remain on stage throughout.

Characterization is not elaborate, but the major figures are satisfactorily delineated by their "humorous" traits, and occasionally the author begins to round out a character. Spirius's fascination with the whipping post suggests a rather sadistic nature, and Onoplutus is both cringing and fearful. These characteristics are generally confirmed by such other contemporary descriptions as we have, especially in the case of Sir Tobie Matthew. When characters are disguised, the author tries to gain dramatic impact from the ironic discrepancies that arise. Jargus, disguised as a Guelf or bishop follower, blesses those who made *bishop* a word of scorn, and Corbus comments, "Most charitably spoken for a Guelf" (1. 896). Rocs is highly suspicious of the scrivener Candle's generosity to Erudius, and is equally horrified when the scrivener demands his fee.

The author's main theme is the absolute necessity for hierarchy in the church and elsewhere. Though of course this was a specific justification of Bishop Smith's authority, it was more: readers of Renaissance literature will recognize the pervasive fear of disorder which Shakespeare articulates most explicitly in *Troilus and Cressida*: "Take but degree away, untune that string,/ And hark what discord follows."[107] In 5.iv, just before the pursuivants arrive, the bishop's opponents begin to reap the rewards of their own teachings. Corbus objects to women's speaking in synods, Rudelbinus defends it, and Spirius tells Rudelbinus that as a layman he does not have the privilege he wants to grant the women. In an impassioned speech Rudelbinus points out that Spirius and his fellows have moved him to speak against a prelate of the church, and now:

Who dares call
Me subject here? Now I have slipped the yoke
Of bishops from my neck with your instinct
(11. 3186-88)

This is an ironic high point of the play, a moment when the interplay of character and situation naturally reveals the self-destructive nature of the anti-bishop position.

Though in fact very little happens, the author attempts to create urgency and suspense in the plot. The day is critical, because the synod is being held. Jargus ascends the chimney after the first mention of the pursuivants in 2.iv, but they do not actually appear until 5.v. In between he tries to escape from his devil's costume and imprisoning chimney, but a series of amusing impediments lead to his own fellows' attempt to exorcise him. The questions of Lucianus and Therulus, who wait anxiously for Jargus's reappearance, enhance our anticipation of his descent. The conclusion is genuinely dramatic. The audience is not sure until the last minute that Erudius will escape from the pursuivants and prison, and the entire final trick, with its thunder and lightning and outsmarting of Rocs by his own superstition, ignorance, and greed, is a worthy climax.

The blank verse line is usually smooth, with an unobtrusive but regular rhythm. However, the author is very insistent upon completing the pentameter, so that when, as frequently happens, a scene ends with an incomplete verse, the first line of the next scene will complete it. Fortunately, there are few instances as awkward as 11. 295-96, where the word *golden* is divided between the lines.

The dialogue varies in quality. Some of the time it is convincingly dramatic, with one person informing and affecting another. Therulus and Lucianus, one a Protestant and the other a Puritan, constantly squabble, partially masking their basic function as expositors. The arguments between the noblemen, in which they weigh conflicting religious and temporal considerations—"My wife solicits me to be a lord" (1. 802)—appear realistic. The line is frequently broken between two or three speakers, accelerating the rhythm. But the playwright had a point to make, and exposing the bishop's enemies as fools and knaves was not enough: the theoretical defense of the bishop had to be presented. In Acts 4 and 5 the speeches become long-winded and the arguments repetitive. This is particularly noticeable in 4.ii, where each of the three women champions her favorite. Though the idea is potentially interesting, the scene is not.

Furthermore, the author's metaphorical and poetic language is uneven. Candle's speech beginning, "I much lament the miserable state/ Of Papists in this land" (1. 1042 ff.) is perhaps the strongest in the play, partly because of its vivid picture of the abuses Catholics suffered. In this passage we see the occasional ease of the poetry, with natural accents and enjambed lines, a comfortable use of standard rhetorical devices like parallelism, strength gathered from emphatic verbs: "beat...beset...break...pillage...dive...search." On the other hand the metaphor of coining in "ancient stamp" and "new-coined" loses its force in "seasick" and "strike them dead," and the intentional slip for the sake of explicating the anagram, "Cross, Rocs I should say," while no doubt helpful if anyone has missed the identification, is heavy-handed. The typical weakness of the drama intrudes in the final lines of this speech. Here the phrases, "jurisdiction, power to bind and loose,/ Commission to approve" appear not for their poetic quality or imaginative appropriateness but for their polemical importance.

Also heavy-handed is the way the author feels compelled to assist the audience to grasp the satire. Not content with the two sets of commentators, he has recourse to a standard technique of polemical drama: he has those satirized confess the virtue of their opponents or of the opposing position in an unguarded moment.[108] Thus Jargus admits that the bishop has no vices, though the Jesuits have invented many (11. 572-76), and Pamoppus says, "The bishop is a burr that will not down...I hold him innocent, yet have so railed/ Upon him...that I feel my mind/ Much troubled at it'' (11. 2682-87). The end of the play, Candle's epilogue to the audience and the lines in which Lucianus and Therulus judge the bishop's cause to be right, is anticlimactic after the bustle of Jargus and the pursuivants, but, once again, the author wanted no ambiguity of judgment.

In a final appraisal of *Hierarchomachia* the contemporary interest in religious argument should be recalled. Sermons were long, and schoolboys were expected to learn their main points by heart after one hearing. Erudius is truly concerned with the state of Candle's soul, and the noblemen's conflict reveals their religious education and involvement. *A Game at Chesse* and other allegorical plays indicate the popular concern with the political-religious quarrels sweeping seventeenth-century Europe. In this light the appeal of *Hierarchomachia* to those able to decipher the allegory would have been strong, and they presumably tolerated what seems to a modern reader verbose and somewhat repetitious discussion.

Today, *Hierarchomachia* offers the fascination of the past. To a student of history, it is an insight into a major religious quarrel with international implications. To a student of the English Catholic church it is a detailed exposure of the attitudes that contributed to the long hiatus between Catholic bishops in England. And to a student of literature it reveals the extent to which seventeenth-century drama flourished under the most adverse circumstances and in the most unexpected places.

8. The Manuscript

The English College copy of *Hierarchomachia* is in excellent condition, although it is missing a quire. It appears to be a fair scribal copy, as is indicated by the spaces left in lines 3472, 3479, and 3490, presumably for words illegible in the scribe's material. Since these were never filled in, the scribe was apparently not able to ask the author's advice. Nonetheless, there are few overt errors; this does not seem to be one of the copies ''very much corrupted and made to speake many absurdetyes'' that the bishop's correspondent complained of.[109] The scribe caught several of his own mistakes; probably he worked from a rather clean source.

The ink and hand are the same throughout, with two possible exceptions: the inserted line 1992, and the letters *ena* that complete the name Odoena in line 2011. Both were apparently additions, written after the body of the page. From the correspondence offering to obtain copies of the play it may be inferred that someone, possibly a priest in hiding, passed his time preparing these manuscripts—or at least that the priests had a professional scribe available for such work.

The manuscript is 32.2 centimeters tall by 20.1 centimeters wide, varying with the untrimmed edge. It consists of eight unsewn quires numbered 1,2,3,4,5,6,8,9 in a hand contemporary with the manuscript. There is an additional marginal 3 on the last page of the third quire.

The quires are not regular in size: the first is a folio in 10 (including the blank cover page); 2,3,4,5, and 6 are folios in 8; and 8 and 9 are folios in 6. The first quire consists of the following:

1^r	Blank except for 1, indicating the first quire
1^v	Blank
2^r	Title page
2^v	Blank
3^r–4^r	*The Author's Apology for this Poem*
4^v	Blank
5^r	*The Persons or Speakers*
5^v	Blank
6^r–10^v	Text, beginning with *The Introduction*.

All the other quires contain only the text of the play. A modern hand has numbered the pages in pencil 1-90, 91x-112x, beginning with *The Introduction* on 6^r and using x to indicate the pages following the break in the manuscript. However, the modern numbering mistakenly omits 108x, and does not number the last page of text or the blank recto and verso following.

The watermark of the manuscript, the same throughout, is described by Heawood as a "pair of Gate-Posts with a device between which may be meant either for a bunch of Grapes or a Fir-cone...." Heawood further remarks that the locale of this watermark is "difficult to determine."[110] But in fact the possible assumptions based on Heawood's research reinforce present theories of the origin of the manuscript. Heawood gives examples of these watermarks as numbers 3485-3535 of his work. Though the watermark in the manuscript is not identical to any of these—it consistently appears upside down—it is closest to numbers 3505, 3506, 3508, and 3531. As shown by Heawood, it consists of two posts with a bar between, which may contain certain letters, beneath which is a hanging pendant and above which, on a support, are grapes or a fir-cone. The bar in the manuscript's watermark appears to contain three letters; on the last sheet, if the watermark is held right side up, these may be read as ?DK. Heawood shows many letters as illegible: 3506, the watermark closest to that in the manuscript, he reads as C ʕ?S.

Of all of Heawood's samples, even those which add decorations not found in our manuscript, only a few do not come from England. One is from Ireland, which may mean that it was carried over from England; one is from Lisbon; and two are from France. England imported its paper in the seventeenth century, and despite the few exceptional provenances, this paper seems to have been made for the English trade. Numbers 3506 and 3531 are both found in Saltonstall's *Mercator* published in London in 1637, 3505 comes from the *Mercator* of 1635, and 3508 comes from an undated Inigo Jones drawing. In general the watermarks come from England in the early seventeenth century, indeed from the 1630s. The coincidence of watermarks would seem to rule out the remote contingency that this manuscript of *Hierarchomachia* was copied outside of England.

9. The Text of This Edition

In this edition of *Hierarchomachia* the spelling has been modernized, except in those few cases which may have represented more than an orthographic variant to the author (e.g., threshall for threshold). The original spelling is also retained where necessary to scansion or wordplay (e.g., amias for amice). The punctuation has been modernized on as regular a system as is possible for long speeches of argumentation originally divided only by commas and semicolons. The general aim throughout has been to assist the modern reader inconspicuously.

The format of the play follows the usual modern practice. Speech prefixes are in the margin; the standard system of indicating a divided pentameter line is adopted. All names are regularized, and abbreviations are expanded. Italic type is retained only when the author uses it for emphasis or for languages other than English. Catchwords have been eliminated.

Our copy of *Hierarchomachia* is not an acting text: it includes very few stage directions, no exits or asides, and only a block entrance at the opening of each scene. The author limits his mention of props to those for the exorcism in 4. v and for Candle's entrance as a scrivener in 5. vii. Most other business—dressing Jargus as a devil, for instance—is obvious from the dialogue. Not wishing to change the nature of the text I have added, in brackets, only a few essential directions, mostly entrances, exits, and asides.

All textual emendations and those modernized spellings where there is any ambiguity of meaning are also enclosed in brackets and explained in the Textual Notes.

NOTES

1. Though all agree on the increase, precise numbers are difficult to establish. Philip Hughes gives 400 secular priests and 14 Jesuits in England in 1598, with an increase of Jesuits to 125 by 1623 (Philip Hughes, *Rome and the Counter-Reformation in England* [London, 1942], pp. 287-88). A lower figure comes from Aveling, who suggests "c. 330-355 in 1609, of which 70-75 regulars" (cited in John Bossy, *The English Catholic Community 1570-1850* [London, 1975], p. 216, n. 35). In 1635 the papal envoy Panzani said that there were about 500 secular priests, 160 Jesuits, 100 Benedictines, 20 Franciscans, and 7 Dominicans in England (Catholic Record Society [C.R.S.], 25: 172). Bossy, the latest to study this question, concludes that "between the death of Elizabeth and the eve of the Civil War, the number of priests on the mission rose from 300 or so to about 750" (Bossy, *The English Catholic Community*, p. 217).

2. *Historical Narrative of John Bennett, Priest, 1621*,C.R.S., 22: 141.

3. John Bossy, "Henry IV, the Appellants and the Jesuits," *Recusant History* 8 (1965): 80-122. Bossy considers the Archpriest controversy again in *The English Catholic Community*, pp. 35-48. See bibliography for other sources.

4. A. F. Allison, "Richard Smith, Richelieu and the French Marriage. The political context of Smith's appointment as bishop for England in 1624," *Recusant History* 7 (1964): 148.

5. Ibid., p. 162.

6. Ludwig von Pastor, *The History of the Popes*, trans. Dom Ernest Graf, O.S.B. (London, 1938), 29:304.

7. Bossy questions whether this agreement with the Benedictines "represented in Bishop's mind the first stage of a compromise with the regulars as a whole, or an attempt to secure Benedictine neutrality in an impending battle with the Jesuits...." (*The English Catholic Community*, p. 53). Cf. Maurus Lunn, O.S.B., "Benedictine Opposition to Bishop Richard Smith (1625-1629)," *Recusant History* 11 (1971): 2-3.

8. Allison, *Richard Smith*, p. 184.

9. Ibid., pp. 148-149.

10. Ibid., p. 189.

11. Bossy writes that the controversy "may perhaps most conveniently be described as an argument about whether the English Catholic community should be governed according to the disciplinary decrees of the Council of Trent or not"(*The English Catholic Community*, p. 53).

12. P. Hughes, *Rome*, p. 350, n. 3.

13. Lunn, "Benedictine Opposition," pp. 7-8.

14. Both letters are reprinted in C.R.S., 22: 148-57.

15. C.R.S., 22: 156.

16. Ibid., 22: 157.

17. Ibid., 22: 157-58. The letter is dated by P. Hughes, *Rome*, p. 354, n.l.

18. P. Hughes, *Rome*, pp. 373-74.

19. Lunn, "Benedictine Opposition," p. 11.

20. Archives of the archbishop of Westminster (AAW) A, 22: 154.

21. P. Hughes, *Rome*, pp. 371-373; Bossy, *The English Catholic Community*, p. 58.

22. "The Note-Book of John Southcote, D.D." C.R.S., 1: 105.

23. AAW, A, 22: 154.

24. P. Hughes, *Rome*, pp. 378-407; Pastor, *History of the Popes*, 29: 307.

25. Father Cyril Murtagh, who discovered the manuscript when he was the archivist of the English College, first identified most of the characters in an article, "Hierarchomachia or the Anti-Bishop," *The Venerabile* 17 (1955): 164-68.

26. Southcot to Blacklo, December 19, 1628, AAW, A, 22: 154.

27. Lunn, "Benedictine Opposition," p.1.

28. W.K.L. Webb, S.J., "Thomas Preston O.S.B., alias Roger Widdrington (1567-1640)," *Biographical Studies* 2 (1954): 216-68.

29. Godfrey Anstruther, O.P., *A Hundred Homeless Years*: *English Dominicans 1558-1658* (London, 1958), pp. 125-33.

30. Godfrey Anstruther, O.P., writes in *The Seminary Priests II: Early Stuarts 1603-1659* (Great Wakering, 1975), p. 120: "George was never at an English seminary but was secretly ordained by card. Bellarmine in Rome, 20 may 1614 together with sir Tobie Mathew, his close friend...." Anstruther dismisses the problems raised in Philippa Revill and Francis W. Steer, "George Gage I and George Gage II," *Bulletin of the Institute of Historical Research* 31 (1958): 141-58, saying "what is there described as his will in 1638 is the will of a namesake, a soap-maker. . . ." (Anstruther, *Seminary Priests*, 2: 121).

31. John P. Feil, "Sir Tobie Matthew and His *Collection of Letters*," Ph.D. diss., University of Chicago, 1962, p. 198. This is the most careful study of Sir Tobie Matthew's life.

32. The letter itself is endorsed with these three names by its recipient. C.R.S., 22: 158.

33. AAW, A, 28:58. Note that the play is always referred to by its subtitle, "The Anti-Bishop" or "Antiepiscopus."

34. Calendar of State Papers, Domestic Series (CSPD), March 26, 1636, 317: 326.

35. John Bossy, "The Character of Elizabethan Catholicism," in *Crisis in Europe 1560-1660*, ed. Trevor Aston (New York, 1965), p. 225.

36. Bossy, *The English Catholic Community*, pp. 153-58.

37. Murtagh, "Hierarchomachia," p. 166, n.1.

38. Feil, "Sir Tobie Matthew," p. 195.

39. Gervas Huxley, *Endymion Porter* (London, 1959), p. 235.

40. Gordon Albion, *Charles I and the Court of Rome* (London 1935), p. 209.

41. Cited in Bossy, *The English Catholic Community*, p. 159.

42. Ibid.

43. *The Lady Falkland: Her Life from a manuscript in the Imperial Archives at Lille* (London, 1861), pp. 10-11. This account is followed by Albion and by Kenneth B. Murdock, *The Sun at Noon* (New York, 1939).

44. Doris Mary Stenton, *The English Woman in History* (London, 1957), p. 137, followed by Bossy, *The English Catholic Community*, p. 159.

45. Albion, *Charles I*, p. 304.

46. This dispute is described at length in Thomas Hughes, S.J., *History of the Society of Jesus in North America* (Cleveland, Ohio, 1907-17), 1: 207-31.

47. Henry Foley, S.J., *Records of the English Province of the Society of Jesus* (London, 1877-83), 7: 624.

48. Bernard Basset, S.J., *The English Jesuits from Campion to Martindale* (London, 1967), p. 181.

49. Foley, *Records*, 7: 624, says that he was readmitted within three years. Basset, *English Jesuits*, p. 181, says the Jesuit General gave permission for his readmission as early as May 15, 1632.

50. It is always difficult to tell whether the letter writers are beginning the year on March 25 or on January 1. Many of these letters have been dated by the archivists at Westminster; I have generally accepted their dates.

51. AAW,A, 27: 19.

52. Ibid., A, 27: 3.

53. Ibid., A, 23: 41; A. F. Allison, "John Gerard and the Gunpowder Plot," *Recusant History* 5 (1959): 62, n. 33.

54. AAW,A, 27: 6.

55. Peter Guilday, *The English Catholic Refugees on the Continent 1558-1795* (London, 1914), p. 323, n. 2; Basset, *English Jesuits*, pp. 207-8.

56. AAW,A, 27: 3.

57. Ibid.

58. AAW,A, 23: 41.

59. Anstruther, *Seminary Priests*, 2: 89.

60. C.R.S., 55: 412; C.R.S., 37, 192; cf. also Anstruther, *Seminary Priests*, 2: 25-28, 144.

61. AAW,A, 27: 127.

62. C.R.S., 40: 1.

63. Ibid., 37: 210.

64. AAW,A, 27: 127.

65. Ibid., 25: 70.

66. Ibid., 27: 127.

67. In the archives of the English College, Scrittura 29.5.1 is such "a relation of the late tumults raysed in the English Colledg, by the way of Apology for the fathers of the Society that haue gouerned the same with the answer to the obiections made against them."

68. The story is told with documents in Charles Dodd, *Church History of England*, ed. M.A. Tierney (London, 1839-43), 5: 94-114, cclxv-cclxxx.

69. AAW,A, 27: 127.

70. Ibid., 27: 126.

71. Ibid., 27: 3.

72. Ibid.

73. Ibid., 27: 6.

74. Ibid., 27: 7.

75. Ibid., 27: 18.

76. Ibid., 27: 19.

77. Allison, "John Gerard," p. 54.

78. Southcot to Fitton, April 16, 1633, AAW,A, 27: 38.

79. Public Record Office, Roman Transcripts. P.R.O. 31/9/17B.

80. AAW,A, 27: 6; 28: 10 (March 4, 1635).

81. Ibid., 28: 58.

82. Murtagh, "Hierarchomachia," p. 168.

83. Oscar James Campbell, *Comicall Satyre and Shakespeare's Troilus and Cressida* (San Marino, Calif., 1938), p. 1.

84. *Ben Jonson*, ed. C. H. Herford and Percy and Evelyn Simpson (Oxford, 1925-52), 3: 428. All citations in the text are to this edition.

85. Campbell, *Comicall Satyre*, p. 54.

86. *Much Ado About Nothing* (3.3 22-23, 68-69), ed. Josephine Waters Bennett, in Alfred Harbage, ed., *William Shakespeare: The Complete Works* (Baltimore, Md., 1969), p. 291.

87. William H. McCabe, "Fatum Vortigerni," *Times Literary Supplement*, August 15, 1935, p. 513. Elsewhere McCabe describes *Astraea*, a college masque whose subject was an allegory of the pacification of Belgium. Masques were commonly allegorical. A sense of the usual dramatic fare at Catholic colleges may be gained from William H. McCabe, "The Play-List of the English College of St. Omers 1592-1762," *Revue de Littérature comparée* 17 (1937): 355-75, and from Suzanne Gossett, "Drama in the English College, Rome, 1591-1660," *English Literary Renaissance* 3 (1973): 60-93.

88. Robert Burton, *Philosophaster*, trans. Paul Jordan-Smith (Stanford, Calif., 1931), p. 29.

89. Ibid., p. 149.

90. [John Hacket], *Loiola* (London, 1648), p. 117.

91. Though Alfred Harbage, *Annals of English Drama*, rev. S. Schoenbaum (London, 1964), p. 113, gives the provenance of the manuscript as "Cambridge (?)," Richard Proudfoot has pointed out to me that the hand in *Periander* is also found in the St. John's, Oxford, manuscript of *Christmas Prince*.

92. R. H. Bowers, "Some Folger Academic Drama Manuscripts," *Studies in Bibliography* 12 (1959): 118.

93. Ibid., p. 120.

94. See, for instance, Rainer Pineas, "The English Morality Play as a Weapon of Religious Controversy," *Studies in English Literature* 2 (1962): 157-80, and idem., *Tudor and Early Stuart Anti-Catholic Drama* (Nieuwkoop [Holland], 1972).

95. E. K. Chambers, *The Elizabethan Stage* (Oxford, 1923), 4: 263, 306.

96. Barnabe Barnes, *The Devil's Charter*, ed. R. B. McKerrow (Louvain, 1904), p. 54.

97. Ibid., p. 15.

98. *The Dramatic Works of Thomas Dekker*, ed. Fredson Bowers (Cambridge, 1964), 2: 497, 496.

99. The latest suggestion is the third Earl of Pembroke. Cf. Margot Heinemann, "Middleton's *A Game at Chess*: Parliamentary-Puritans and Opposition Drama," *English Literary Renaissance* 5 (1975): 232-50.

100. J. W. Harper, ed., *A Game at Chess* (London, 1966), p. xiii.

101. Gerald Eades Bentley, *The Jacobean and Caroline Stage* (Oxford, 1941-68), 4: 872. The Spanish ambassador may be guilty of special pleading, but cf. Heinemann's evidence of the crowds.

102. Cited by Harper, *Game at Chess*, p. xii. For priests in the audience of the Jacobean theater, see I. J. Semper, "The Jacobean Theater through the Eyes of Catholic Clerics," *Shakespeare Quarterly* 3 (1952): 45-51.

103. R. C. Bald, ed., *A Game of Chesse* (Cambridge, 1929), p. 88.

104. Ibid., pp. 11-12.

105. R. C. Bald, "An Early Version of Middleton's 'Game at Chesse,' " *Modern Language Review* 38 (1943): 177-80.

106. Bald, *Game at Chesse*, pp. 62-63.

107. I.iii. 109-10; ed. Virgil K. Whitaker, in Harbage, *Shakespeare*, p. 986.

108. Cf. Pineas, *Tudor and Stuart Anti-Catholic Drama*, passim.

109. AAW,A, 27: 6.

110. Edward Heawood, *Watermarks* (Hilversum [Holland], 1950), p. 26.

Hierarchomachia
or
The Anti-Bishop

Vindiciæ ✝ Sacræ.
compiled in
A
Comik Satyre.
entituled
Hierarchomachia,
or
The Anti-Bishop.
Written by one
Reuerardus:
that is,
Re vera } Ardens.
seu
Rei veritatis
A louer of Truth.
Against
Certaine new-found
Reformers:
and
Anarchists of this
time, of whom it
was longe since
prophecied.

And out of your owne-selues shall arise Men
speaking peruerse things, to drawe awaie dis=
ciples after them selues. Actes, 20. ver. 30.

Vindiciae Sacrae
Compiled in
A
Comic Satire
entitled
Hierarchomachia,
or
The Anti-Bishop,
Written by one
Reverardus:
that is,
Re vera }
seu } *Ardens.*
Rei veritatis }
A lover of truth
Against
Certain new-found
Reformers
And
Anarchists of this
time, of whom it
was long since
prophesied:

And out of your own selves shall arise men speaking perverse things, to draw away disciples after themselves. Actorum 20. versus 30.

The Authors Apologie for this Poem. To the Reader.

Good Reader;

My endeavor in this Comick Satyre, is to vindicate a truth, suppressed, and almost borne downe by a strong hand. The occasion a Controversie which hath sett a foote among Catholicks betweene their Sheppard and his flock, the Clergie and the Laity committed to his charge, wherein much abuse, and iniurie is offered to mens consciences. yet, neither side faultie, if both may be credited. The matter is now come to this height, that either a Soveraigne custome of the Church, must be abrogated, or a new forme of Government introduced, which may bring a world of badd consequences if it be passed over in silence, and the secret underminers of Hierarchie not touch'd their owne. I intended this worke, as a private satisfaction to myselfe, expressing those strange apprehensions I had of the dignitie of this opposition, which brought with it into my fancie the [illegible] of particular men, whom I knew to be the chiefe instruments, and setters on of this scandalous affront. yet I spare them not for it. let them thanke themselves, that spare not by their example to incense the zeale of the most submisse spirit, and make it sensible of a wronge offered to the very heart, and soule of Religion. The historicall passage of this Satyre are partly true, and partly fabulous, yet for the most part coming so neere the truth, as human conjecture could leade me, not being able to judge of the inward intentions of the men, but by their outward actions, nor of the causes, but by their effects. In which, conjecturall

The Author's Apology for this Poem. To the Reader.

Good Reader:

My endeavor in this comic satire is to vindicate a truth suppressed and almost borne down by [a] strong hand. The occasion a controversy lately set afoot among Catholics, between the shepherd and his flock, the bishop and the laity committed to his charge, wherein much abuse and injury is offered to men's consciences, yet neither side faulty, if both may be credited. The matter is now come to the height, that either a known custom of the church must be abrogated, or a new form of government introduced, which may bring a world of bad consequences if it be passed over in silence and the secret underminers of hierarchy not told their own. I intended this work as a private satisfaction to myself, expressing some strong apprehensions I had of the indignity of this opposition, which brought with it into my fancy the persons of particular men whom I know to be the chief instruments and setters-on of this scandalous affront. If I spare them not for it, let them thank themselves, that spare not by their example to incense the zeal of the most remiss spirit and make it sensible of a wrong offered to the very heart and soul of religion. The historical passages of this satire are partly true and partly fabulous, yet for the most part coming so near the truth as human conjecture could lead me, not being able to judge of the inward intentions of the men but by their outward actions, nor of the causes but by their effects. In which conjectural manner of proceeding, I take the libertie of a Poet, that is sometimes to faine more of the persons, then they may happily deserve, yet not more then the matter itselfe may iustly beare. For that, though I seeme to make them odious, or ridiculous by my fictions, it is with relation to a truth, implied in the cause itselfe, which they defend, and of which I dare boldly affirme, though not so much of them, that it is irreligious, and therefore liable to the worst of censures. For it is an abetting the Subiect in disobedience to his Spirituall Pastor, which in temporall causes, and against Princes, were high treason to attempt; what then is this, observing the proportion betwixt God and man, the soule and the bodie, but the highest oppression thereof. I leave them notwithstanding, that may seeme to be aimed and pointed at in this Comedie, in theire full freedome to take to themselves as much, or as little of the imputation laid upon them, as they list or can with a safe conscience, and wish them to be the lesse troubled, the more they finde themselves inwardly free from blame. For to an innocent man nothing can prove so glorious in the end, as to have his actions throughly tried, and his verie thoughts put to the test. In which respect I should not be much moved, to see my name brought on the stage, though to noe other end, then to serve as a scar-crowe, to affright the Spectators from doing ill. To all obiections whatsoever, that may bee made against me concerning this work, my present defence is

Pictoribus atq; Poetis
Quidlibet audendi semper fuit aequa potestas.
Painters and Poetts still
Have licence to be bould, and faine at will.

Bon

manner of proceeding, I take the liberty of a poet, that is sometimes to feign more of the persons than they may happily deserve, yet not more than the matter itself may justly exact. So that, though I seem to make them odious or ridiculous by my fictions, it is with relation to a truth implied in the cause itself which they defend, and of which I dare boldly affirm, though not so much of them, that it is irreligious and therefore liable to the worst of censures. For it is an abetting the subject in disobedience to his spiritual pastor, which in temporal causes and against princes were high treason to attempt; what then is this, observing the proportion betwixt God and man, the soul and the body, but the highest expression thereof? I leave them notwithstanding, that may seem to be any way pointed at in this comedy, in their full freedom to take to themselves as much or as little of the imputation laid upon them as they list or can with a safe conscience, and wish them to be the less troubled, the more they find themselves inwardly free from blame. For to an innocent man nothing can prove so glorious in the end as to have his actions thoroughly tried and his very thoughts put to the test. In which respect I should not be much moved to see my name brought on the stage, though to no other end than to serve as a scarecrow to affright the spectators from doing ill. To all objections whatsoever that may be made against me concerning this work, my present defence is:

Pictoribus atque poetis
Quidlibet audendi semper fuit aequa potestas.
Painters and poets still
Have license to be bold and feign at will.

Both with others; to witt, of Chamber & bedd,
I haue in a manner performed; yet am I not
such an hauer of priuiledge, that I will not
willingly submitt myselfe to the Judgement
of good men; or refuse to be tryed by God,
and my Countrey; And soe I make an end
with this protestation: That noe spleene, or
malice to the men I seeme here perticulary
to taxe, much lesse to their callinge, and institute, both which I carry reuerence, and respect,
hath moued me to write this inuectiue; but
onely an auersion I haue, as is said before,
from the opposition itselfe, and the vnworthy
manner of resisting in it, as if it were a
lawfull and a meritorious deede, hath in a
manner extorted from me this courage to
strike at a notorious abuse; though withall
I cannott refuse peirce through the sides both
of the Authors, and the Abettors Complott.
ffarwell.

Your freind and
Wellwisher.

Reuerardus.

Both which offices, to wit, of painter and poet, I have in a manner performed; yet am I no such enhancer of privileges that I will not willingly submit myself to the judgment of good men, or refuse to be tried by God and my country. And so I make an end with this protestation: that no spleen or malice to the men I seem here particularly to tax, much less to their callings and institutes, both which I much reverence and respect, hath moved me to write this invective; but only an aversion I have, as is said before, from the opposition itself and the unworthy manner of persisting in it, as if it were a lawful and a meritorious act, hath in a manner extorted from me this courage to strike at a notorious abuse; though withal I cannot choose pierce through the sides both of the authors and the abettors themselves. Farewell.

Your friend and
wellwisher,
Reverardus.

The persons or Speakers.
Grex.

1. Thorulus; a Protestant } Ministers.
2. Lucianus; a Puritan. }
3. Erudius; a Guelf, or follower of the Bishop.
4. Candle; a Neutralist, or time Critick.
5. Bolnutus; Mr. Ghibellin, and kt. of ye goulden fleece.
6. Jargus; his second.
7. Onoplutus; his procurator.
8. Coredurus; Mr. Ghibellin of the kts. of Malta.
9. Spirius; his second.
10. Sapertonus; a Ghibellin writter of that Order.
11. Dauus; his vndertaker.
12. Nicodimus; Mr. Ghibellin of ye kts. of St. James.
13. Pamoppus; his second.
14. Polinodus; als Nodipol. } lay Champions for the Ghibellins.
15. Corbus. }
16. Rudelbinus. }
17. Bittomattus; a concealed Ghibellin.
19. Aggaeus, his politick freind.
19. Nicetta. } Ladies diversly affected, ye { 1. To ye Bps. Cause.
20. Valeria. } { 2. To ye kts. of Malta.
21. Celia. } { 3. To those of ye golden fleece.
22. A Seruant.
23. Roes. } Pursuants.
24. Milston. }
25. Finger. }
26. Amoy. }
27. Constable with Officers.

Hierarchomachia or The Anti-Bishop

The Persons or Speakers

Grex

1. *Therulus, a Protestant* } *Ministers*
2. *Lucianus, a Puritan* } *Ministers*

3. *Erudius, a Guelf, or follower of the bishop*
4. *Candle, a neutralist, or time critic*
5. *Bolnutus, Master Ghibelline and Knight of the Golden Fleece*
6. *Jargus, his second*
7. *Onoplutus, his procurator*
8. *Coredurus, Master Ghibelline of the Knights of Malta*
9. *Spirius, his second*
10. *Sapertonus, a Ghibelline writer of that order*
11. *Davus, his undertaker*
12. *Nicodimus, Master Ghibelline of the Knights of Saint James*
13. *Pamoppus, his second*
14. *Polinodus, alias Nodipol* } *Lay Champions for the Ghibellines*
15. *Corbus* } *Lay Champions for the Ghibellines*
16. *Rudelbinus* } *Lay Champions for the Ghibellines*
17. *Bitomattus, a concealed Ghibelline*
18. *Aggeus, his politic friend*
19. *Nivetta* } *Ladies diversely affected the* { 1. *to the bishop's cause*
20. *Valeria* } *Ladies diversely affected the* { 2. *to the Knights of Malta*
21. *Celia* } *Ladies diversely affected the* { 3. *to those of the Golden Fleece*
22. *A Servant*
23. *Rocs* } *Pursuivants*
24. *Milston* } *Pursuivants*
25. *Finger* } *Pursuivants*
26. *Amoy* } *Pursuivants*
27. *Constable with Officers*

The Introduction

Therulus ~ Lucianus.

Th. Lucian, a word. Lu. who calls? Th. 'Tis Therulus.
Lu. What newes? Th. have you not heard what stirrs of late
Are raisd in Brittriana? Lu. No, nor care.
Th. Thou knowest the manie fractions of this Land,
That like so manie severall springs have flow'd
Even through the vaines, and sinewes of our State
Thou knowest as well how these, and they have sway'd
The comons who have declinde of free will
To shune and Libertie, but to doome
And heavenly things we have not lost a part
For feare to erre, but by meere constraint
And force of heavenly power and to our hate
Wee have not only drawen the multitude
But those that sitt at helme and guide our State,
Although with different mindes, as they are mov'd
With time, or money, or with their owne conceipte.
Our adverse partie though with forraine fraude
They strengthned are, yet are they bound to the lawes,
And cannot interrupt, or stopp our course.
Lu. All this I knowe and more; but what's the newes?
Th. 'Tis true, I had forgott. why we are friends.
Lu. The divell we are. Th. Beleeve it, though our streames
Of doctrine from diverse sources runn,
And thou dost hold the head of little ruffe,
Starcht beards, prunde night-capps, yea's and nay's
With their turnd upp, and nothing stone, but nositers.
And I from Parliament am taught by faith
To oppose Religion hand in hand with the State
As kinge and times direct, which thou abhorr'st.
Yet now against a common adversarie

'Tis

Hierarchomachia or The Anti-Bishop

The Introduction

Therulus, Lucianus.

Therulus. Lucian, a word.
Lucianus. Who calls?
Therulus. 'Tis Therulus.
Lucianus. What news?
Therulus. Have you not heard what stirs of late
Are raised in Bintriana?
Lucianus. No, declare.
Therulus. Thou knowest the many fractions of this land,
That like so many several springs have flowed
Even through the veins and sinews of our state;
Thou knowest withal how thou and I have swayed
The Commons with our doctrine of free will
To sin and liberty, but to divine
And heavenly things we have not left a gap
For grace to enter—but by mere constraint
And force of heavenly power—and to our parts
We have not only drawn the multitude
But those that sit at helm and guide our state,
Although with different minds, as they are moved
With thine, or mine, or with their own conceits.
Our adverse party, though with foreign friends
They strengthened are, yet are they bound with laws,
And cannot interrupt or stop our course—
Lucianus. All this I know and more, but what's the news?
Therulus. 'Tis true, I had forgot. Why we are friends.
Lucianus. The devil we are.
Therulus. Believe it, though our streams
Of doctrine from divided sources run,
And thou beest held the head of little ruffs,
Starched beards, perfumèd night-caps, yea's and nay's
With eyes turned up and nothing seen but whites,
And I from parliaments am taught by faith
To join religion hand in hand with state
As kings and times direct, which thou abhorr'st,
Yet now against a common adversary

Tis fitt wee ioyne. The Papists haue obtain'd
A Bishop for their head. Lu. The Lord forbide
That ragg of Popery ~~[illegible]~~ renew'd againe.
Doth the right wor:ll his Maiestie
And our beloued Brethren the Lords,
That sitt in Councell, sleepe? Th. Not sleepe, but winke
A while at this, or for a time connive;
But now they are awake. Lu. They did as were?
Th. Many than; the Papists nowe deuided are
Into two factions, much like this and mine:
One for the Bp stands, the other strives
him to suppresse, and his authoritie;
For though the Pope hath plac'd him at the sterne
To rule the lay-Catholiks with full scope,
And with as ample faculties, as may
Any Bishopps or Archbpps power compare
Over their flocke. yea, though three gentle Cardinalls,
And 3. Popes Bulls haue fortified his claime,
Of Prelacie, and seeme to approue,
And made it cleere as heauen, in London here
Not to be question'd; yet sublimer witts
Are found, that slight him. Those affect a State
In theire affaires, that smells of Anarchy,
Much like to this. Lu. A godly, pious care,
And edifying much, were it not spoilt
With Romish superstition: but proceede
I longed to heare how this hath vext the State,
That are not wont to favour Anarchies,
And for this cause haue sleight'd me, and made
Our Tribe of Levi oft to hold their tongues,
A most ungodly practise, but goe on.
Th. These Anarchiste or Antihierarchiste
Are subdevided into three Commaunds.
The first, and strongest side, though least knowne
Unto the Christian world, Bolandist rules.

The 2d.

'Tis fit we join. The Papists have obtained
A bishop for their head.
Lucianus. The Lord forbid!
That rag of popery renewed again!
Doth the right worshipful his Majesty,
And our belovèd bretheren, the lords
That sit in council, sleep?
Therulus. Not sleep, but wink
A nod or so, or for a time connive;
But now they are awake.
Lucianus. Pray say, as how?
Therulus. Why thus: the Papists now divided are
Into two factions much like thine and mine:
One for the bishop stands, the other strives
Him to suppress, and his authority.
For though the pope hath placed him at the stern
To rule the lay-recusants with full scope,
And with as ample faculties as may
With bishop's or archbishop's power compare
Over their flocks; yea, though three general councils
And three pope's bulls have fortified his claim
Of prelacy and virtue to approve,
And made it clear as heaven, in common sense
Not to be questioned, yet sublimer wits
Are found that [slight] him. These affect a state
In church affairs that smell of anarchy,
Much like to thine.
Lucianus. A godly project sure,
And edifying much, were it not choked
With Romish superstition, but proceed.
I long to hear how this hath waked the state,
That are not wont to favor anarchies,
And for this cause have silenced me, and made
Our tribe of Levi oft to hold their tongues—
A most ungodly practice—but go on.
Therulus. These anarchists or antihierarchists
Are subdivided into three commands.
The first and strongest part, though latest known
Unto the Christian world, Bolnutus rules;

The second Creatures. and the last,
And least in number are Nicodemus:
For other Captaines dare not ioyne, for feare
This may be counted Schisme in after times,
And their Credits may become a blurre.
Lu. A foolish feare forsooth. yf it be schisme
To roote out Bishops, and sett Elders upp
To fill their places, I am much deceaued.
Why then, and I would further, wee abiur'd
And shooke the Popes authoritie to clowts,
And yet wee holde ourselues no schismaticks.
Th. Unles to one another, wee are none.
Lu. Tis true, thou art a Consubstantialist,
And therefore damn'd. Th. Thou art an Arrian.
A Jewe, a Turke, an Atheist. Lu. hould, noe more
Wee shall fall out, and marr our sport in hand.
Goe forward with the free-fold Anarchists.
Th. All these by priviledge are growne so great,
That notwithstanding their religious vowes,
That pleade the contrary they doe pretend
An equall portion with the Ministers private
Under the Lay-Covenant, with [illegible]
They strengthen thus. That they had leave to preach,
Teach, and administer the Sacrament
Before his coming. therefore why not still?
As for the generall Councell, that commands
The Bishops approbation should be askt,
Before they heare Confessions of the Lay,
Tis not regarded they saie, when the Lawe,
Because not published, and if published,
Tis by a power that contradicts the State.
Lu. There's come in the State a prettie close,
Me thinks the State should much commend them for't
To gratifie them for their witte pardes.
Th. Their writers printed [illegible]; for such their follies,

The

The second Coredurus; and the last
And least in number, one Nicodimus.
For other captains dare not join, for fear
This may be counted schism in aftertimes,
And so their credits may receive a blur.

Lucianus. A foolish fear, forsooth. If it be schism
To root out bishops and set elders up
To fill their places, I am much deceived.
Why thou and I went further, we abjured
And shook the pope's authority to clouts,
And yet we hold ourselves no schismatics.

Therulus. Unless to one another, we are none.

Lucianus. 'Tis true, thou art a consubstantialist,
A therefore damned.

Therulus. Thou art an Arian,
A Jew, a Turk, an atheist.

Lucianus. Hold, no more.
We shall fly high and mar our sport in hand.
Go forward with thy threefold anarchists.

Therulus. All these by privilege are grown so great
That notwithstanding their religious vows
That plead the contrary, they do pretend
An equal portion with the bishop's power
Over the lay-recusants, which pretense
They strengthen thus: that they had leave to preach,
Teach, and administer the sacraments
Before his coming, therefore why not still?
As for the general council that commands
The bishop's approbation should be asked
Before they hear confessions of the lay,
'Tis not received, they say, within the land,
Because not published, and if published,
'Tis by a power that contradicts the state.

Lucianus. O here comes in the state, a pretty close.
Methinks the state should much commend them for't
To gratify them for their witty pains.

Therulus. Their witty pains indeed; for by this fetch

The Lay are strucke with feare, as they suppose,
And dare not shewe their heads, in his behalfe.
Yea, some affected partially to them,
Or els affrighted with the onely words
Of power, and State, forgetting that the cause
Is for Religion, and the roote of Scismes
Wch they want powre to bynde, as well as loose
Can hardly stand (this saith the Hierarchists)
They in a publicke writing without name,
Yet in the name of all, though some knowe of it,
Proscribe the Bishop, and renounce his power
Irrevocably, resolutely bent
Never to yeeld a iot. Lu. My spirit sinks.
Th. And myne I trowe, I should be sorry els.
Nowe then the State, that hitherto sat still
To see the issue, having found the knott,
That heretofore was hard to loose, not broke,
Now readie by contention to dissolue
(As common policie them taught) struck in,
And siding with the weaker cause, have made
The poize runne even, that wch advantage drewe
The other scale, that now the Bishops part
Inclines against. Wch action I approve
Against the Papists, though amongst ourselves
The practise were unlawfull. Lu. Not a iot.
I would our Bishops to this passe were brought
Those great Arminian Bulls and Scripture Rams.
Th. Ware, least thou fore stirr choller. Lu. I have done,
A word, or two in zeale, and I have done.
But now, what did the State; what said the King?
Th. Two severall Proclamations from the Kinge
Were by the Lords sent out to apprehend him;
But yet he is not found. Lu. Tis pittie sure,
I longue to see him marche up Holborne hill,
And one to followe after, and be hang'd.

Th. You

The lay are struck with fear, as they suppose,
And dare not show their heads in his behalf.
Yea, some affected partially to them,
Or else affrighted with the only words
Of *power* and *state*, forgetting that the cause
Is for religion and the good of souls,
Which without power to bind as well as loose
Can hardly stand (thus say the hierarchists)—
They in a public writing without name,
Yet in the name of all, though few knew of it,
Proscribe the bishop and renounce his power,
Irrevocably, resolutely bent
Never to yield a jot.

Lucianus. My spirit right.

Therulus. And mine I trow, I should be sorry else.
Now then the state, that hitherto sat still
To see the issue, having found the knot
That heretofore was hard to loose, not broke,
Now ready by contention to dissolve,
(As common policy them taught) struck in,
And siding with the weaker cause have made
The poise run even, that with advantage drew
The other scale, that now the bishop's part
Inclines again. Which action I approve
Against the Papists, though among ourselves
The practice were unlawful.

Lucianus. Not a jot.
I would our bishops to this pass were brought,
Those great Arminian bulls and scripture rams.

Therulus. Peace, lest thou stir choler.

Lucianus. I have done.
A word or two in zeal, and I have done.
But now what did the state? What said the pope?

Therulus. Two several proclamations from the king
Were by the lords procured to apprehend him,
But yet he is not found.

Lucianus. 'Tis pity sure;
I long to see him march up Holborn hill,
And ours to follow after and be hanged.

Th. You Sir are rude: and worke upon my spleene.
Lu. forbeare, the qualme is past, a pang of zeale
Possest my part. Th. The Divell take such panges.
Well, to be breif, The Pope, to whom this cause
Is nowe referr'd, stands doubtfull what to doe
For though he much distaste these Anarchists,
That calle his Bishops in question, wch in former
Times ordinarie power over the Lay,
And thus in secret seeme to undermine
His power, and Judgment in creating them;
Yet for respect he beares unto the State,
Who are become a partie, he forbeares,
To censure them (for seeing not constrain'd
Are loath directly to oppose that cause
An other Princes plotts) the sporte remaines,
While matters are suspended, to observe
The strange invented plotts of Anarchists
To shift their Bishopp off, their dreames, and tales
Of newe decrees against him, all to gull,
And stupefie the Laitie, that expect
Some miracles be done in their behalfe;
The wiser sort saie little, but see more,
And much suspect all is not gould, that shines;
The summe of this exprest in lively showes
Shall in a Comedy to day be showne.
Within this place. Say, will you sitt by me,
And see it acted. Lu. Though it be prophane
To see these common plaies, yet for this once
My Spirit moves me to sitt downe. Th. Then knowe
(For I have read the play) in fained names
This Storie is contriv'd, least you mistake
Those of the Bishopps side are called Guelfes,
The other Ghibellins (of two factious States,
That sometime wasted Italie with warrs
These sorts of Ghibellins, knights of St James

Are

Therulus. You still are rude and work upon my spleen.
Lucianus. Forbear, the qualm is past, a pang of zeal
Possessed my heart.
Therulus. The devil take such pangs!
Well, to be brief: The pope, to whom this cause
Is now referred, stands doubtful what to do,
For though he much distastes these anarchists
That call his brief in question, which in terms
Gives ordinary power over the lay,
And thus in secret seem to undermine
His power and judgment in creating him,
Yet for respect he bears unto the state,
Who are become a party, he forbears
To censure them (for princes not constrained
Are loath directly to oppose that cause
Another prince protects). The sport remains,
While matters are suspended, to observe
The strange invented plots of anarchists
To shift their bishop off, their dreams and tales
Of new decrees against him, all to gull
And stupefy the laity, that expect
Some miracles be done in their behalf.
The wiser sort say little but see more,
And much suspect all is not gold that shines.
The sum of this expressed in lively scenes
Shall in a comedy today be shown
Within this place. Say, wilt thou sit by me
And see it acted?
Lucianus. Though it be profane
To see these common plays, yet for this once
My spirit moves me to sit down. [*They sit.*]
Therulus. Then know
(For I have read the play) in feignèd names
This story is contrived. Lest thou mistake,
Those of the bishop's side are callèd Guelfs,
The other Ghibellines (of two factious states
That sometime wasted Italy with wars).
Three sorts of Ghibellines, Knights of Saint James

Are nam'd, of Malta, and the Goulden ffleece,
Under these heads: Nicodemus of St. James,
Of Malta Coredurus; of the goulde
En ffleece Bolnutus. for the Guelfes are stil'd
[illegible] with their Leaders of the holy Ghost:
But now the Musicke sounds, the Prologue comes.

The Prologue.

The Author of this Comedy instil'd
The Antichrist, bade me to explaine
his purest meaning to your nobler thought,
Gentle Spectators first he bids you frame
This climate, under the Antarticke pole,
Where our Antipodes a famous Ile
Call'd Bintriana hath, and there our Scene
Whose subiect is a Bishop in disgrace,
Scorn'd, and neglected by his owne flocke,
Strange president: The Spirits, that him oppose,
Are in this present Comedy describ'd.
The Author grounds it here upon report
And here, in knowledge, being full inform'd
Both of the men, and actions: for whose sake
he wisheth all were fictions here set downe,
And nothing reall, but his paines to write
he onely is compell'd to paint them forth,
That stick up [illegible] in their [illegible] fame,
That wound his credit, take away his right,
And all to further their preposterous ends.
Yet are their names obscur'd, their deeds made knowne
That none can take ought ill, but what's his owne.
Warrs without blood are these, yet wound they deepe.
Tis pittie from one such [illegible] worlds should weepe.
The Author takes his leave, and saies in these
he studies as much their profit, as to please.

Actus

Are named, of Malta, and the Golden Fleece,
Under three heads: Nicodimus of Saint James,
Of Malta Coredurus, of the Gold-
En Fleece Bolnutus. For the Guelfs are styled
Knight with their leader of the Holy Ghost:
But now the music sounds, the prologue comes.

The Prologue

Prologue. The author of this comedy enstyled
The Anti-Bishop sends me to explain
His honest meaning to your nobler thoughts.
Gentle spectators, first he bids you frame
This climate under the Antarctic pole,
Where our antipodes, a famous isle
Called Bintriana, lies, and there our scene,
Whose subject is a bishop in disgrace,
Scorned and neglected by his proper flock,
Strange precedent! The chief that him oppose
Are in this present comedy described.
The author grounds it part upon report
And part in knowledge, being full informed
Both of the men and actions, for whose sake
He wisheth all were fictions here set down,
And nothing real but his pains to write.
He only is provoked to paint them forth
That stick up censures in their bishop's fame,
That pound his credit, take away his right,
And all to further their preposterous ends.
Yet are their names obscured, their deeds made known
That none can take aught ill, but what's his own.
Wars without blood are these, yet wound they deep.
'Tis pity from one faith such works should creep.
The author takes his leave, and says in these
He seeks as much your profit, as to please.

Actus Primus.

Scena Prima.

Erudius Candle.

Pray, gentle Candle hould, forbeare extreames,
Bee not so passionate. Can. Erudius
I pray, stand a side, and give my fury vent,
Or els my hart will breake: Shall I endure
To see religion by these dayes abus'd,
And yet stand mute, and patient like an Asse:
Eru. I prithee what religion dost thou meane:
For thou hast none. Can. I tell thee to have none
Is better, then have one in these daies.
Eru. Sure thou mistak'st? Can. Erudius, art thou sure?
Are these myne eyes? is this the aire? that heaven?
Eru. Admit they were, what then? Can. Admit they were,
Is it not plaine. Eru. how plaine? mayst thou not sleepe,
And apprehend all these; and thinke thou see;
Then wake, and finde thy selfe deceav'd? Can. how's this,
Why sure I live, and breath, past all receipt.
Eru. yet some imagine they are dead, that live.
Can. Some melancholy fooles: Eru. Thou art more madd,
That think'st thou art alive, when thou art dead.
Can. Dead? Eru. yes. Thou only hast a walking tongue,
That like a Ghost doth haunt the world, and wails
That cries upon the vice of every man;
As it would blast them with a poisonous breath,
When all the rest, that was of thee lyes dead
Intombd in thine owne ordure, and rakt up
In ashes of selfe-ignorance, and pride.
Ca. Why this discourse will make me madd indeede.
Er. Art thou a likely man to taxe the age
Of follies, and abuses, that art thyselfe

Tho

Actus primus

Scena prima

Erudius, Candle.

Erudius. Pray, gentle Candle, hold, forbear extremes,
Be not so passionate.
Candle. Erudius,
Pray stand aside and give my fury vent,
Or else my heart will break. Shall I endure
To see religion by these apes abused,
And yet stand mute and patient like an ass?
Erudius. I prithee what religion dost thou mean?
For thou hast none.
Candle. I tell thee to have none
Is better than have any in these days.
Erudius. Sure thou mistak'st.
Candle. Erudius, art thou here?
Are these mine eyes? Is this the air? that heaven?
Erudius. Admit they were, what then?
Candle. Admit they were,
Is it not plain?
Erudius. How plain? Mayst thou not sleep
And apprehend all these and think them so,
Then wake and find thyself deceived?
Candle. How's this?
Why sure I live and breathe past all conceit.
Erudius. Yet some imagine they are dead, that live.
Candle. Some melancholy fools.
Erudius. Thou art more mad,
That think'st thou art alive when thou art dead.
Candle. Dead?
Erudius. Yes. Thou only hast a walking tongue,
That like a ghost doth haunt the world and rail,
That tires upon the vices of each man
As it would blast them with a poisonous breath,
When all the rest that was of thee lies dead,
Entombed in thine own ordure, and racked up
In ashes of self-ignorance and pride.
Candle. Why this discourse will make me mad indeed.
Erudius. Art thou a likely man to tax this age
Of folly and abuse, that art thyself

The most abused man, and dost commit
The greatest follie, that the world hath knowne.
Ca. As how? Ex. To saie there is not God. Ca. I'le sweare
I never said so; only that 'tis best
To be of noe Religion in these daies.
Ex. As much to say, there is no God. Ca. graunt that,
And I'le confesse, I am a carrion Atheist.
Ex. What is the king to thee, if not ador'd
With due respect, and reverence of a kinge?
What God, if not acknowledg'd? Ca. Still the same.
Ex. Is he the same to thee, whom thou denyest?
Ca. To me he is not. Ex. Thou to thee noe God,
Thou noe Creator, thou art then no man,
Because noe Creature, thou art then starke dead,
Nay thou art nothing, but by wanting forme
Of grace, and of Religion thou art made
A thing worse nothing, worse then foole, or asse.
Ca. So that Religion is the forme thou saist,
That makes, or unmakes man. Ex. Fitt for this end,
Where mist, the whole miscarries. Ca. heare you Sere,
What is Religion, but an idle sound,
A name, a forme of speech, got in the braine,
Begott by fancie upon ignorance,
Maintain'd by policie to master fooles,
And keepe the world in awe? Ex. A rare discourse,
Goe on. Ca. were it a substance, else confin'd
In circumstance of tyme, or place, or man,
It would be found. Ex. And is to those, that seeke.
Ca. Why, I have sought it amongst all the sects,
That raigne this day, and fill the world with lyes.
More then patience, I finde no right to truth
In anie man, or woman. Ex. yet thou think'st
'Tis truth thou speak'st it. Ca. And will maintaine it so.
Ex. Thou art then neither man nor woman Sere,
But some hobgoblin, there's no truth in man.

Ca. Why

The most abusèd man, and dost commit
The greatest folly that the world hath known?
Candle. As how?
Erudius. To say there is not God.
Candle. I'll swear
I never said so, only that 'tis best
To be of no religion in these days.
Erudius. As much to say, there is no God.
Candle. Prove that,
And I'll confess I am a carrion corpse.
Erudius. What is the king to thee, if not adored
With due respect and reverence of a king?
What God, if not acknowledged?
Candle. Still the same.
Erudius. Is he the same to thee, whom thou deni'st?
Candle. To me he is not.
Erudius. Then to thee no God,
Then no creator, then art thou no man
Because no creature, then art thou stark dead,
Nay, thou art nothing. Thus by wanting form
Of grace and of religion thou art made
A thing worth nothing, worse than fool or ass.
Candle. So that religion is the form, thou sayst,
That makes or unmakes man.
Erudius. Fit for his end,
Which missed, the whole miscarries.
Candle. Hold you there.
What is religion but an airy sound,
A name, a form of speech hatched in the brain,
Begot by fancy upon ignorance,
Maintained by policy to master fools
And keep the world in awe?
Erudius. A rare discourse,
Go on.
Candle. Were it a substance, else confined
In circumstance of time, or place, or men,
It would be found.
Erudius. And is to those that seek.
Candle. Why, I have sought it among all the sects
That reign this day and fill the world with lies.
More than patience, I find no right to truth
In any man or woman.
Erudius. Yet thou think'st
'Tis truth thou speak'st.
Candle. And will maintain it so.
Erudius. Then art thou neither man nor woman sure,
But some hobgoblin; there's no truth in man.

Ca. Fye on't, this consistent confirmes me quite.
Er. But say, what figures doe these Pretenders prove?
Ca. One saies he hath the Spirit; but who knowes
Whether the same be black, or white – not I.
Another pleads the word: I take his word,
Just as his honestie, not worth a ~~[struck]~~ strawe.
A third referrs me to the Church, and there
He leaves me to looke out I know not what,
Nor here, nor where, nor when, where am I lost,
As in a Labyrinth; at last stepps forth
A learned Papist bidding me inquire
For a direct Succession of Men
Under one head, united in one lawe,
Consenting in one faith deriv'd from Christ,
And ruled by his substitute the Pope.
The Pope, said I? what is he? Man or God?
Man he replies. Then may he be deceav'd.
In human things he may; what warrant then
have I to trust his judgment in divine?
Christ's promise made to Peter, next to him
As his Successor, then the holy Ghost
Sent as a seale of a Truth unto his Church
Not to be cancell'd, while the world endures.
Then shewes me certaine Markes to finde this Church,
Soe visible, and plaine, as nothing more.
There, I confesse, I was overcome'd, and joy'd
To see this Storie of the world, the truth
Contained in her whole, and proper picture.
But ~~[struck]~~ here. Er. Then plaid'st the foole againe, I feare.
Ca. I staid not long before I tooke disgust
Not at the faith, and Church, but at the men,
That both profest, yet in their lives were foes
denying Christ, his Church, their faith and all
On all occasions. Most were vulgar men,
And of the baser ranke, not mov'd the same,
The Gentrie, that knowe more, yet did the same,

Those

Candle. Pox on't, this sophistry confounds me quite.
Erudius. But say, what signs do these pretenders show?
Candle. One says he hath the spirit, but who knows
Whether the same be black or white? not I.
Another pleads the word: I take his word,
Just as his honesty, not worth a straw.
A third refers me to the church, and there
He leaves me to look out I know not what,
Nor how, nor where, nor when; here am I lost
As in a labyrinth. At last steps forth
A learned Papist bidding me inquire
For a direct succession of men
Under one head, united in one law,
Consenting in one faith derived from Christ,
And rulèd by his substitute the pope.
"The pope?" say I. "What is he? man or god?"
"Man," he replies. "Then may he be deceived."
"In human things he may." "What warrant then
Have I to trust his judgment in divine?"
"Christ['s] promise made to Peter, next to him
As his successor, then the Holy Ghost
Sent as a seal of a truth unto his church,
Not to be canceled while the world endures."
Then shows me certain marks to find this church
So visible and plain as nothing more.
Here, I confess, I was convinced, and joyed
To see this phoenix of the world, the truth,
Containèd in her sole and proper sphere.
But here—
Erudius. Thou played'st the fool again, I fear.
Candle. I stayed not long before I took disgust
Not at the faith and church, but at the men
That both professed, yet in their lives were Jews,
Denying Christ, his church, their faith and all
On all occasions. Most were vulgar men
And of the baser rank, nor moved they much
The gentry, that knew more, yet did the same.

These Haggards me to see their best expresse.
There gameing, whoreing, drinking, and the like.
But then the pride of smaller schooles we dumbe.
Er. A happie chance, couldst thou haue so remain'd.
Ca. Now I together for example should I goe:
Er. Whereto thyselfe, thou shouldst haue first begun,
The rest would followe soone. Ca. The diuell as soone;
Next I survey the clergie, their worth
With scholars, and Teachers. Er. What of these?
Ca. Faith, these are men. Er. Why there you found itt a towne
What wouldst thou more? Ca. Such men, Erudius.
Er. As were not theire. Ca. Nay worse. Er. As haue their faults.
Ca. not small ones, my Erudius. Er. Well forbeare.
Here's companie will interrupt our talke.
Ile finde a tyme to rid thee of these doubts,
And sett thy soule at libertie againe.

Scena Secunda.

Bolnutus, Targus. Erudius. Candle.

Targus. Ta. My Lord. Bol. Knowe you these two?
Ta. not well.
Bo. Are they beleeuers? Tar. yes the one, but stands not
well affected to our cause, a Guelfe.
The other is a Neutralist, or Critick,
But rather more inclined to the Guelfs.
Bol. Then let them passe untill we finde a tyme
To fitt their turnes. Tar. It seemes they meane to stand,
And stare vs in the face, I'le drawe. Bol. fforbeare,
The lawe forbidds such trialls; speake them faire.
Tar. Gentlemen; by your leaue. Erud. Our leaue you haue
With our best wishes. Cand. Lett's stand a side.
Bol. Why, sure he is a ffreind. Tar. Beleiue it not
Is he a ffreind, that is not wholly ours.
Bol. I grant, we ought not to admitt such ffreinds
Because we should resemble God, that saies
He is against him, that not with him fights.

yet for

These staggered me to see their vast excess,
Their [gaming], whoring, drinking, and the like.
But then the pride of females struck me dumb.
Erudius. A happy chance, couldst thou have so remained.
Candle. Now whither for example should I go?
Erudius. Why to thyself. Thou shouldst have first begun,
The rest would follow soon.
Candle. The devil as soon.
Next I survey the clergy, which consists
Of seculars and regulars.
Erudius. What of these?
Candle. Faith, these are men.
Erudius. Why here thou found'st a truth—
What wouldst thou more?
Candle. Such men, Erudius.
Erudius. As were no gods.
Candle. Nay worse.
Erudius. As have their faults.
Candle. Not small ones, my Erudius.
Erudius. Well, forbear.
Here's company will interrupt our talk.
I'll find a time to rid thee of these doubts
And set thy soul at liberty again.

Scena secunda

Bolnutus, Jargus, Erudius, Candle.

Bolnutus. Jargus.
Jargus. My lord.
Bolnutus. Know you these two?
Jargus. Not well.
Bolnutus. Are they believers?
Jargus. Yes, the one, but stands
Not well affected to our cause, a Guelf.
The other is a neutralist or critic,
But rather more inclined to the Guelfs.
Bolnutus. Then let them pass until we find a time
To fit their turns.
Jargus. It seems they mean to stand
And stare us in the face; I'll draw.
Bolnutus. Forbear,
The law forbids such trials; speak them fair.
Jargus. [*To Candle and Erudius*.] Gentlemen; by your leave.

(*text continued on following page*)

Yet for our ends we often tymes are forc'd
To use indifferent freinds, but how like mules
To travaile for us, with small thankes, but still
Without reward. Tar. A christian policie.
Bol. But Sirra, we are alone; have you receiv'd
The letters, that were sent from forraigne parts?
Tar. I have. Bol. What newes? Tar. Tis writt fro Rome, y^t they
Absolve the Bishopps cause against our plea,
Our informations cannott worke effect
For by the Crowne he is equall made
In power with Bishopps in their diocesse.
Bol. Tut, I will put a spoke into this wheele,
If Coredurus will but second me,
Shall stoppe his course. But here our gaine consists
To drawe this Coredurus to our part,
With all his knights of Malta, for till nowe
Wee never could induce them, nor they us;
The plott lyes in my head to make us freindes.
What newes from other parts? Tar. ffrom Flanders these
The Nunns, that hitherto were rul'd by us
Are in revolt, and would put off our yoake;
They have solicited the Guelfes to ioyne
Whoe favour'd by the ordinary, have
made entrie in our place. Bol. Have they so?
Worke braines as thou wilt want, and I shall crosse
Their newe designes. Are here noe voices left
Amongst the Nunns to stickle for us? Tar. Yes.
But three above the rest, that roare it out
As if they with our Spirit were possest.
Bol. Soft Targus, tis not ours, to roare so lowde,
Wee best can bite in secret, and unseene;
Lett's pardon out the nuns that in our place
confesse

Erudius. Our leave you have
With our best wishes.
Candle. [*To Erudius.*] Let's stand aside.
Bolnutus. Why, sure he is a friend.
Jargus. Believe it not.
Is he a friend that is not wholly ours?
Bolnutus. I grant we use not to admit such friends
Because we should resemble God, that says
He is against him that not with him fights.

Yet for our ends we oftentimes are forced
To use indifferent friends, but how like mules:
To travail for us with small thanks, but still
Without reward.
Jargus. A Christian policy.
Bolnutus. But since we are alone: have you surviewed
The letters that were sent from foreign parts?
Jargus. I have.
Bolnutus. What news?
Jargus. 'Tis writ from Rome, the pope
Abets the bishop's cause against our plea.
Our informations cannot work effect,
For by the breve he is equal made
In power with bishops in their diocese.
Bolnutus. Tut, I will put a spoke into this wheel,
If Coredurus will but second me,
Shall stop his course. But here our gain consists
To draw this Coredurus to our part,
With all his knights of Malta, for till now
We never could endure them, nor they us;
The plot lies in my head to make us friends.
What news from other parts?
Jargus. From Sluxber these:
The nuns, that hitherto were ruled by us,
Are in revolt and would put off our yoke;
They have solicited the Guelfs to join,
Who, favored by the ordinary, have
Made entry in our places.
Bolnutus. Have they so?
Work brain as thou wert wont, and I shall cross
Their new designs. Are there no voices left
Among the nuns to stickle for us?
Jargus. Yes.
But three above the rest, that roar it out.
As if they with our spirit were possessed.
Bolnutus. Soft, Jargus, 'tis not ours to roar so loud;
We best can bite in secret and unseen.
Let's harken out the men that in our place

Confesse those Names, and were they Saints Ile finde
A waie to bringe their Credit on the Stage,
And spott them with Aspersions, that shall dye
their soules in graine. But first there must be found
Some man of valiant ingenuous at home
That dares so farr be ours, as right or wronge
Shall not disturbe him from the first conceipt
That what wee doe, is iust, in all respects;
And that to contradict it were a Crime.
This man with my Instructions shalbe sett
To bringe this Stratagem about. No more;
Here's Coredurus with his frend-selfe,
Lett's heare their talke, You enter at our Cue.

Scena tertia.

Coredurus, Spirius, Bolnutus, Iargus.

Spirius, my word is past. Spi. Recall it back,
Make you so precious of a blast of aire?
What else are words? Cor. Why, they are Relatives,
And sett a morall value on the man
Whose words they are. Should I be false of word
I were unfitt for humane intercourse.
Spir. True, were they with advantage to be kept
But when with prejudice they are observ'd
And threaten losse, who keepes them is a foole.
Cor. What prejudice to me to be approv'd
And by a lawfull Bishop? Spir. Yes of Clownes.
Admitt he were, why, we are made his sheepe
By auncient Charter, Ordinaries beinge,
Invested with Archbishops power, in time
of vacant Seas, with right to binde or loose
In either Courts, we have bene little sheepe;
And shall

Confess these nuns, and were they saints, I'll find
A way to bring their credit on the stage
And spot them with aspersions that shall dye
Their souls in grain. But first there must be found
Some man of valiant impudence at home
That dares so far be ours as right or wrong
Shall not disturb him from the fixed conceit
That what we do is just in all respects,
And that to contradict it were a sin.
This man with my instructions shall be sent
To bring this stratagem about. No more;
Here's Coredurus with his second self.
Let's hear their talk, then enter at our cue.

Scena tertia

Coredurus, Spirius, Bolnutus, Jargus.

Coredurus. Spirius, my word is passed.
Spirius. Recall it back;
Make you so precious of a blast of air?
What else are words?
Coredurus. Why, they are relatives,
And set a moral value on the man
Whose words they are. Should I be false of word
I were unfit for [human] intercourse.
Spirius. True, were they with advantage to be kept.
But when with prejudice they are observed
And threaten loss, who keeps them is a fool.
Coredurus. What prejudice to me to be approved
And by a lawful bishop?
Spirius. Yes, of clouts.
Admit he were, why, we are made his peers
By ancient charter, ordinaries born,
Invested with archbishop's power in time
Of vacant sees, with right to bind or loose
In either court. We have been little popes,

And shall not to a Delegate hand places
And stoope to his Comand! Ile first goe turke.
Bol. Wee must holde vp his humour in his still,
And sooth his humor of Bishops come
With Cardinalls power, to serue our ends
Els I could laugh out right at his conceipts
That dreames of miters & knights, and crosier staues.
Cor. How can wee thus oppose the Bishops Armes,
But all the world will mock vs: and in scorne,
In steede of Malta, call vs knights of Malt.
Spi. A fico for the world, lett malt goe steepe
Wee are exempted from the common forme
Of swearing Obedience, such as Bishops vse
On subiects to exact: Cor. Exemptions cease
That are repeal'd by Councells, and Popes Bulles.
Spir. Lett Bulls and Councells doe their worst Ile finde
A starting hole to sett vs free. Cor. As how?
Spir. Why thus: The Councell they doe make alleadge
Ile stand too't, neither hath, nor can, nor ought
To be receiu'd within this land: Cor. How soe?
Suppose it should be publisht. Spir. Tis a toy,
Who publish it? Cor. The Bishop. Spi. By what power?
Cor. The Popes. Spir. Wee will oppose. Cor. With what? Spir. The lawe.
Cor. That's a voide. Spir. The State. Cor. Doth it become our vowes,
To argue thus? is this our Roman faith &—
Spir. Who faith and vowes with enemies abhorres
Deserues to dye a slaue. Cor. What Enemies
haue wee to feare? Spir. The Bishop. Bol. Be still I
Iargas: and I the Bishop. Cor. Wee are ouer-heard.
Bol: Nay, feare not, Cardinall will ioyne
our cause we feare A Bishops wisdome
to pawne our rights and giue into our hands,
The order, and call vs Renegats.

Abr Eniges

And shall we to a delegate give place
And stoop to his command? I'll first go thrash.
Bolnutus. [*Aside.*] We must hold up this humor in him still,
And soothe this lunacy of bishops born
With ordinary power, to serve our ends;
Else I could laugh outright at his conceit
That dreams of mitered knights and cradle popes.
Coredurus. How can we thus oppose the bishop's power
But all the world will mock us? and in scorn,
Instead of Malta, call us Knights of Malt.
Spirius. A *fico* for the world, let malt go steep.
We are exempted from the common form
Of church obedience, such as bishops use
On subjects to exact.
Coredurus. Exemptions cease
That are repealed by councils and popes' bulls.
Spirius. Let bulls and councils do their worst, I'll find
A starting hole to set us free.
Coredurus. As how?
Spirius. Why thus: The council they do most allege,
I'll stand to't, neither hath, nor can, nor ought
To be received within this land.
Coredurus. How so?
Suppose it should be published.
Spirius. Pish, a toy;
Who publish it?
Coredurus. The bishop.
Spirius. By what power?
Coredurus. The pope's.
Spirius. We will oppose.
Coredurus. With what?
Spirius. The law.
Coredurus. That's void.
Spirius. The state.
Coredurus. Doth it beseem our vows
To argue thus? Is this our Roman faith?
Spirius. Who faith and vows with enemies observes
Deserves to die a slave.
Coredurus. What enemies
Have we to fear?
Spirius. The bishop.
Bolnutus. So say I.
Jargus. And I the bishop.
Coredurus. We are overheard.

(*text continued on following page*)

For thinges misdone that are exempt from Lawe
And Comon order; not like other mens;
Tis not to be put up: Spir. Lett's rather thrash.
Jar. Content, lett's rather thrash. Cor. But how can wee
Remove this Mountaine, or withstand a power
Soe backt by Custome, Scriptures, Councells, Popes,
And left by Christ to rule his Spouse the Church?
Bol. I grant, tis hard directly to oppose
Soe sterne a title, least the world crie shame;
But indirectly there are hundred wayes
To fobb him off, and strengthen our pretence
With publick zeale of State, and of our Cause:
First wee'l accuse the man. Cor. Of what? Bol. Lett's thinke,
hath he noe vices? Spir. There's the spight on't, none.
Bol. Speake Jary, knowst thou none? Jar. ffaith none
Wee have invented manie some yeares since
To have disgrac'd him with the Pope at Rome,
And with the Cardinalls, but none would take,
He was made Bishop in dispight of us. —
Bol. Soft then, lett's make him odious to the State.
Jar. That's easlie done. Cor. Not with such ease, I feare,
He had not entred without their consent
Or tacit voice; they know of two extreames
The least was best; and that licentious times,
And spiritts, that would spurne against a State
Would by the Churches censure be restrain'd
And kept in awe; such is a Bishops power.
Jar. The more's the pittie. This onlie should be ours.
Spir. And ours; But I have hammer'd in this braine
A plott to bringe the State about for us,
And dash the Bishopps cause. Jar. For God's sake how?
Spir. The warr betwixt Liege, and our State,

Shall

Bolnutus. Nay, fear not, Coredurus, we will join;
Our cause is fair. A bishop to intrude
Upon our rights and pry into our ways,
To oversee and call us to accompt

For things misdone that are exempt from law
And common order, not like other men;
'Tis not to be put up.
Spirius. Let's rather thrash.
Jargus. Content, let's rather thrash.
Coredurus. But how can we
Remove this mountain, or withstand a power
So backed by custom, scriptures, councils, popes,
And left by Christ to rule his spouse the church?
Bolnutus. I grant, 'tis hard directly to oppose
So clear a title, lest the world cry shame;
But indirectly there are sundry ways
To job him off and strengthen our pretense
With public zeal of state and of our cause.
First we'll accuse the man.
Coredurus. Of what?
Bolnutus. Let's think,
Hath he no vices?
Spirius. There's the spite on't, none.
Bolnutus. Speak, Jargus, know'st thou none?
Jargus. Faith, none.
We have invented many, some years since,
To have disgraced him with the pope at Rome,
And with the cardinals, but none would take;
He was made bishop in despite of us.
Bolnutus. Soft then, let's make him odious to the state.
Jargus. That's easily done.
Coredurus. Not with such ease, I fear:
He had not entered without their consent
Or tacit voice. They know of two extremes
The least was best, and that licentious pens
And spirits, that would spurn against a state,
Would by the church's censure be restrained
And kept in awe; such is a bishop's power.
Jargus. The more's the pity. This eclipseth ours.
Spirius. And ours. But I have hammered in this brain
A plot to bring the state about for us,
And dash the bishop's cause.
Jargus. For God's sake how?
Spirius. The war betwixt Lialga and our state

Shall helpe this proiect. Bol. Right, my very thought.
Jar. Soe your goode wills may iumpe in one conceit
Spir. Goe too, you have not all the braines, tis mine,
I said this plott, is mine. Bol. I grant it; on.
Should I denie, hee'le strike me. Jar. Hee's all fire;
Good captaine on. Spir. Then thus the Bishop came
Till knowne, first from Liege, where hee liv'd
There made, and there intruded on our Land.
Jar. Not that, intruded. Spir. He was graced too
By the chiefe favorite here. Jar. Still better, on.
Spir. Nowe were it hard, thinke you by words cast out
Or private writings to wronge the State,
And put a iealousie into their heads
That he may have, or els hath had, or hath
Some correspondence with our forraigne foes?
Bol. A case most facil; but could we make good
The least surmise of this, or shew it plaine
He were undone; and we for ever made.
Jar. Wee'le doe our best. Cor. He is too wise for that.
Bol. It is enough, the State but once suspect
His cake is dough. Jar. I see, we shall not thrash
For Spirus hath knockt the Bishop downe;
Me thinkes I see him sprawle. Spir. Content with me!
Bol. Tripes! Why, we of policie are knowne,
Aswell as learning, to be Maisters. Jar. Right,
Say Statists too, you shall not speake amisse.
Cor. Religious policie you meane. Bol. Most true.
Cor. Then wee may venture to be holie, and rogue.
Spir. May spurr them on in case they should prove dull.
Jar. That's not our fault, we can ride poste for neede.
Bol. And will to further such a pious cause.
Cor. But for the laities, how may they be drawne
To leave the Bishops side? Bol. That care be mine.
Spir. And mine. Jar. And mine. Bol. Well said; lett's all concurre.
Cor. About it then. Spir. My braines begin to stirr.
Scena 4a.

Shall help this project.
Bolnutus. Right, my very thought.
Jargus. See how good wits may jump in one conceit.
Spirius. Go [to], you have not all the brains, 'tis mine,
I say this plot is mine.
Bolnutus. I grant it; on.
[*Aside*.] Should I deny, he'll strike me.
Jargus. [*Aside*.] He's all fire;
[*To Spirius*.] Good captain, on.
Spirius. Then thus: the bishop came,
'Tis known, first from Lialga, where he lived,
There made, and thence intruded on our land.
Jargus. [Note] that, intruded.
Spirius. He was gracèd too
By the chief favorite there.
Jargus. Still better; on.
Spirius. Now were it hard, think you, by words cast out
Or private writings to incense the state,
And put a jealousy into their heads
That he may have, or else hath had, or hath
Some correspondence with our foreign foes?
Bolnutus. A way most facile, but could we make good
The least surmise of this, or show it plain,
He were undone and we forever made.
Jargus. We'll do our best.
Coredurus. He is too wise for that.
Bolnutus. It is enough the state but once suspect:
His cake is dough.
Jargus. I see we shall not thrash,
For Spirius hath knocked the bishop down;
Methinks I see him sprawl.
Spirius. Contest with us?
Bolnutus. Or us? Why we of policy are known,
As well as learning, to be masters.
Jargus. Right,
Say fathers too, you shall not speak amiss.
Coredurus. Religion's policy you mean.
Bolnutus. Most true.
Coredurus. Then we may venture to be halves, and join.
Spirius. Nay spur them on in case they should prove dull.
Jargus. That's not our fault; we can ride post for need.
Bolnutus. And will to further such a pious cause.
Coredurus. But for the laity, how may they be drawn
To leave the bishop's side?
(*text continued on following page*)

16

Scena quarta.

Candle. Crudius.

What said you to these lights? these burning lampes
That beautifie the church? what art thou stun'd?
Cru. I knowe not what to said, I stand amaz'd,
Wee dreampt: t'was sure a vision that wee sawe.
Can. I and a strange one too, why thou canst dreame
As well as I, thou wake, and be dream'd.
Cru. Why so I am; It was a dreame. Can. Art sure
Th'art yet awake? Cru. I know not, I thinke yes;
I'me sure, the men appear'd not yester-night,
The same they proud to day. They seemed Saints
They were so modest, so retir'd; their speech
Soe grave, their weapons so discreete, and all
Their actions soe reform'd, and sett in print;
That either then I was awake, now sleepe;
Or then I was asleepe, and wake but nowe
Can. Just so; good morrowe &c. t'is time to rise.
I'me gladd I caught you napping; what excuse,
What glosse can serve to iustifie these men?
And staie me from mine error of Beleife.
Cru. I cannot staie him, whom the divell detaines
Not thee whom folly, and distrust guides.
Hadst thou one sparke of Grace, or were thy faith
Not meerely humane, I could cleere this mist,
And make thine eyes behold the Sunn againe.
Can. Doe so, I longue to see these clouds dispel'd.
Cru. When Pine-trees shake, and loftie Cedars nod,
Wee see t'is but a tempest moves the aire,
The earth standes firme, and solid. Can. but he thinks
That grace, the earth by flatterers had defac'd.
Cru. True, for these greate ones, that like Cedars spread
Their branches o're the church, doe some tymes reele
And totter

Bolnutus. That care be mine.
Spirius. And mine.
Jargus. And mine.
Bolnutus. Well said; let's all concur.
Coredurus. About it then.
Spirius. My brains begin to stir. [*Exeunt.*]

Scena quarta

Candle, Erudius.

Candle. What say you to these lights? these burning lamps
That beautify the church? What, art thou stunned?
Erudius. I know not what to say, I stand amazed.
We dreamt: 'twas sure a vision that we saw.
Candle. Aye, and a strange one too. Why thou canst dream
As well as I, then wake and be deceived.
Erudius. Why so I am; it was a dream.
Candle. Art sure
Th'art yet awake?
Erudius. I know not; I think yes;
I'm sure the men appeared not yesternight
The same they prove today. They seemèd saints,
They were so modest, so retired; their speech
So grave, their judgments so discreet, and all
Their actions so reserved and set in print,
That either then I was awake, now sleep,
Or then I was asleep, and wake but now.
Candle. Just so; good morrow, sir, 'tis time to rise.
I'm glad I caught you napping; what excuse,
What gloss can serve to justify these men?
And stay me from mine error of belief?
Erudius. I cannot stay him whom the devil drives,
Nor thee whom folly and distrust pursues.
Hadst thou one spark of grace, or were thy faith
Not merely human, I could clear this mist
And make thine eyes behold the sun again.
Candle. Do so: I long to see these clouds dissolved.
Erudius. When pine trees shake and lofty cedars nod,
We see 'tis but a tempest moves the air;
The earth stands firm and solid.
Candle. But the fruits
That grace the earth lie scattered and defaced.
Erudius. True. So these great ones, that like cedars spread
Their branches [o'er] the church, do sometimes reel

And totter with the winde, by passions rais'd
That strippes them of their leaves, deflowres their workes;
Yet faith that is the rocke, unmoved standes
Con-centred, with a rocke, that never swarves.
Can. You meane the Church. Eru. I doe. Can. I know your rocke;
'Tis now become a rocke of scandall. Eru. True,
For such blinde fooles as thou to dash upon;
And will bring ruine, and eternall losse
To all, that shall oppose it. Can. Never I,
I'le rather not approach, but stand a loofe,
For feare I split my vessell. Eru. Thinke not so
To save thy selfe. Can. Why not. Eru. Because upon
This rocke, the Church is built that only saves;
Can. What would'st thou have me doe in two extreames?
Eru. Thou maist approach it, but approach it not.
Can. By heaven I will not, I'me not such an one.
Eru. Then let us goe, I hope this storme is past.

Grex

Lucianus . Therulus:

Farewell, I must be gone. The. Stay, what's the cause?
Luc. A vowe to sweare by heaven, and I will by.
The. I prethy stay, restraine thy raptious zeale,
The oath is modest, in respect of those
Our gallants sweare, you cannot passe the streetes,
But boyes and women, will outbrave this oath;
What thinkst thou then of the player, [illegible] this plott
Against the Bishopp, and could wish my braine
Against our Bishopps were forsaking bread;
Twere meate and drinke to me. The. [illegible], mai'st thou speake
[illegible] thine owne [illegible], as I beleeve thou wilt
And see thy errour. The [illegible] doe beginne.

Actus 2.

And totter with the wind by passions raised,
That strips them of their leaves, deflowers their works;
Yet faith, that is the root, unmovèd stands,
Con-centered with a rock that never swerves.
Candle. You mean the church.
Erudius. I do.
Candle. I know your rock;
'Tis now become a rock of scandal.
Erudius. True,
For such blind fools as thou to dash upon,
And will bring ruin and eternal loss
To all that shall oppose it.
Candle. Never I;
I'll rather not approach, but stand aloof,
For fear I split my vessel.
Erudius. Think not so
To save thyself.
Candle. Why not?
Erudius. Because upon
This rock the church is built that only saves.
Candle. What wouldst thou have me do in two extremes?
Erudius. Thou mayst approach it, but reproach it not.
Candle. By heaven I will not; I'm not such an one.
Erudius. Then let us go, I hope this storm is past. [*Exeunt*.]

Grex.

Lucianus, *Therulus*.

Lucianus. Farewell, I must be gone.
Therulus. Stay, what's the cause?
Lucianus. A wretch to swear by heaven, and I sit by!
Therulus. I prithee stay, restrain thy captious zeal.
The oath is modest in respect of those
Our gallants swear; you cannot pass the streets
But boys and women will outbid this oath.
What think'st thou of the play?
Lucianus. I take this plot
Against the bishop, and could wish my brain
Against our bishops were so well employed;
'Twere meat and drink to me.
Therulus. So mayst thou choke
With thine own wish, as I believe thee. Sit
And see the rest. The second act begins.

Actus Secundus.

Scena prima.

Polinodus. Larguus.

You neede not spurr a horse that's free: Noe more,
Ile make the Lawe your packhorse; It shall waite
Upon the golden fleece that you adore
Let conscience roare, or crumple; stand or fall
My soule is safe, tis pinnd upon our skirts
Whom God hath made the Atlas of his Church,
Whose Secretaries to the holy Ghost
That knowe his will, may doe it when you please
By speciall priviledge, which none but you
Can challenge or pretend, you are my all
If you mistrust not, noe more can I.
Lar. Thankes Polinodus for your liberall praise
As for the point you touch of priviledge
To doe Gods pleasure, as it seemes ours
It is a secret knowne to none, but those
Of our Society, not all (the most
Noe doubt will contradict it) but to some
Within this land, and not in every case
Nor every where, but heere, and in the case
Of Bishopps powre, and practise to approve
Which none else can question, whom you knowe
To be the only Ministers under Heaven.
Pol. I knowe it reverend Larguus. Lar. May those knights
Of Malta, that assist us, are [illegible]
In this alone that it is, for [illegible] they [illegible]
[illegible] their [illegible]; and when they all have done
Tis in our power to cause them to [illegible]
[illegible] stand [illegible] [illegible] before,
When wee have wrought [illegible] we care not much,
To gauge the [illegible] against [illegible]
There to rest idle, and at ease, while wee

Shall reape

Actus secundus

Scena prima

Polinodus, Jargus.

Polinodus. You need not spur a horse that's free. No more,
I'll make the law your packhorse; it shall wait
Upon the golden fleece that you adore.
Let conscience reach or crumple, stand or fall,
My soul is safe, 'tis pinned upon [your] skirts
Whom God hath made the Atlas of his church,
Chief secretaries to the [Holy] Ghost,
That know his will, may do it when you please
By special privilege, which none but you
Can challenge or pretend. You are my all;
If you miscarry not, no more can I.
Jargus. Thanks Polinodus for your liberal praise.
As for the point you touched of privilege
To do God's pleasure, as it seconds ours:
It is a secret known to none but those
Of our society, not all (the most
No doubt will contradict it) but to some
Within this land, and not in every case
Nor everywhere, but here, and in the case
Of bishop's power and practice to approve,
Which we—none else—can question, whom you know
To be the only minions under heaven.
Polinodus. I know it, Reverend Jargus.
Jargus. [Nay], those Knights
Of Malta, that assist us, are excused
In this alone, that 'tis for us they sweat
More than themselves; and when they all have done,
'Tis in our power to leave them to their chance,
And stand at distance with them as before.
When we have wrought our ends, we care not much
To hang the instrument against the wall,
There to rest idle and at ease, while we

Shall reape the profitt of their paines, and ours.
Let this suffice; will Corbus come? Pol. I sent
For him, and Rudelbinus; in this place
Wee are to meete, heere at the Divells bush.
Retire you to this Lobby, shift yourselfe
Into a Guelfish habitt; you may seeme
A reverend &c. one of the Bishopps traine;
That done, be vigilant, and you shall heare
How like a Champion Ile defend your cause
And drawe the Laiety with a chaine of Steele
Into our Contoure; Corbus, welcome friend;
And Rudelbinus welcome.

Scena Secunda

Corbus. Rudelbinus. Polinodus.

Wee come at
your Summons Polinodus, and are come
To argue with you in the Bishopps case;
you knowe the cause. Rud. But who may heere direct
our conference in this point? Pol. For that my care
Hath fore-provided; here's a reverend Guelfe
Within this roofe, shall satisfie your doubts
Of conference, if anie shall arise;
For mine, it is of proofe, and made of Steele.
Cor. And mine the same, a thing wee deale in [illegible].
Rud. Sitt downe, and Rudelbinus first begin
Pol. A Bishopp or noe Bishopp, what's your voice?
Rud. A Bishopp mine, Cor. and mine a Bishopp. Pol. Good,
That cannot be denied, and therefore mine.
The second point; what power wee shall allowe
And grant him over us. Rud. This not [illegible]
To limitt that wee are not sheepe. Pol. What then?
Suppose the sheepe would be a wolfe.
Cor. Woe worth it. Ru. Suppose the skie should fall. P. Why then
May you in [illegible] [illegible] [illegible] then [illegible].

Rud. So [illegible]

Shall reap the profit of their pains and ours.
Let this suffice. Will Corbus come?
Polinodus. I sent
For him and Rudelbinus; in this place
We are to meet, here at the Devil's Bush.
Retire you to this lobby, shift yourself
Into a Guelfish habit; you may seem
A reverend sir, one of the bishop's train.
That done, be vigilant, and you shall hear
How like a champion I'll defend your cause
And draw the laity with a chain of steel
Into our sentence. [*Exit Jargus.*] Corbus, welcome friend;
And Rudelbinus, welcome.

Scena`secunda

Corbus, Rudelbinus, Polinodus.

Corbus. We received
Your summons, Polinodus, and are come
To argue with you in the bishop's case.
You know the law.
Rudelbinus. But who may here direct
Our conscience in this point?
Polinodus. For that my care
Hath fore-provided; there's a reverend Guelf
Within this roof shall satisfy your doubts
Of conscience, if any shall arise;
For mine, it is of proof and made of steel.
Corbus. And mine the same, a thing we deal in much.
[*Polinodus.*] Sit down, and Rudelbinus first begin:
A bishop or no bishop, what's your voice?
Rudelbinus. A bishop mine.
Corbus. And mine a bishop.
Polinodus. Good;
It cannot be denied, and therefore mine.
The second point: what power we shall allow
And grant him over us.
Rudelbinus. 'Tis not in us
To limit that; we are no popes.
Polinodus. What then?
Suppose the pope commit us to a wolf.
Corbus. Well urged.
Rudelbinus. Suppose the sky should fall.
Polinodus. Why popes
May err in choosing pastors o'er their flock.

Rud. The Popes said that saints would steale the lambes,
Ah Popes may erre, and all the Clergie too,
That haue their pardes for sin, may not woe
That thus oppose him, unles he permitt?
Cor. A schere'd repulse, me thinks my friend he's gon'd,
Ile helpe him out; but Polynodus speake,
you knowe the lawe, what stuff it in this case.
Pol. A Premunire; losse of Goods and lands,
Besides imprisonment for terme of life
Will followe, if we once receiue his powre.
Cor. Marry God sheild, Ile shutt him out of dores
If he come neere me first. Rud. Soe will not I;
T'were good we warn'd him first. Pol. Doe so that please;
I haue shooke hands with him long since. Cor. And I.
Rud. Saies not the lawe the same against a Preist
T'is premunire, losse of goods and lands;
haue you shooke hands with them? you shutt your dores.
Cor. Tush thinks to ouerwrith vs. Pol. you are quick;
T'is time, we haue pull'd on our selues this yoake
A little more then words. Rud. Is't call'd a yoake
To harbour Iesuits, the comfort of our soules?
Pol. Some are I grant a comfort, others none;
I neuer yet tooke comfort in a Guelfe,
Nor he from me releife; if I could chuse,
had I a dozen sonnes, none should be Guelfes.
Rud. your reason &c. Pol. For reason let that passe,
It is my nature &c. Rud. A good one. Cor. yes,
But marke it well. Rud. I doe. Pol. Some men there are
haue woone my heart. Cor. And mine, the Ghibellins
Are wondrous winning men. Rud. And getting too.
Pol. &c. if they doe soe, all they gett's their owne.
Rud. It seemes then by their winnings you are lost
And by their gettings, others are the worse.
Pol. Be plaine, I understand you not. Rud. Why then.
you won by them, are lost unto the Guelfes,
Soe by their gettings others are the worst.

the worst

Rudelbinus. So foxes say that fain would steal the lambs.
If popes may err, and all the clergy too
That gave their voices for him, may not we
That thus oppose him, only to surmise?
Corbus. A shrewd repulse, methinks my friend is [gagged];
I'll help him out: but Polinodus speak,
You know the law, what saith it in this case?
Polinodus. A *premunire*, loss of goods and lands,
Besides imprisonment for term of life,
Will follow if we once receive his power.
Corbus. Marry, God shield! I'll shut him out of doors
If he come near me first.
Rudelbinus. So will not I;
'Twere good we warned him first.
Polinodus. Do so that please;
I have shook hands with him long since.
Corbus. And I.
Rudelbinus. Says not the law the same against a priest?
'Tis *premunire*, loss of goods and lands;
Have you shook hands with them? You shut your doors.
Corbus. Tye thinks to overwrites us.
Polinodus. You are quick.
'Tis true, we have pulled on ourselves this yoke
A little more than words.
Rudelbinus. Is't called a yoke
To harbor priests, the comfort of our souls?
Polinodus. Some are, I grant, a comfort, others none;
I never yet took comfort in a Guelf,
Nor he from me relief. If I could choose,
Had I a dozen sons none should be Guelfs.
Rudelbinus. Your reason sir.
Polinodus. For reason, let that pass;
It is my nature, sir.
Rudelbinus. A good one.
Corbus. Yes,
But mark it well.
Rudelbinus. I do.
Polinodus. Some men there are
Have won my heart.
Corbus. And mine; the Ghibellines
Are wondrous winning men.
Rudelbinus. And getting too.
Polinodus. Sir, if they do so, all they get's their own.
Rudelbinus. It seems then by their winning you are lost,
And by their gettings others are the worse.
Polinodus. Be plain, I understand you not.

(*text continued on following page*)

The worse for you whom Ghibellins have gott.
Pol. I see you are conceited. Cor. Soe are wee,
That only for conceit are call'd the witty.
Rud. Well, whether will thou then? the proverb saies
And so am I, what will you I should doe?
I would not stick to ioyne, were I assur'd
By such Dimittis, my soule were free
My goods, and lands, and children touch me neere,
My wife solliciteth me to be a Lord,
I were a foole to stand in myne owne light,
If Confessours and Dimittis give way.
Pol. Dimittis as sound as any Bell,
Shall be your Sheete; neither Maior, nor Sheriff,
Nor Bishops Officer shall staie your course.
Cor. Soft, if you meane the Inquisitours, they may,
For they can staie both Lords and Ladies too;
They are the Bugbeares of the tyme. Pol. 'Tis true
Next to the Bishopp most I feare those Roagues.
Rud. I'le be noe Irish Baron for that trick.
Pol. Nor Scottish I advise you, but behould
Here comes the reverend Guelfe. I would you of,
Would all the rest were like him, Factions would ceast,
And then betwixt a Guelfe and Ghibellin
Would be noe odds. Rud. Nor is, unless he makes even
Ends. I have seene this suspitious face
Among the Ghibellins, or I mistake
Whom you speake ~~the~~ marke.

Scena tertia.

Jargus. Corbus. Polinodus. Rudelbinus.

God save you Knights;
Or Gentlemen, or both. Cor. Or neither Sr
For some of us are minded to be Lords.
Jar. I crie you mercie then. Pol. You're welcome Sr.
Ghibellins Example hath possest this Knight,
Whether

Rudelbinus. Why thus:
You won by them are lost unto the Guelfs;
So by their gettings others are the worse.

The worse for you whom Ghibellines have got.
Polinodus. I see you are conceited.
Corbus. So are we,
That only for conceit are called the wits.
Rudelbinus. Wit [whither] wilt thou then? the proverb says,
And so am I; what will you I should do?
I would not stick to join were I assured
By sound divinity my soul were free.
My goods, and lands, and children touch me near;
My wife solicits me to be a lord;
I were a fool to stand in mine own light
If conscience and divinity give way.
Polinodus. Divinity as sound as any bell
Shall be your passport; neither mayor, nor sheriff,
Nor bishop's officer shall stay your course.
Corbus. Soft, if you mean the pursuivants, they may:
For they can stay both lords and ladies too;
They are the bugbears of the time.
Polinodus. 'Tis true,
Next to the bishop most I fear those rogues.
Rudelbinus. I'll be no Irish baron for that trick.
Polinodus. Nor Scottish I advise you—but behold,
Here comes the reverend Guelf I told you of.
Would all the rest were like him, jars would cease,
And then betwixt a Guelf and Ghibelline
Would be no odds.
Rudelbinus. Nor is, where he makes even.
Sure I have seen this supercilious face
Among the Ghibellines, or I mistake.
When speaks the oracle?

Scena tertia

Jargus, Corbus, Polinodus, Rudelbinus.

Jargus. God save you, knights,
Or gentlemen, or both.
Corbus. Or neither, sir.
For some of us are minded to be lords.
Jargus. I cry you mercy then.
Polinodus. You're welcome, sir.
A foolish scruple hath possessed this knight,

Whether he may resist the Bishopps power,
Sent hither by the H. ghost to governe soules.
Tar. If it be burdensome he may. Rud. The yoake
Of Christ is sweete, such is a Bishopps power.
Tar. It is unnecessary for these tymes.
Rud. In times of greater hazard it was thought
most necessary. Tar. Times and men are chang'd.
Rud. Into the worse I feare, but must the Church
Then change her government. Tar. If men be found
That can supplie a Bishopps want, it must.
Pol. Indeede some Ghibellines supplie that want
most richlie; they are priviledg'd to doe
more, then I le brag of; neither Prince nor Pope
Can equall them in spirit, though in power.
But 'tis a secret this, and knowne to fewe
yet take it on my credit, 'tis most true.
Cor. And myne most cleare. Rud. Your credits both are good
But this exceedes all credit, were it true,
And were it cleare, all wonder; make this good,
I'le burne my Library. Pol. 'Twere pittie &c.
It is a verie faire one. Cor. There are witts
can, if they list, make stranger matters good
And those not farr to seeke. Rud. My paines are sav'd
I have them in the worde alreadie &c.
I will dispute no further in this case;
I am convinc'd, although against my will
Two credits here are pawn'd to warrant one;
Now if the third will stake his soule, I le joyne.
Tar. my soule for yours, you may forsake the Guelfes
Reject the Bishopp, vilifie his power
And call it monstrous, lawlesse, and assum'd
A noveltie not knowne these fortie yeares.
Pol. You might put him to that, and yet not lye.
Cor. A goodly tyme. Tar. Once a goulden age
Wherein the name of Bishopp was not heard
Nor suffer'd to take footing in this land.

Thankes

Whether he may resist the bishop's power,
Sent hither by the pope to govern souls.
Jargus. If it be burdensome he may.
Rudelbinus. The yoke
Of Christ is sweet; such is a bishop's power.
Jargus. It is unnecessary for these times.
Rudelbinus. In times of greater hazard it was thought
Most necessary.
Jargus. Times and men are changed.
Rudelbinus. Into the worse, I fear, but must the church
Then change her government?
Jargus. If men be found
That can supply a bishop's want, it must.
Polinodus. Indeed some Ghibellines supply that want
Most richly. They are privileged to do
More than I'll brag of; neither prince nor pope
Can equal them in spirit, though in power.
But 'tis a secret this and known to few,
Yet take it on my credit, 'tis most true.
Corbus. And mine most clear.
Rudelbinus. Your credits both are great,
But this exceeds all credit, were it true;
And were it clear, all wonder. Make this good,
I'll burn my library.
Polinodus. 'Twere pity, sir,
It is a very fair one.
Corbus. There are wits
Can, if they list, make stranger matters good,
And those not far to seek.
Rudelbinus. My pains are saved,
I have them in the wind already, sir;
I will dispute no further in this case,
I am convinced, although against my will.
Two credits here are pawned to warrant one;
Now if the third will stake his soul, I'll join.
Jargus. My soul for yours, you may forsake the Guelfs,
Reject the bishop, vilify his power,
And call it monstrous, lawless, and assumed,
A novelty not known these forty years.
Polinodus. You might put ten to that, and yet not lie.
Corbus. A goodly time.
Jargus. To us a golden age
Wherein the name of bishop was not heard
Nor suffered to take footing in this land,

Thankes to those cloister Spiritts, that have made
It odious heere, and beggar'd it abroade
With pittiable slanders, and reports,
Would beate a dogg off, much more fright the Sheepe;
From feeding it amongst vs, till of late;
I would that late had never beene. Pol. Amen.
Iar. Alas Sr, I am but a Guelfe, and poore
And therefore not regarded in these daies;
Were I a Ghibellin, I might be rich
And fitt for a Ladies counsells, and exploits
Of higher name, and ranke. Rud. me thinks I smell
The powder treason in these rash exploites.
Well, God forgive them if they did amisse
I would not iudge them guiltie for a world
I'me sure that Ghibellins were counted then
More daungerous farr then Guelfes, vnto the State,
And were more hated then the Bishopp now.
But lett that passe, vnconstant times I see
Doe roule like flouds, and in their currents woe.
Now Sir, what meanes have wee to gaine this prize
And here with most advantage, wee may crosse
The Bishopps designe. Pol. Tis first thought fitt by such
As are Superiors. Rud. Who are those I praie?
You meane noe Bishopp sure. Cor. No, God forbidd.
Pol. The Ghibellins I meane. Cor. Nay then saies true
Wee must be boyes againe, and goe to schoole
If wee doe well. Rud: yes, and be whipt, goe on,
you lost at; Tis thought fitt. Pol. Wee waive our minds
Unto this man; the picture of that thinge
Men call a Bishopp, now a word of Warne.
Iar. God rest their Soules that made it so, say I
Cor. Most charitably spoken for a Guelfe.
Pol. And this in answere to a letter fram'd
By him of late, and sent to vs. Rud. you meane
De Gerlay, Archbishopp, but not to vs.

Pol. In them

Thanks to those choicer spirits that have made
It odious here, and beggared it abroad
With profitable slanders and reports
Would beat a dog off, much more fright the pope
From sending it among us till of late.
I would that late had never been.
Polinodus. Amen.
Jargus. Alas, sir, I am but a Guelf, and poor,
And therefore not regarded in these days;
Were I a Ghibelline, I might be rich
And fit for a lady's counsels, and exploits
Of higher name and rank.
Rudelbinus. Methinks I smell
The powder treason in these rank exploits.
Well, God forgive them if they did amiss,
I would not judge them guilty for a world.
I'm sure that Ghibellines were counted then
More dangerous far than Guelfs unto the state,
And were more hated than the bishop now.
But let that pass, unconstant times I see
Do rove like floods, and in their currents we.
Now say, what means have we to play this prize,
And how with most advantage we may crush
The bishop's claim.
Polinodus. 'Tis first thought fit by such
As are superiors—
Rudelbinus. Who are those I pray?
You mean no bishop sure.
Corbus. No, God forbid.
Polinodus. The Ghibellines I mean.
Corbus. Nay, he says true:
We must be boys again and go to school
If we do well.
Rudelbinus. Yes, and be whipped. Go on,
You left at: 'Tis thought fit—
Polinodus. We write our minds
Unto this man, the picture of that thing
Men call a bishop, now a word of scorn.
Jargus. God rest their souls that made it so, say I.
Corbus. Most charitably spoken for a Guelf.
Polinodus. And this in answer to a letter framed
By him of late and sent to us.
Rudelbinus. You mean
To the lay Catholics, but not to us.

Pol. In them too all I meane. Rud. Then [illegible] blinde
We catholiques, that knowe we are in harte
Such as these [illegible]? Cor. Sr the best of witts
Our Ghibellines will make it good, [illegible].
Rud. But will they make us good, that should be? Cor. yes,
For els, that they are none. Rud. A [illegible] worke.
Cor. And this you knowe is held a paradox.
Rud. Pray God it prove so. Cor. To the point. Pol. This man
To prove he is our head, church first,
Pope Urbans Bull, yea the wordes that give
him ordinary power, then he cites
Two Generall Councells, Lateran and Trent
That also of Vienna. Cor. To what end?
Pol. To shew his full commission to approve
With Bulls of other Popes to back his clayme.
Tar. But you may bringe forth rammes shall beate them back.
Rud. Pray name those rammes. Tar. I speake by metaphor,
Els sure they have not hornes, their names are these
Bolnudus master of the goulden Fleece
Of Malta Corcdurus, and the [illegible]
Nicodimus [illegible] captaine of the [illegible],
Besides the State. Rud. I now hitt the marke
Those other rammes were fumblers, but for them
they can but beate backe, the Bishop without rammes
And they must stand [illegible], [illegible].
Tar. And [illegible] [illegible] not [illegible], I hope.
As all the world may witnesse [illegible]
Rud. And better now [illegible]
[illegible] shall not [illegible]
In answering this letter? Pol. [illegible]
[illegible] Cor. A curious one, no doubt.
Pol. [illegible] you be Ordinarie as you said,
Then have you power to doe a world of things
That may be prejudiciall to our State
You may doe this [illegible] I knowe not what.
Rud. [illegible] you may [illegible] what hath bene done,
That must be [illegible]. Pol. [illegible] knowe.

Cor. That's

Polinodus. In them to us I mean.
Rudelbinus. Can any think
Us Catholics, that know we are in heart
Such bishop haters?
Corbus. Sir, the best of wits,
Our Ghibellines, will make it good we are.
Rudelbinus. But will they make us good, that hold so?
Corbus. Yes,
Or else that they are none.
Rudelbinus. A bloody word.
Corbus. And this you know is held a paradox.
Rudelbinus. Pray God it prove so. To the point.
Polinodus. This man,
To prove he is our head, produceth first
Pope Urban's brief, yea the words that give
Him ordinary power, then he cites
Two general councils, Lateran and Trent,
That also of Vienna.
Corbus. To what end?
Polinodus. To show his full commission to approve,
With bulls of other popes to back his claim.
Jargus. But you may bring forth rams shall beat them back.
Rudelbinus. Pray name those rams.
Jargus. I speak by metaphor—
Else sure they have no horns—their names are these:
Bolnutus master of the Golden Fleece,
Of Malta Coredurus, and for need
Nicodimus chief captain of Saint James,
Besides the state—
Rudelbinus. I now hit the mark.
Those other rams were fumblers, but for them—
They can but beat back the bishop without rams,
And they must stand our friends, else we are gone.
Jargus. And we, we have deserved no less, I hope,
As all the world may witness for us now.
Rudelbinus. And better now than never, as before;
But to conclude, what way shall we observe
In answering this letter?
Polinodus. We'll begin
With this conceit.
Corbus. A curious one, no doubt.
Polinodus. "If you be ordinary, as you say,
Then have you power to do a world of things
That may be prejudicial to our states.
You may do this or that, I know not what."
(*text continued on following page*)

Cor. That's left unto the witts to studie out.
Pol. I that, he may erect Tribunalls, Courts
Of Justice, Cancell or examin wills
If they proue faultie. Rud. I should thinke this fitt,
Were it reform'd in breef, and in case
The Comon lawe, that calles the Catholicke
Should faile to doe vs right. I see noe cause
But if a priuate freind, or Priest, may serue
To right our differences that occurre
By telling what in Conscience must be done.
But he may doe the same, although his powre
Be more coercitiue, I must confesse.
Iar. O Lord that word hath strucke me to the heart.
Cor. Helpe Sir to hould the reuerend Ghost that sinkes.
Rud. A suddaine qualme belike. Pol. How doe you Sir?
Iar. The very apprehension of that word
Co-er-citiue, dismaies me; I am well
But for that saying. There is in me such
Antipathy of nature from that word.
Pol. [illegible] tis an old disease, that haunts vs all,
I am not at this instant free. Cor. Nor I
It makes me [illegible] when I thinke vpon't;
My bodie loues [illegible], noe restraint.
Pol. But to be briefe, I thinke tis best we drawe
Our busines to a point of State, for once
After our hartie commendations thus
Neuer to change our mindes, or our wordes.
Cor. Nowe as you loue me, lett that be the word,
Recede; tis exquisitely good, it seemes;
And cannot misse, but strike the matter dead
Tis something to resist a Bishopps powre
Because coercitiue. Iar. Hould o my heart.
Cor. I crie you mercie Sir, I had forgott
But neuer to recede, may still goe on.
Pol. Why there's the point of honor. Iar. That's to say
Perseuerance. Rud. The [illegible] contrary wais.
Iar. I hope

Rudelbinus. So you may play the fool. What hath he done
That must be told?
Polinodus. Nay, nothing yet we know.

Corbus. That's left unto the wits to study out.
Polinodus. Aye, that he may erect tribunals, courts
Of justice, cancel or examine wills
If they prove faulty.
Rudelbinus. I should think this fit,
Were it reformed in secret, and in case
The common law, that balks the Catholics,
Should fail to do us right. I see no sense
But if a private friend or priest may serve
To right our differences that occur,
By telling what in conscience must be done,
But he may do the same, although his power
Be more coercitive, I must confess.
Jargus. O Lord, that word hath struck me to the heart!
Corbus. Help, sirs, to hold the reverend Guelf that sinks.
Rudelbinus. A sudden qualm belike.
Polinodus. How do you, sir?
Jargus. The very apprehension of that word,
Co-er-citive, dismayed me; I am well
But for that saying. There is in me sure
Antipathy of nature from that word.
Polinodus. Pray, 'tis an old disease that haunts us all,
I am not at this instant free.
Corbus. Nor I;
It makes me costive when I think upon't;
My body loves much opening, no restraint.
Polinodus. But to be brief, I think 'tis best we draw
Our business to a point of state, so end
(After our hearty commendations) thus:
Never to change our minds or once recede.
Corbus. Now as ye love me let that be the word,
Recede; 'tis exquisitely good, it seems,
And cannot choose but strike the matter dead.
'Tis somewhat to resist a bishop's power
Because coercitive.
Jargus. Hold, O my heart!
Corbus. I cry you mercy, sir; I had forgot—
But never to recede, nay, still go on.
Polinodus. Aye, there's the point of virtue.
Jargus. That's to say
Perseverance.
Rudelbinus. The clean contrary way.

Jar. I hope you thinke not so Sr. Rude faith, there came
The burden of that songe, into my heade
Just as you spake: But shall wee sett our names
To this defiance? Pol. Noe. Rud. Then t'will be call'd
A Libell. Jar. A most pious one, noe doubt,
And very profitable for your soules.
Cor. If that's suspect'd, or else. Rud. T'were hard to graunt.
Cor. Wee would not undertake it. Pol. Let it goe
Then in the name of all. Rud. What all? Pol. The lay.
Rud. That little were too vast, besides the scorne
Of thousands would looke back upon this act
That knowe it not, or knowing would oppose;
Then some of us may chaunce to get the name
Of Nodipol foolang; or in fine
Some squint ey'd Squire, the finder of a rare
Tale goode tis dangerous to provoke good witts.
Cor. Good witts? I hope wee want not such ourselves
But if you meane by good, the lamer sort
Of comon witts, not stupid nor yet dull,
yet not so quicke to apprehend things right
or sound their depth, but with some odds of tyme
As hindred by affection, or conceit
Wee make men stumble into strange Apologies.
Rud. As wee are made to stumble into this.
Cor. Ile undertake ten thousand such are founde
Will swallowe this device, and prayse the plott,
Some Lords and Ladies too, but Ladies most,
Whom none can satisfie but Thelemites
(I meane in doubts of conscience) otherwise
Noe changes of fashions, which yet could [illegible]
If after they repent, be theirs the shame
Meane tyme, our turnes be serv'd. Rud. you have describ'd
A sort of people able to bring in
All kinds of schisme, and error to the church.
Cor. It may be wee are those; but that which brought
our Thelemites, that hang themselves [illegible] ever.
Rud. [illegible] thinke so but conspiracies, [illegible]
Echo

Jargus. I hope you think not so, sir.
Rudelbinus. Faith, there came
The burden of that song into my head
Just as you spake. But shall we set our names
To this defiance?
Polinodus. No.
Rudelbinus. Then 'twill be called
A libel.
Jargus. A most pious one no doubt,
And very profitable for your souls.
Corbus. Aye, that's supposed, or else—
Rudelbinus. 'Twere hard to grant.
Corbus. We would not undertake it.
Polinodus. Let it go
Then in the name of all.
Rudelbinus. What all?
Polinodus. The lay.
Rudelbinus. That little were too vast. Besides, the scorn
Of thousands would look back upon this act
That know it not, or knowing would oppose;
Then some of us may chance to get the name
Of Nodipol Foolano; or in fine
Some squint-eyed squire, the finder of a hare.
Take heed, 'tis dangerous to provoke good wits.
Corbus. Good wits? I hope we want not such ourselves.
But if you mean by good the tamer sort
Of common wits, not stupid nor yet dull,
Yet not so quick to apprehend things right
Or sound their depth, but with some odds of time—
As hind'red by affection, or conceit—
We make men stumble into strange exploits.
Rudelbinus. As we are made to stumble into this.
Corbus. I'll undertake ten thousand such are found
Will swallow this device and hug the plot,
Some lords and ladies too, but ladies most,
Whom none can satisfy but Ghibellines
(I mean in doubts of conscience)—otherwise
No change of fashions ever yet could tire—
If after they repent, be theirs the shame;
Meantime our turns be served.
Rudelbinus. You have described
A sort of people able to bring in
All kind of schism and error to the church.
Corbus. It may be so are these, but that 'tis thought
Our Ghibellines, that teach them, cannot err.
Rudelbinus. If any think so but themselves, 'tis well,

Els I should hardly place them in my Creede;
They haue bene causers of much good they saie
Within his Land; some answere for their endes.
If they endure the test, and proue good goulde
In his last triall, and like counterfeit kinges,
Are overthrowne the Bishop, horse and man
With Crosiars-staffe, and Miter in the dust.
And yet gett praise on earth, tis match'd in heauen;
I'le burne my Bookes, and onely studie them,
And their historicall actions, while I breathe.
What newes with you Sr.

Scena quarta.

Seruant. Rudelbinus. Polinodus.
Corbas. Tarzus.

Ser. Wee are afraide;
The horse with officers will be beset;
And Roes, Milston leade them, with a route
Of Bills and Staves; they seeke for Priests they saie
And are call'd Pursevants, or hounds of State.
Rud. Haue they possest the dore? Ser. not yet, Rud. Away.
Shift for your selues my freindes, I must be gon.
Pol. Tis premunire, losse of goods and landes,
If you be taken with vs; Sr. farewell.
Cor. Convey me Susan to the posterne gate,
Where I am fear'd to take my last leaue.
Tar. O for a mouse-hoale now to hide my selfe
To be a Ghibelline's not proofe I see.
O staie my freindes from running: whither flie
Whilst I [illegible] the Bishop from my sight;
Hauing had this feined habit of a Guelfe
[illegible] from betraide.

Scena quinta.

Else I should hardly place them in my creed;
They have been causers of much good, they say,
Within this land; some answer for their ends.
If they endure the test and prove good gold
In this last trial, and like vent'rous knights
Can overturn the bishop, horse and man,
With crosier's staff and miter in the dust,
And yet get praise on earth, reward in heaven,
I'll burn my books and only study them
And their heroical actions while I breathe. [*Enter Servant.*]
What news with you, sir?

Scena quarta

Servant, Rudelbinus, Polinodus,
Corbus, Jargus.

Servant. Sir, we are afraid
The house with officers will be beset;
One Rocs, Milston lead them with a rout
Of bills and staves; they seek for priests, they say,
And are called pursuivants or hounds of state.
Rudelbinus. Have they possessed the doors?
Servant. Not yet.
Rudelbinus. Away!
Shift for yourselves my friends, I must be gone. [*Exit.*]
Polinodus. 'Tis *premunire*, loss of goods and lands,
If you be taken with us, sir, farewell. [*Exit.*]
Corbus. Convey me, sirrah, to the postern gate;
Sir, I am forced to take my hasty leave. [*Exeunt.*]
Jargus. O for a mousehole now to hide myself!
To be a Ghibelline's no proof I see
To stay my friends from running; why they fly
As if I were the bishop, from my sight;
Pray God this feignèd habit of a Guelf
Prove not my bane. Who's here? I am betrayed. [*Enter Candle.*]

Scena quinta.

Candle. Fargus.

I much lament the miserable state
Of Papists in this Land, and Romish Priests
That finde not cause or respit from the cry
Of full mouth'd Pursivants, that beate all passes,
Besett their waies, breake houses, pillage roomes,
Dive into privies, search the very beddes
Of women great with childe, and with the fright
Make them miscarry; strippe their cloathes from maids
Under pretence to finde some Agnus Dei's
Or other Reliques. What they finde, as plate
Or Jewells, or whole summes of ready cash
Within the house, t'is theirs, for ever lost
Unto the owners. there's no Judge, that dares
Controll them for't, or stand a Papists friend,
The law denying favour, least the world
Judge him Protector of an odious cause.
Well may the Papists hope for heaven, for since
They have their Purgatory here; nor neede
They feare a second triall after death,
If they could not agree among themselves,
And beare with patience this [illegible] distresse,
Rets. I thanke their Milstone the divell and all,
For hell's broake loose, if they but once appeare
And shew their faces [illegible] in the streetes
[illegible] they meane to [illegible] children [illegible]
And women squeake to see their goggle eyes
That glare as they would sett the world on fire.
Were it not for such rascalls as these, long since
I might have [illegible] good [illegible] in my soule
And beene a Papist of the [illegible] straine;
None of these [illegible] Spiritts, that confound
Hierarchicall order, and begin to girde
[illegible] Sea-sicke, to heare the very name,

Ex. ambo.

Scena quinta

Candle, Jargus.

Candle. I much lament the miserable state
Of Papists in this land, and Romish priests
That find no cause or respite from the cry
Of full-mouthed pursuivants that beat all paths,
Beset highways, break houses, pillage rooms,
Dive into privies, search the very beds
Of women great with child and with the fright
Make them miscarry, strip the clothes from maids
Under pretense to find some *Agnus Dei's*
Or other relics. What they find, as plate
Or jewels or whole sums of ready cash
Within the house, 'tis theirs, forever lost
Unto the owners. There's no Juda that dares
Control them for't, or stand a Papist's friend,
(The law denying favor,) lest the world
Judge him protector of an odious cause.
Well may the Papists hope for heaven, for sure
They have their purgatory here; nor need
They fear a second trial after death
If they could not agree among themselves,
And bear with patience this almighty Cross—
Rocs I should say—Milston, the devil and all—
For hell's broke loose if they but once appear
And show their fiery noses in the street
Or house they mean to rifle; children, boys,
And [women] squeak to see their [goggle] eyes
That glare as they would set the world on fire.
Were it not for such rubs as these, long since
I might have writ good Christian in my soul
And been a Papist of the ancient stamp,
None of these new-coined spirits that confound
Hierarchic order and begin to pick
And grow seasick to hear the very name

Of Bishopps, both Generall and Particular
But Jurisdiction, power to binde and loose,
Commission to approve, those strike them dead
And the [illegible] my distresse have not discharg'd.
A Ghibellin, there's [illegible] on the ground,
See how he lifts his hands, and prayes at heaven,
And does his followers [illegible] against the clergy.
[illegible], I will [illegible] him for his owne, not [illegible]
To ridd him wholie from his feares, his plot
Was first begun by me, nor shall it dye
Thus in the infancie. [illegible], stand up,
Take heart of grace (a thing it seemes you want
By, faith, as well as I.) take courage [illegible].
Jar. I thanke you kindly, twas a suddaine qualme
I feare is the [illegible], but your laste words
have struck the fright more inward, there it lyes
And makes my heart to quake and pant for life,
[illegible] in the [illegible], yea the racke,
And Gallowes, for a worde, in a just cause,
And for Religion as they have done
Of our forefathers, Martirs, for their faith;
yet in the cause of Bishopps and their power
I am turn'd cowarde, and I know not how;
[illegible], there's some secrett in't. Can: Some secret guilt
That clogs your cause, or else some want of faith,
Or [illegible] of selfe-love, or pride, or [illegible];
It may be covetousnes, and feare to [illegible]
Some goulden mountaines fabrick'd in your braine
Whereof for future ages, is it not?
Jar. Faith, some such thinge [illegible], and fills my thought
With much distraction. Can: But here's hope that praier
And discipline, and [illegible] may subdue
And [illegible]. Jar. [illegible] of [illegible],

And [illegible]

Of bishop, vicar-general, and the like—
But jurisdiction, power to bind and loose,
Commission to approve, these strike them dead—
And see if my discourse have not dispatched
A Ghibelline, there's Jargus on the ground;
See how he tilts his heels and spurns at heaven:
So do his fellows kick against the church.
Well, I will daw him for this once, not so
To rid him wholly from his fears; this plot
Was first begun by me, nor shall it die
Thus in the infancy. Arise, stand up,
Take heart of grace (a thing it seems you want
By fits, as well as I). Take courage, sir.

Jargus. I thank you kindly, 'twas a stomach qualm.
I feared the pursuivants, but your last words
Have struck the fright more inward; here it lies
And makes my heart to quake and pant for life.
I could endure these harpies, yea the rack
And gallows for a need, in a just cause
And for religion, as the rest have done
Of our forefathers, martyrs for their faith;
Yet in this cause of bishops and their power
I am turned coward and I know not how;
Sure, there's some secret in't.

Candle. Some secret guilt
That clogs your cause, or else some want of faith
Or sickness of self-love, or pride, or so;
It may be covetousness and fear to mar
Some golden mountain's fabric, which your brain
Projects for future ages, is it not?

Jargus. Faith, some such [thing] cries buzz, and fills my thought
With much distraction.

Candle. But there's hope that prayer,
And disciplines, and hairshirts may subject
And tame this fury.

Jargus. They are out of date,

And seldome vs'd by vs, but to slow fleash
Or stupifie the body, the inward man
Wee striue to mortifie. Can. You striue in vaine,
The scoure the inward man cannot indure
A [illegible] yet his pointe [illegible]
But leaving this discourse, you must desist
Some monies to [illegible] for the [illegible] straite
The man's [illegible] officers that [illegible] the Priests
Take it you are one. Jac. You may mistake,
I am not what I seeme. Can. True, you say right,
You are a wolfe, I tooke you for a lambe,
Or rather thus, you seeme to be a Guelfe
But a Ghibellin. Jac. In odious thinge,
This single word doth include the night
But in thinge favourable, sith the lawes,
All this word Monke, or Monke doth not include
A Priest or Abbott; so a Guelfe or Priest
Includes not Ghibellin; and in this sence
I am not Priest. Can. Indeede you shall be none
I'm not sure at all, that I can see
Because you should a Priest, an odious thing,
But more a Bishop, and his Coadiutor
And nothing favourable but your ende.
It may be this hath made you oft denie
Before the Magistrate, that you are Priests,
Because the name is odious, and containes
Most of your tribe, and some could wish in thinge
More favourable, it were so indeede;
And you were none at all, for what say they
Is Priesthood in you, but a stale to drawe
Upon scare on simple soules, that you with ease
May spoile their bodies of the golden fleece.
Sheep [illegible] a [illegible], thrust into a waterman's lande,
[illegible] with your [illegible] the [illegible] that give you life;

And all

And seldom used by us but to scare fleas
Or stupefy the itch; the inward man
We strive to mortify.
Candle. You strive in vain:
It seems this inward man cannot endure
A bishop's presence yet, his power much less.
But leaving this discourse, you must devise
Some means to save yourself; the house will straight
Be crammed with officers that search for priests—
I take it you are one.
Jargus. You may mistake;
I am not what I seem.
Candle. Troth, you say right,
You are a wolf, I took you for a lamb;
Or rather thus, you seem to be a Guelf,
But a Ghibelline—
Jargus. In odious things
The simple never doth include the mixed,
But in things favorable, saith the law,
As this word clerk, or monk doth not include
A priest or abbot; so a Guelf or priest
Includes no Ghibelline; and in this sense
I am no priest.
Candle. Indeed you should be none
In any sense at all that I can see,
Because you hold a priest an odious thing,
But more a bishop and his faculties,
And nothing favorable but your ends.
It may be this hath made you oft deny
Before the magistrate that you are priests,
Because the name is odious and contains
None of your tribe; and some could wish in things
Most favorable it were so indeed
And you were none at all; for what, say they,
Is priesthood in you but a stale to draw,
Then seize on simple souls, that you with ease
May spoil their bodies of the golden fleece?
Or like a sword, thrust into a madman's hand,
Wherewith you strike the root that gave you life

And above blacke loyns of the noblest braines,
That was a Bishop renowned, his throne
[illegible] Bishop makers, haters I should saie
Thou are [illegible]; for this you all deserve
That [illegible] should hate you, whom you would disgrace,
And Bishops whom you quarter, hange and drawe
As if they were at Tyburne in your hands
Even at his power, to be depos'd (craft of
I should have said) And [illegible] here,
You now should wish to see your Bishop hang'd
Whom you have sought to strangle at his birth,
And [illegible] and have long since consp'd
To extinguish the name of Bishop from the earth.
Jac: O God forbid that we should wish him harme,
Or seeke his death, we leave that to the lawe;
But if the State would please to keepe him safe,
Or banish him, That [illegible] may be [illegible]
[illegible] we desire no more.
Can: I would I were a Statesman for your sakes,
You should have your desire. Jac. And you no doubt,
A great reward [illegible] for your good will.
Can: He should be safe, and you should take his place,
For you should be profess'd, and [illegible] before.
Jac: [illegible] the Bishops [illegible] ungodly right.
Can: [illegible] the [illegible], where you doe more good
Then [illegible] and [illegible] soules
[illegible] you make Christian [illegible] till
You should triumph, and plant the Bishops [illegible],
In great necessity, and for a time.
But [illegible] Christian [illegible] that you make
[illegible] factious, and [illegible] to be [illegible]
[illegible] makes you [illegible] from [illegible];

And

And at one blow lop off the noblest branch
That makes a bishop reverenced, his power?
Such bishop makers, haters I should say,
You are esteemed; for this you well deserve
That priests should hate you, whom you would disgrace,
And bishops whom you quarter, hang and draw
As if they were at Byturne in your hands
Even at this hour, to be deposed (cast off
I should have said). And 'tis no marvel sure
You now should wish to see your bishop hanged,
Whom you have sought to strangle at his birth
And entrance here; and have long since conspired
To [sponge] the name of bishop from men's hearts.
Jargus. O God forbid that we should wish him harm
Or seek his death, we leave that to the law;
But if the state would please to keep him safe,
Or banish him, that so we may be rid
Of this vexation, we desire no more.
Candle. I would I were a statesman for your sakes;
You should have your desire.
Jargus. And you, no doubt,
A great reward in heaven for your good will.
Candle. He should be safe, and you should take his place,
For you should be preferred and go before.
Jargus. Before the bishops, 'twere a goodly sight.
Candle. Yes, to the Indies, where you do more good
Than stay to brabble here and hazard souls.
In kingdoms you make Christian 'tis thought fit
You should triumph and play the bishop's part,
In great necessity, and for a time;
But not in Christian kingdoms that you mar
With factions and ambitions to be great,
Which makes you tyrants of an holy cause;

And striuing to usurpe an others right,
Deserue to lose your owne; like those dogs
The Judges to your [illegible] places.
There you proue Saints, where Sadduces and Scribes,
There Pharisees, and there Samaritanes.
'Tis therefore fittest you should change the aire,
And there be still imploy'd; this is your doome,
Unlesse you would amend; and better brooke
What you pretend in shew, but least obserue,
Obedience to superiours, and higher powers;
And yet you beare your bones to kisse the ground,
When you but nodd; and if they once repine,
[illegible] you [illegible] till you driue
Them out of doores like dirt, for some cause
Of slight contempt; some matter of small weight.
Whereas in [illegible] that [illegible] the life
And soule of discipline, on which depends
The beauteous structure that adornes the Church,
And makes like to Angells hierarchie,
The only proppe, and Atlas of the world,
There (I abhorre to speake it) you contend
With Lucifer to raise your thoughts aboue
Not only humane, but diuine degrees,
And makes [illegible] Tyrants, by [illegible] your aymes,
[illegible] you [illegible] short, and [illegible]
[illegible] 'tis Gods glory, you aduance
In all our actions; 'tis the Motto, stile
And glosse of all our works. Can then the glosse
Proue currant [illegible] it [illegible] the text?
Or God be glorified by euill workes?
[illegible] God worketh good of euill, so doe wee.
He does it not [illegible] but for his sake.

And al

And striving to usurp another's right
Deserve to lose your own, like Aesop's dog.
The Indies is your only place:
There you prove saints, here Sadducees and scribes;
Here Pharisees, and there Samaritans.
'Tis therefore fittest you should change this air
And there be still employed; this is your doom,
Unless you could amend and better brook
What you pretend in show, but least observe,
Obedience to supreme and higher powers;
And yet you teach your boys to kiss the ground
When you but nod; and if they once repine,
Add penance upon penance till you drive
Them out of doors like outcasts, for some cause
Of slight contempt, some matter of small weight.
Whereas in serious things that touch the life
And soul of discipline, on which depends
The beauteous fabric that adorns the church,
And makes like to angels—hierarchy,
The only prop and Atlas of the world—
Here (I abhor to speak it) you contend
With Lucifer to raise your thoughts above
Not only human, but divine decrees,
And makes heaven's throne by level with your aims;
But look you light not short and catch a fall.
[*Jargus.*] Alas, sir, 'tis God's glory we advance
In all our actions; 'tis the motto, style,
And gloss of all our works.
Candle. How can the gloss
Prove current, when it falsifies the text?
Or God be glorified by evil works?
Jargus. God worketh good of evil, so do we.
Candle. He does it not.
Jargus. Nor we, but for his sake,

And ad maiorem Dei gloriam:
Which takes the edge of evill from our workes.
Car. O does it so? Sure if you were at Rome,
Thou durst not stand to this. Jar. Welcome to Sr.
The case is alter'd here, for London sakes;
But not at Rome. Car. Well for this quaint conceipt,
I shall goe neere to fitt you with an oath
Shall alter you, and make your workes appeare
In their true colours: Sr I wish yourselfe,
And for your safetie have devis'd a waie,
To fright the Pursevants, if they should come
To finde you out, that so you may escape.
Jar. I rest, much bound unto you for your care.
Car. While I step in for this disguise, you may
Commit yourselfe unto this honest paire,
And make a trinitie of Anarchists,
Though not in doctrine; and so expect
My fast returne. Jar. Must I be forc'd to take
For harbor here?

Grex

Theralus. Lucianus. Targus.

I cannot call to minde,
That I did reade this passage, in the Play.
Lu. This Candle is a wagg, and faine would ioyne
A Ghibellin with us, in our consort.
The. Art thou content: Lu. I like him for his stuffe.
The. And I mislike him, not although this stuffe
[illegible] my stomacke-holds were it not some
[illegible] Bishops of the greatest number, I
May hope to [illegible], [illegible] our Judges.

Lu. And

And *ad majorem Dei gloriam*;
Which takes the edge of evil from our works.
Candle. Oh, does it so? Sure, if you were at Rome
You durst not stand to this.
Jargus. Believe it, sir.
The case is altered here, so Ploydon says,
But not at Rome.
Candle. [*Aside.*] Well, for this quaint conceit
I shall go near to fit you with a case
Shall alter you and make your works appear
In their true colors. Sir, I wish you well,
And for your safety have devised a way
To fright the pursuivants if they should chance
To find you out, that so you may escape.
Jargus. I rest much bound unto you for your care.
Candle. While I step in for this disguise, you may
Commit yourself unto this honest pair,
And make a trinity of anarchists—
Though not in unity—and so expect
My short return. [*Exit.*]
Jargus. Must I be forced to seek
For harbor here?

Grex.

Therulus, Lucianus, Jargus.

Therulus. I cannot call to mind
That I did read this passage in the play.
Lucianus. This Candle is a wag, and fain would join
A Ghibelline with us in one consort.
Therulus. Art thou content?
Lucianus. I like him for his cause.
Therulus. And I mislike him not, although this case
Concerns my copyhold, were it put home
Unto our bishops; of whose number, I
May hope to prove a primate ere I die.

Lu. And I an Elder of the Sinagogue.
Th. Of Zeners bellowes, Sir, I would you take your place.
Lu. your good example Sir hath made you friends.
Sur. I will accept your offer, and sitt downe.
Th. He commes the stoole hee hath made a stage,
And his broad Arke, and place the Coere,
To take your rest at volume, in the worke.
I rolle the Curtaine. Lu. Tis pretty sure,
He meanes to make a Comedie of Ruth
Or of Susanna. Surely with the Elders.
He cannot else but take and [illegible]
Th. The Musicke, now make way for the [illegible].

Actus tertius

Scena prima

Candle, Targus

See, this goes well; I'le suite him in his kinde,
To make our sport compleate; there wanted two,
A Divell, and a foole; the Divell is found,
And here's his Coate: the foole I play my selfe,
Rather then faile to finde one in this place,
That better can performe the part; this here,
In such a throng; if all should prove so wise,
As none could act the part, he oft hath plaid.
If all should faile, here comes a Drone behinde
Of learned Gnidos, [illegible] it to the life,
Who being held for wise, and knowing more
then knows not this, that they imployed a knave,
Or will not knowe it, which is worse, because
they thinke that Goodnesse and the strength of friends
Whereof the Gaolers are [illegible], will serve
To bolster

Lucianus. And I an elder of the synagogue.
Therulus. Of Jews belike; [*To Jargus.*] Sir, will you take your place?
Lucianus. Your good example, sir, hath made you friends.
Jargus. I will accept your offer and sit down.
Therulus. It seems the poet here hath made a stop
To end his second [Act], and placed you here
To take you up at retrieve in the next.
I relish the conceit.
Lucianus. 'Tis pretty sure;
I mean to make a comedy of Ruth
Or of Susanna shortly, with the like;
It cannot choose but take and fructify.
Therulus. The music now makes way for the third Act.

Actus tertius

Scena prima

Candle, Jargus.

Candle. So, this goes well; I'll suit him in this kind.
To make our sport complete there wanted two,
A devil and a fool; the devil is found
And here's his coat; the fool I play myself,
Rather than fail to find one in this place
That better can perform the part; ['tis] hard,
In such a throng, if all should prove so wise
As none could act the part he oft hath played.
If all should fail, here comes a crew behind
Of learned ones shall act it to the life;
Who being held for wise and knowing men,
Yet know not this: that they impugn a truth,
Or will not know it, which is worse, because
They think that greatness, and the strength of friends,
Whereof the Guelfs are poorly backed, will serve

To boulster all their actions, and smooth ther
The wrinckled browes of Heaven, which makes
Religion monstrous in all sortes of men,
That must be effected with neglect of right.
But to my taske etc. the [illegible] is here,
You must be speedie. [illegible] What a divells [illegible]
[illegible] my gravitie, this change [illegible]
Cap. Remember etc. you are to deale with ffriends
ffor [illegible] and [illegible] divells [illegible]
In your shape you cannott putt them off;
[illegible] his [illegible] [illegible] [illegible] should, [illegible]
[illegible] a man, if they should bring me forth;
And now I thinke on it, [illegible] is said to leade
A dogge a longe with him [illegible] out [illegible]
Cap. Tis true, but Phisitians [illegible] winde
They are more subtile in their [illegible] then hares,
And if he could, you shall not take the ground,
And [illegible] the stopp in daunger of his Nose
But you shall mount the chimney, poore and stand
And stand upon that shelfe, an [illegible] for [illegible]
And [illegible] Baron, till the storme be past
In case you should be [illegible], you may leape downe
And fright with [illegible] but you drive them [illegible],
Or make your owne escape, [illegible] for feare.
[illegible] [illegible] [illegible] [illegible] put it on,
[illegible] to play the Divills part.
Cap. [illegible] but you have practis'd it before.
[illegible] now [illegible]. [illegible]. My [illegible]
[illegible] [illegible] [illegible]
[illegible] [illegible] [illegible] [illegible]
[illegible] [illegible] [illegible]
[illegible] [illegible] [illegible] [illegible]
[illegible]

To bolster all their actions and smooth up
The wrinkled brows of policy, which makes
Religion monstrous in all sorts of men
That most affect it with neglect of right.
But to my task: [*To Jargus.*] Sir, the disguise is here,
You must be speedy.

Jargus. What, a devil's coat?
Will it become my gravity, this change?

Candle. Remember, sir, you are to deal with friends—
For pursuivants are worse than devils here—
In your shape you cannot put them off;
In this you may.

Jargus. Pray God they smell me not
To be a man—if they should urge me hard—
And now I think on't, Rocs is said to lead
A dog along with him to wind out priests.

Candle. 'Tis true, but Ghibellines he cannot wind:
They are more subtle in their trains than hares;
And if he could, you shall not take the ground
And play the fox in danger of his nose.
But you shall mount this chimney piece and stand
Upon that shelf, an harbor for salt eels
And rusty bacon, till the storm be past.
In case you should be spied, you may leap down
And fight with firebrands till you drive them hence
Or make your own escape, while they for fear
Creep into several holes.

Jargus. Come, put it on,
I'll learn this once to play the devil's part.

Candle. No doubt but you have practiced it before,
It fits you now so well.

Jargus. My hand once in,
I purpose to go through stitch, but say,
Where are these Gogmagogs?

Candle. About the door
They hover yet, straight ready to chop in
At the least watchword. Rocs his nose appeared

Out at an alehouse lattice as I came,
And like a blazing comet struck me blind,
That for a time I was constrained to grope
And feel my way; whether his eye or face
Had dazzled me (for both are fiery red,
And like a glass enamored of the sun
Project a brightness that outdares the sight)
I know not well. I'm sure what I beheld
Was not an angel's face, but such as yours:
I mean a bad one, such as you appear
Now to my fancy.
Jargus. Devils of this kind
Must thus be conjured, else our prayers and fasts
Will hardly drive them out.
Candle. You need not [woo]
My softness to believe you in this point.
I think your prayers and fastings have small force
To drive them forth, that are yourselves possessed
With greater spirits, covetousness and pride,
Two sakers, rather sackers of the world;
So proper chiefly to your rulers here
As shadow to the substance of a man,
Or moisture to the main and ocean sea.
Else you would never in so just a claim
Confront your bishop, and oppose his power
Upon such slender terms; you sure would spare
To lay flat violent hands upon the text
And sense of briefs and wrest them as you do;
Then fill the world with clamors, yea with threats,
And make the pope to stagger and demur,
Whether in these extremes of time and friends,
Whereof you plead advantage, he were best
To yield so far to you as not to tax
And censure you as yet, or you to him
In free acceptance of his second self

I meane your Bishopp there; but there's noe hope
You should venture to share a godly worke,
Least your beginning with your ends should square,
And you committ an Act against your will;
That lookes noe further then the love of God,
The rules of Charitie; and good of soules;
Which you professe in words, but in your deedes
Performe it with a world of base respects,
And reservations more then base respects.
But harke: I heare some trampling, to your Mass
Mount up my sister of piety. Goe, its a body's [illegible],
Here, let him stand whilst I [illegible] and devine.
But staie! this enters first; tis, tis, my friend
Eradius, thou art welcome to our sporte.

Scena Secunda.

Erudius. Carello

What sporte? Car. Why, the game made a Gorkin, hee
hath newly cast his feathers, and will prove
A killing Bird, when he shall come to game.
Er. I understand you not. Car. Why the Saint
Or Chimney, Targas, in a Divells Coate [illegible]
Hath taken Sanctuarie, to avoide
The Pursevants, whom he imagines nowe
About the house, and ready for to seize him
By my invention he is thus surprized
With Saint Francis Shoes, and from a Ghibellin
Translated to a Divell. For you knowe
By nature, the corruption of the one
Must needes begett the other, as things best
declined into the worst; I'me sure the Ghibellin
Was Divelish.

[illegible]

(I mean your bishop here); but there's no hope
You should concur to such a godly work,
Lest your beginning with your ends should square
And you commit an act against your wills,
That looks no further than the love of God,
The rules of charity, and good of souls,
Which you profess in words, but in your deeds
Perform it with a world of base respects
And reservations, more than those respects.
But hark, I hear some trampling, to your mew.
Mount up, my bird of prey. [*Exit Jargus.*] So, he is lodged;
There let him stand until I call him down.
But stay! Who enters first? Oh, 'tis my friend. [*Enter Erudius.*]
Erudius, thou art welcome to our sport.

Scena secunda

Erudius, Candle.

Erudius. What sport?
Candle. Why, I have made a jerkin, he
Hath newly cast his feathers and will prove
A killing bird when he shall come to hand.
Erudius. I understand you not.
Candle. Within this vault
Or chimney, Jargus in a devil's coat
Hath taken sanctuary to avoid
The pursuivants, whom he imagines now
About the house and ready for to search;
By my invention he is thus surprised
With panic fears, and from a Ghibelline
Translated to a devil. For you know,
By nature the corruption of the one
Must needs beget the other, as things best
Decline unto the worst; I'm sure the plot

Was divellish, he and others handled last,
And well deserv'd his vengeance. Ex. I must confesse
Because against a Bishopp, tis not lesse
Then if it were committed against the State
Off God himselfe, whom Bishopps represent
In his full power, and government of Prelates
As Kinge of minds and bodies; which two spheres
Ought not to be contemn'd, or spurn'd against,
For God sustaines their quarrell, as his owne:
And in this sence he well may be compar'd
Unto the divell, that doth either wronge
Though with pretence and shew of greater good,
Nor can the Ghibellinis pretend that good
In Bishopps want, which will not freely flowe;
Were there noe Ghibellin within this land,
Or Antihierarchist in all the world.
For Ghibellin and Antihierarchist
Are words accounted convertible termes.
Cap. The same that Antichristian. Ex. Except
Some few religious Ghibellins indeede,
That keepe their vowes, sustain'd, and take the part
Of none but Gods anointed, while the rest
Laugh them to scorne, and in our London taverns
Singe Pæans, and applaude their good successe
In working mischiefe, and disgrace to Guelfs.
Cap. Never, tell them [illegible], this place for me
I have [illegible] a place of [illegible]
Where he may doe his pennance in the smoake
A while, in soote and ashes. Come, tis time
Wee quitt this place, and take an other stand
From whence wee may descrie a knot of fowle
That hither come in flocks. To day is held
A generall meeting of these states of knights.
For tis a darke and dangerous path they treade,
And [illegible]

Was devilish he and others handled last,
And well deserves this change.
Erudius. I must confess,
Because against a bishop, 'tis no less
Than if it were commenced against the state
Of God himself, whom bishops represent
In his full power and government of souls,
As kings of lives and bodies; which two powers
Ought not to be contemned or spurned against,
For God sustains their quarrel as his own;
And in this sense he well may be compared
Unto the devil that doth either wrong,
Though with pretense and show of greater good.
Nor can the Ghibellines pretend that good
In bishops' want which will not trebly flow
Were there no Ghibelline within this land,
Or Antihierarchist in all the world.
For Ghibelline and Antihierarchist
Are now accounted convertible terms.
Candle. The same that Antichristian.
Erudius. Except
Some few religious Ghibellines indeed,
That keep their vows unstained and take the part
Of none but God's anointed, while the rest
Laugh him to scorn and in our common tears
Sing paeans and applaud their good success
In working mischief and disgrace to Guelfs.
Candle. Well, let them brag that win; I'm sure for one
I have procured a place of little ease,
Where he may do his penance in the smoke
Awhile, in soot and ashes. Come, 'tis time
We quit this place and take another stand,
From whence we may descry a knot of fowl
That hither come in flocks. Today is held
A general meeting of these states of knights,
For 'tis a dark and dangerous path they tread

And leaded to hell, & Guile. ffor, heauen protects
Noe disobedience to superior powers,
But loves subordination, wch those men
Striue to abolish. In this place theyr neste,
An ordinary harbor for such birds
As flye by twilight; you must knowe besides
That Woodmen heere may haue an actiue voice,
And passe their verdict on the Bishopps head.
Some companie appeares; lett's be gone.

Scena Tertia.

Dauus. Spirus. Sapertonus. Coreditus.

Viua la Malta. Spir. Now braue Spiritts on
Dauus and Saperton, my valiant Dons,
A warre of honor calls vs to the field
Against an airie Bishopp. Sap. Would there were
Whole Airies of them, I shall neede noe Armes
Offensiue, or defensiue, but my pen.
Dau. And I noe other but my Spectacles.
Cor. That neither pen nor Spectacles will serue
Without some further Glorie. Sap. Not serue?
Were Bellarmine aliue, or Lessius here
Before my face, how would they sweat for feare,
Least they should heare the thunder of my pen?
Dau. Or see the lightning of my Spectacles?
Spi. Or feele the rodds that I haue laide in pisse,
To tickle the Hierarchie? Cor. Wee must not thinke
The Bishopp such a schooleboy, to be aw'd
With fruitlesse words. Spi. Wee'le stripp him of his gowne
And leaue it naked like a Mutton's taile;
And then lett me alone to lay it on,
Myne Arme is vs'd to bambasts of this kinde.

Sa. As for

And leads to hell, I think. For heaven protects
No disobedience to superior powers,
But loves subordination, which these men
Strive to abolish. In this place they meet,
An ordinary harbor for such birds
As fly by owl-light; you must know besides
That women here may have an active voice
And pass their verdict on the bishop's head.
Some company approach; let's be gone. [*Exeunt.*]

Scena tertia

Davus, Spirius, Sapertonus, Coredurus.

Davus. *Viva La Malta.*
Spirius. Now brave spirits on!
Davus and Saperton, my valiant dons,
A war of honor calls us to the field
Against an airy bishop.
Sapertonus. Would there were
Whole airies of them, I shall need no arms
Offensive or defensive but my pen.
Davus. And I no other but my spectacles.
Coredurus. Soft, neither pens nor spectacles will serve
Without some further policy.
Sapertonus. Not serve?
Were Bellarmine alive, or Lessius here
Before my face, how would they sweat for fear
Lest they should hear the thunder of my pen?
Davus. Or see the lightning of my spectacles?
Spirius. Or feel the rods that I have laid in piss
To firk the hierarchy?
Coredurus. We must not think
The bishop such a schoolboy, to be awed
With fruitless words.
Spirius. We'll strip him of his power
And leave it naked like a cuckoo's tail,
And then let me alone to lay it on:
Mine arm is used to combats of this kind.

1 · 40

Sa. As for his powre, if you have power to strive,
I'le laie it bare, and naked to your hand;
I meane any man shall doe it. Dec. And my tongue
Shall strip him both of creditt, and of freinds.
Cor. But will it not provoke the Pope thinke you,
To take his part when he shall see his powre
Thus left by us. Spi. The Pope must be content
To beare with patience, what he cannot mend;
The best is, we have found the State inclin'd
To our proceeding then, what neede we feare.
Cor. Some sharpe reproofe, or censure for our paines?
Sap. Tut, feare not that, we have the grey-goose winge
Shall fight our quarrell even against the Pope,
He must be told his owne, and his decrees
Without a generall councell doe not binde
But by discretion; It remaines in us
To make them currant, or to clippe their winge
As in my writinge I have largely prov'd
And made it evident unto the State.
Cor. But all the rest of Christendome besides
Will run you little thankes, for by your grounds
New heresies may springe and braving schismes
Before a generall councell cut them downe
And that may prove too late, when they growe high
And swell in multitudes above their bankes,
Like full gorg'd rivers; here some other meane
Was left by Christ, wch you would faine conceale
To staie the deluge then so longe a tyme
Wherein a generall councell may be call'd
Else woe be to the Church. Sap. The Church must beare,
And when one, in his owne conducte
may be suppos'd uncertaine where or how,
That may support her in a time of neede;
But this my learning never yet could finde
Or conscience grant.

Scena.

Sapertonus. As for his power, if you have power to strike
I'll lay it bare and naked to your hand;
I mean my pen shall do it.
Davus. And my tongue
Shall strip him both of credit and of friends.
Coredurus. But will it not provoke the pope, think you,
To take his part when he shall see his power
Thus lashed by us?
Spirius. The pope must be content
To bear with patience what he cannot mend;
The best is, we have found the state inclined
To our proceeding; then what need we fear?
Coredurus. Some sharp reproof or censure for our pains?
Sapertonus. Tut, fear not that, we have the grey-goose wing
Shall fight our quarrel even against the pope.
He must be told his own, and his decrees
Without a general council do not bind
But by discretion; it remains in us
To make them current or to clip their wings,
As in my writings I have largely proved
And made it evident unto the state.
Coredurus. But all the rest of Christendom besides
Will con you little thanks, for by your grounds
New heresies may spring and branch themselves
Before a general council cry them down,
And that may prove too late, when they grow high
And swell in multitudes above their banks
Like full-gorged rivers; sure some other mean
Was left by Christ (which you would fain conceal)
To stay this deluge, than so long a time
Wherein a general council may be called,
Else woe be to the church.
Sapertonus. The church must bear,
And pardon me; in this some providence
May be supposed, uncertain where or how,
That may protect her in a time of need;
But this my learning never yet could find,
Or conscience grant. [*Exeunt.*]

Scena quarta

Candido with Euridias from above

Tis mervaile, for the one
Is blinde, the other halfe, his learning's blinde,
His Conscience lame. Eur. Why, with friends [illegible]
Not naturall defects. Can. And therefore both
The worse supported; speake softly, least they heare.
Can. Why, now are you in private to consult
Behould in ther Chayre, before they passe
They le leave a taste behinde of their designes:
Bolnubus is the first, the other [illegible]
I have not seene, Can. first, then I'll informe you
Of knowledge in the man. Eur. yet hee's reported,
He that with strings [illegible] Bolinubus so,
And various postures both of face and legge
The Generall Procurator for the Kings
That guild their floore, and Onoplatus [illegible],
Which some interpret, a [illegible]; or [illegible]
That seemes to beare his wings upon his eares,
Like to another Midas, or Mid-asse.
As for my part, I thinke the man not badde,
Nor much to be envi'd for high conceit,
Or straines of witt, or learning, only I speake
Against the Bishopp, putts him in esteeme,
And honour with the Master Ghibellin;
Which makes him much imploy'd, he seldome goes
Without some pockett papps to bestowe
On everie one he meets, that seemes to snappe
At Bishopps not his owne but other mens;
Nor yet to be admir'd, but by himselfe;
And when he speakes, or writs unto a friend,
He dropps such sentences, would make one sicke,
Which he

Scena quarta

Candle with Erudius from above

Candle. No marvel, for the one
Is blind, the other halts: his learning's blind,
His conscience lame.
Erudius. Both artificial sure,
Not natural defects.
Candle. And therefore both
The less excused.
Erudius. Speak softly lest they hear.
Candle. They now are gone in private to consult. [*Enter below Bolnutus, Onoplutus, Nicodimus, Pamoppus.*]
Behold another troop. Before they pass
They'll leave a taste behind of their designs.
Bolnutus is the first, the other three
I have not seen; canst thou instruct my want
Of knowledge in the men?
Erudius. Yes, by report:
He that with cringes courts Bolnutus so,
And various postures both of face and leg,
Is general procurator for the knights
That gild their fleece, and Onoplutus called,
Which some interpret, a rich ass, or one
That seems to bear his riches in his ears
Like to another Midas or Mid-Ass.
As for my part, I think the man not bad,
Nor much to be envied for high conceit
Or strains of wit or learning, only zeal
Against the bishop puts him in esteem
And favor with the master Ghibelline,
Which makes him much employed; he seldom goes
Without some pocket papers to bestow
On everyone he meets that seems to snap
At bishops (not his own but other men's,
Nor yet to be admired but by himself);
And when he speaks or writes unto a friend
He drops forth sentences would make one sick,

Which he distinguisheth with Rumors and paines;
As such, the Bishopp is not well advis'd,
His words ridiculous, his claime absurd,
he makes himselfe contemptible. Can. Enough.
Passe to the other two, my stomacke heaves
At those old Sawyers, fruits of a narrowe witt.
Eru. The other two are Courtiers of S.t James,
A Stocke of auncient kingship, and in those raines
haue since beheld the Ambition, and disgrac'd
Their noble Ancestors, which were esteem'd
The Stewards of the Church, and Hierarchie
In former tymes, as by these two of late
Are like to be infring'd, and his for want
Of good advise, and knowledge of those Causes,
That being over credulous afore
The Counsell of an Enemie before
The Bishopps right, whom now they will oppose
The Companie, and so are like to speede;
Their names Pamophus, and Nicodimus;
The laste is first in place, and more retir'd,
And temperate by nature, then the first
Who is more cholericke, yet both are bold
In their opposition to the Bishopps course,
And more on trust, then knowledge of the truth.
Ca. A favorable censure, now they speake.

Scena quinta.

Bolnubus. Onoplutus. Nicodim. Pamoph.
Candle. Erudius.

I wonder Targus hath not yet appear'd
I thought to finde him here, you must supplie
his absence Onoplutus, till he comes
And take his office. Ono. I am resolv'd to take

more then

Which he distinguisheth with hums and haws,
As thus: "The bishop is not well advised,
His power ridiculous, his claim absurd,
He makes himself contemptible—"
Candle. Enough,
Pass to the other two, my stomach heaves
At these old saws, fruits of a narrow wit.
Erudius. The other two are vent'rers of Saint James,
A stock of ancient knights, and in these wars
Have run besides the cushion and disgraced
Their noble ancestors, which were esteemed
For pillars of the church and hierarchy
In former times; which by these two of late
Are like to be infringed, and this for want
Of good advice and knowledge of themselves,
That being over-credulous prefer
The counsel of an enemy before
The bishop's right, whom now they will oppose
For company, and so are like to speed.
Their names Pamoppus and Nicodimus;
The last is first in place and more retired
And temperate by nature than the first,
Who is more choleric, yet both are led
Upon persuasion to the bishop's war,
And more on trust than knowledge of the truth.
Candle. A favorable censure! Now they speak.

Scena quinta

Bolnutus, Onoplutus, Nicodimus, Pamoppus.
Candle [*and*] *Erudius* [*from above*].

Bolnutus. I wonder Jargus hath not yet appeared;
I thought to find him here. You must supply
His presence, Onoplutus, till he comes
And take his office.
Onoplutus. I am used to take

More then I came to give. Bol. I iudge you fitt
To serve my turne, the better to perswade
These worthie knightes to leave the Bishopps side,
That takes from him more then he would give.
Nil. He saith it is his right. Bol. See let him saie;
I'me sure the custome hath bene, ours to take;
Nor will we change our custome for a songe;
Give vs possession, let him challenge right
And gett it when he can. Pa. If you take all
And are too loath to give a little back
How shall we hope for favour at your hands
When wee shall stand in neede. Pro. Bee but good boyes,
And please Bolnutus well, you neede not feare,
But then you must forsake the Bishopps part,
And stiffly stand for vs. Pa. For that your purse
May make vs sure, with only gold you friends
You knowe our natures never yet could strike
An harmonie in Schooles, yet there your purse
May chaunge to tune vs to another key;
Some works we doe for charitie, but moste
For Benefactors. Pro. Sr you must comply
With ministers, reforme them how you please.
Bol. Lett me alone to leade them wth sure baits;
And hooke them to our cause with golden hopes;
My noble friends, our purse, and hearts are yours,
You shalbe your owne carvers in them both;
What would you more? Ca. To make the bargaine sure
T'were good they had them both within their hands.
Ex. What wouldst thou have their hearts out? Ca. Otherwise
Their purse will never followe; 'Tis their life.
Bol. Against the way, how we may pleasure you,
You may condemne our purses, and our selves.

Fin. 3 sce

More than I love to give.
Bolnutus. I judge you fit
To serve my turn, the better to persuade
These novice knights to leave the bishop's side,
That takes upon him more than he would give.
Nicodimus. He saith it is his right.
[*Bolnutus.*] So let him say;
I'm sure the custom hath been, ours to take;
Nor will we change our customs for a song;
Give us possession, let him challenge right
And get it how he can.
Pamoppus. If you take all
And are so loath to give a little back,
How shall we hope for favor at your hands
When we shall stand in need?
Onoplutus. Be but good boys
And please Bolnutus well, you need not fear;
But then you must forsake the bishop's part
And stiffly stand for us.
Pamoppus. For that your purse
May make us sure, which only gets you friends.
You know our natures never yet could strike
An harmony in schools, yet here your purse
May chance to tune us to another key;
Some works we do for charity, but most
For benefactors.
Onoplutus. [*To Bolnutus.*] Sir, you must comply
With promises, perform them how you please.
Bolnutus. [*To Onoplutus.*] Let me alone to lead them with such baits,
And hook them to our cause with golden hopes.
[*To Nicodimus and Pamoppus.*] My noble friends, our purse and hearts are yours,
You shall be your own carvers in them both;
What would you more?
Candle. To make the bargain sure
'Twere good they had them both within their hands.
Erudius. What, wouldst thou have their hearts out?
Candle. Otherwise
Their purse will never follow; 'tis their life.
Bolnutus. Devise the way how we may pleasure you;
You may command our purses and ourselves.

Ans. I see he loves you, now he offers faire
Take benefitt of time, the Treasure yett.
Bel. Wee'l leave you to consider well the point

Scena Sexta

Nicodimus. Pamophus. Candle. Erudius.

Pamophus, What doe you advise i' th' businesse
Shewes difficultie, and requires some weight
More then wee have; I feare to sift the thing
In question of the Bishopps right wee see
It is oppos'd by such as will not spare us
To shake us off, when they have felt their hands.
As for their purses they weigh no more
Then courtiers friendshipp, or [illegible] promise,
That still come short, and waste [illegible] fees
More then three quarters, ere the whole be gott,
Besides much time, and labour spent in vaine;
Another thing that moves me most to fight
Under the Bishopps Banner, is the shame
That may arrive to us, should wee prevaile.
For you must know one of your Order first
Procur'd to sett his Theodore upp,
And brought the Hierarchie into the land;
A man of lasting memorie, my friend
And honour'd by the Gaeles, from whom he reapt
Most noble favours, whilst he in his sett
Repair'd againe, that they obteyn'd their [illegible]
Of Rome, and freedome, and of scattered troopes
Grewe to a Bodie, were instiled Knights,
Under one Leader of the holy Ghost,
Whose chiefe Lieutenant in the charge of Soules
The Bishopp is esteem'd; and shall wee strive
To put his fabricke downe with our owne hands

was first

Onoplutus. I see he loves you; now he offers fair
Take benefit of time, the iron's hot.
Bolnutus. We'll leave you to consider well this point [*Exeunt Bolnutus and Onoplutus.*]

Scena sexta

Nicodimus, Pamoppus, Candle [*and*] *Erudius* [*from above*].

Nicodimus. Pamoppus, what do you advise? This case
Shows difficulty and requires some reach,
More than we have, I fear, to sift the truth
In question of the bishop's right. We see
It is opposed by such as will not spare
To shake us off when they have got their ends.
As for their promises, they weigh no more
Than courtier's friendship or exchequer pays,
That still come short and waste in under fees
More than three quarters ere the whole be got,
Besides much time and labor spent in vain.
Another thing that moves me most to fight
Under the bishop's banner is the shame
That may accrue to us should we prevail.
For you must know one of your order first
Concurred to set his predecessor up
And brought the hierarchy into this land;
A man of lasting memory, my friend,
And honored by the Guelfs, from whom he reaped
Most noble favors, which he in this sort
Repaid again, that they obtained their suit
Of Rome, and freedom, and of scattered troops
Grew to a body, were enstylèd knights,
Under one leader of the Holy Ghost,
Whose chief lieutenant in the charge of souls
The bishop is esteemed; and shall we strive
To put this fabric down, which with our hands

Was first preferr'd. La. you put me in a maze;
I neuer thought this busines so intricate,
Bee sworne vpon our honors; yet you knowe
Wee haue you here, and deepely are ingag'd
In credit on the other side, you aske
My best aduise in this; the same demaunde
I make to you; your place bespeakes you wise,
I am your shadowe, you the hand that waits
And turnes vpon the weather of your breath;
Allott me but my place, point me the waie
My zeale is goode-nimble, and moues wingedly on,
Nor goes it further then the p^r^sent tence,
And there my grammer ends. Can. 'tis well it ends
Before the perfect comes. Er. The perfect, why?
Ca. Because the p^r^sent ends in O. and M.
Vt kno, knas, knaui, followes by the rule
Which makes the perfect tence. Er. The p^r^sent tence
As now you did pronounce it, fitts your selfe.
Ca. But smarts not where it hitts. Er. your
Are now too bitter. Candler, I must flye
your companie vnlesse you would refraine.
Ca. Faith pardon me, this once I must confesse
I prest the letter of his words too hard;
And like a foole in labour for a iest,
Made haste to be deliuered out of tyme.
But I recall my words, and heere absolue
The one, and other from the house infect'd
Howeuer it may seeme a simple part
To leaue their Bishopp in such slender groundes.
Ni. I am not yet resolu'd what course to take,
Wee are but fewe; our credit yet hath scarce
Weigh'd forth, and little acquaintance with the world

Though

Was first upreared?
Pamoppus. You put me in a maze;
I never thought this business to entrench
So near upon our honors; yet you know
We have gone far, and deeply are engaged
In credit on the other side. You ask
My best advice in this; the same demand
I make to you; your place bespeaks you wise,
I am your shadow, yea, the vane that waits
And turns upon the weather of your breath;
Allot me but my place, point me the way,
My zeal is hoodwinked and runs mainly on,
Nor goes it further than the present tense,
And there my grammar ends.
Candle. 'Tis well it ends
Before the perfect comes.
Erudius. The perfect—why?
Candle. Because the present ends in *O* and *As*,
Ut kno, *knas*, *knavi*, follows by the rule
Which makes the perfect tense.
Erudius. The present tense,
As now you did pronounce it, hits yourself.
Candle. But smarts not where it hits.
Erudius. You
Are now too bitter, Candle, I must fly
Your company unless you could refrain.
Candle. Faith, pardon me, this once I must confess
I pressed the letter of his words too hard,
And like a fool in labor for a jest
Made haste to be delivered out of time.
But I recall my words, and here absolve
The one and other from the sense inferred,
However it may seem a simple part
To leave their bishop on such slender grounds.
Nicodimus. I am not yet resolved what course to take.
We are but few, our credit yet hath scarce
Peeped forth and took acquaintance with the world;

Though knowne abroade, wee are but strangers heere.
But this to ioyne with rebells at first dashe,
Will disadvantage vs, for after tymes;
And men will saie; tis pittie those greate knights,
That haue deserv'd so well in other places,
Should loose their fame, and reputacion heere
Through idle managing their cause at first.
Pa. I knowe not what to saie to mens reports,
Nor care I what men saie, name but the part
Wee shall incline to, and let me alone,
To laie about me, light it where it may:
Or if you shame to speake, giue me but leave
To name the side, our question's at an end.
Ni. Then name it hardly. Pa. Wee are Ghibellines
And will maintaine their cause, and bidd farewell
Vnto the Guelfs, and pull their Bishopp downe,
Soe speede vs God, our Ladie, and St James.
Ca. The divell rather is your only Saint,
That must advance his cause. Er. I pray thee peace.
Ca. I cannot hold. thinks he the Gus are proude
And factious like himselfe, yet may as well
Thinke God will favour him, or Saints will fall,
As hope to speede in this by other meanes,
Then by the divells. Er. Silence Spiritus comes
See how hee'l worke these vessells into froth.
Ca. Indeede his witt is barmy, and soone workes
Like squibbs of bottle ale, about the Towne.

Scena Septima.

Spiritus. Ramoppus. Nicodemus. Candle. Erudio.

What still consulting? come, resolue for shame
The field is won; and you are still in doubt
wch parte

Though known abroad, we are but strangers here.
But thus to join with rebels at first dash
Will disadvantage us for aftertimes,
And men will say: " 'Tis pity these green knights,
That have deserved so well in other parts,
Should lose their fame and reputation here
Through idle managing their cause at first."
Pamoppus. I know not what to say to men's reports,
Nor care I what men say; name but the part
We shall incline to and let me alone
To lay about me, light it where it may—
Or if you shame to speak, give me but leave
To name the side, our question's at an end.
Nicodimus. Then name it hardly.
Pamoppus. We are Ghibellines
And will maintain their cause, and bid farewell
Unto the Guelfs, and pull their bishop down,
So speed us God, our Lady, and Saint James.
Candle. The devil rather is your only saint
That must advance this cause.
Erudius. I prithee, peace.
Candle. I cannot hold! Thinks he the saints are proud
And factious like himself? He may as well
Think God will favor him, or saints will fall,
As hope to speed in this by other means
Than by the devil's.
Erudius. Silence, Spirius comes
See how he'll work these vessels into froth.
Candle. Indeed his wit is barmy and shoots corks
Like squibbs of bottle ale about the town.

Scena septima

Spirius, Pamoppus, Nicodimus; Candle [and] Erudius [from above].

Spirius. What, still consulting? Come, resolve, for shame!
The field is won, and you are still in doubt

Which side to take, beware each other side
Doe we will you for Neutralls in the end;
And so betwixt two stooles you kisse the ground,
Pa. With what? Sp. Even with that part I might affront
To you the Maister of this Chorticle commands.
Spi. And then beware a new come Ca. 'Tis but the Cast,
'Tis well we scape a flaying. Pa. Spirits,
Wee are not Tenants to the Whipping Post,
Nor you the Beadle, though you have taught Schooles,
And borne some office in the Comon wealth.
Once Constable, and twice an Under-Sheriffe;
How spell you that. Ca. In English it spells knave,
I know not what it spells in other partes,
For change of Aire doth seldome alter myndes.
Ex. But grace may curbe nature as in him
And others of his ranke, may be presum'd.
Ca. That this is but presumption may appeare,
Even in the Whispers that he now impugnes.
Ex. You are not made a Judge. Ca. Not I. The cause
Itselfe informes a Jury, though I were dumbe.
Pa. Nay Captaine, if you summe, the knowne tongue
To have about with you, were it at Cuffs
Or Cudgells, either for a bloodie pate,
Because most hold you valiant; so am I
As Hercules: but try me every ward.
Spi. What not in getting boyes, or tossing Balls,
Wherewith he knocks the lustie Centaures downe?
I hope you'l leave him here. Why, he could spin,
And reele, and keepe a house. Pa. But these are tales
I take not notice; In all things else
I hould my selfe as tall a man as he.
Spi. As lustie, you would say, but not so tall;
For he was created of a Giants size,
You're but a dwarfe; but sure you are as fraile
As hee

Which part to take. Beware lest either side
Do vomit you for neutrals in the end,
And so betwixt two stools you kiss the ground.
Pamoppus. With what?
Spirius. Even with that part I most affect
To get the mast'ry of.
Candle. The tail he means.
Spirius. And then beware a whipping.
Candle. That's the least:
'Tis well we 'scape a fleaing.
Pamoppus. Spirius,
We are no tenants to the whipping post,
Nor you the beadle, though you have taught schools
And borne some office in the commonwealth.
Once constable and twice an under-sheriff;
How spell you that?
Candle. In English it smells knave,
I know not what it spells in other parts,
For change of air doth seldom alter minds.
Erudius. But grace may enter nature, as in him
And others of his rank may be presumed.
Candle. That this is but presumption may appear
Even in the bishop's case he now impugns.
Erudius. You are not made a judge.
Candle. Not I, the cause
Itself infers as much, though I were dumb.
Pamoppus. Nay, captain, if you fume, then know I long
To have a bout with you, were it at cuffs
Or cudgels, either for a bloody pate,
Because men hold you valiant; so am I,
As Hercules, but try me every way.
Spirius. What, not in getting boys or tossing pots,
Wherewith he knocks the lusty centaurs down?
I hope you'll leave him there. Why, he could spin,
And reel, and keep a wench.
Pamoppus. Tut, these are tales,
I take no notice; in all things else
I hold myself as tall a man as he.
Spirius. As lusty, you would say, but not so tall;
For he was counted of a giant's size,
You're but a dwarf; but say you are as frail

As he was fain'd, would you not thinke [illegible] storme
To lett the Bishop call you to accompt?
Pa. And I should see him hang'd, or banish'd first;
There's all the harme I wish him from my heart;
When he is dead I'le quitt him all the rest
Of old accompt betweene vs from this houre
Even to the generall daie. Spi. Most noblie spoake,
I now begin to honor thy brave minde.
Pa. But Spirius, two scruples yet remaine
That vex vs both; the one, how we may trust
Bolnutus, or his promise of Ransom
ffor our good wills, and not to see vs want:
The other, how to settle vp the Arch,
According our credit breakes, should we continue
The Bishops overthrowe whom first we raisd.
Spi. You shall be held the warrelike of this age
In maistering Bishops as he was esteem'd
The setter vp, and puller downe of kinges,
In former tymes, what honor would you more?
Pa. ffaith, that's enough, a conscience lesse would serve
Ten dam'd tenn thousand soules were but this [illegible]
ffulfill'd in thought, for I suppose the deede
Is but an Embrion yet, and so must out;
Beside your case is comon with our kinges
Who had as ample share in setting vp
His Predecessor as your selues, nay more,
In speech and writing, we bestow'd the name
Of Cardinall on him, though wee were none
Would take our words, and faine helpe our hands
Because we since have found [illegible] [illegible] thrive
Under an Arbiter as before;
Noe more can you. Pa. Tis time we bustle then
And buckle to this geere. Spi. The time is past
Where you consult and [illegible]. Pa. Here's my hand

Wee'l make

As he was feigned, would you not think full scorn
To let the bishop call you to accompt?
Pamoppus. Sure I should see him hanged or banished first;
There's all the harm I wish him from my heart;
When he is dead I'll quit him all the rest
Of old accompt between us from this hour
Even to the general day.
Spirius. Most nobly spoke!
I now begin to honor thy brave mind.
Pamoppus. But Spirius, two scruples yet remain
That vex us both: the one, how we may trust
Bolnutus or his promise of reward
For our good wills, and not to see us want;
The other, how to solder up the crack
Wherewith our credit breaks, should we contrive
The bishop's overthrow whom first we raised.
Spirius. You shall be held the [warlocks] of this age
In mastering bishops, as he was esteemed
The setter up and puller down of kings
In former times; what honor would you more?
Candle. Faith, that's enough, a conscience less would serve
To damn ten thousand souls, were but the sin
Fulfilled in thought, for I suppose the act
Is but an embryon yet and so must end.
[*Spirius.*] Besides, your case is common with our knights.
We had as ample share in setting up
His predecessor as yourselves, nay more:
In speech and writing we bestowed the name
Of ordinary on him, though we now
Would eat our words and fain belie our hands,
Because we since have found we cannot thrive
Under an overseer as before;
No more can you.
Pamoppus. 'Tis time we bustle then
And buckle to this gear.
Spirius. The time is past
While you consult and trifle.
Pamoppus. Here's my hand.

Would make him a poore Bishop ore wee knowe.
Ni. Can he be poorer then our selues? Spi. Wee yes,
I haue knowne begging ffryers, as rich as Monkes;
And Bishops poorer then them both. Ni. They were
Some Grecians sure of Chalcedon, or so
That onely had the name; or els were sent
To Jewes and Turkes; that would not owne him. Spi. Right,
Euen such is hee, and such are wee. Ni. Not Turkes
Nor Jewes I hope. Pa. Sure wee beleiue in Christ.
Spi. I see you mou'd, you mistake my words;
My meaning was not, that wee are the same,
But very like to them, not in beleife
But fact; as not acknowledging the powre
Of Bishops ouer vs, which in itselfe
Is more vnchristian to deny, in him
I hold a sinne to graunt; In him he meanes
Pro hic et nunc, whereas in secula
Bole but Seculorum, let the Clerke say Amen
Ca. Soe said the Clerke, that sleeping [illegible] a knock,
He cry'd Amen, and dyed. Ve. His ending word
Out-liu'd his fate, which tongue the Clerks from'd
To his Creators Will; his liuing ~~[illegible]~~ dies,
Nor ended it so, but with the Speakers shame.
Ni. But yet wee thinke wee should beleiue the Pope.
Spi. His Conscience [illegible] may erre,
And he mistake grossly; Ill [illegible]
To put such precious liquor in a Spunge,
Such power into a bubble, that with ease
Wee can dissolue, and blowe into Ayre.
Ve. Soft; t'is but as you finde the State inclin'd
To fauour you and giue your followers leaue;

Should

We'll make him a poor bishop ere we leave.
Nicodimus. Can he be poorer than ourselves?
Spirius. Why yes,
I have known begging friars as rich as monks,
And bishops poorer than them both.
Nicodimus. They were
Some Grecians, sure, of Chalcedon, or so,
That only had the name; or else were sent
To Jews and Turks that would not own him.
Spirius. Right,
Even such is he, and such are we.
Nicodimus. Not Turks
Nor Jews, I hope.
Pamoppus. Sure we believe in Christ.
Spirius. I cry you mercy, you mistake my words;
My meaning was not that we are the same,
But very like to them, not in belief
But fact: as not acknowledging the power
Of bishops over us, which in itself
It were unchristian to deny, in him
I hold a sin to grant; in him I mean
Pro hic et nunc, if not *in secula*.
Bolnutus. Put *seculorum* to't, I'll say amen.
Candle. So said the clerk that sleeping caught [a] knock;
He cried, "Amen," and died.
Erudius. His ending voice
Outlived his fate, whose tongue the echo seemed
To his Creator's will; this living dies,
Nor ends it so but with the speaker's shame.
Nicodimus. But yet methinks we should believe the pope.
Spirius. His reverend paternity may err,
And he mistaketh grossly if he think
To put such precious liquor in a sponge,
Such power into a bubble, that with ease
We can dissolve and lessen into air.
Erudius. Soft, 'tis but as you find the state inclined
To favor you and give your bellows vent;

Should they withhold their influence, you'ld shrinke,
And vanish into froth, while he may stand
Like an vnshaken rocke, that splitts the wrath
Of angrie Neptune, and outbraues the windes.
Spi. Now to your other doubt, your want of meanes
And trusting to Bolnutius words, I graunt
They are but slender warrants; their rewardes
Come alwaies halting after longe expence
Of tyme, and labour; and the least distast
Cutts off all hope of payment, but in some
Wille there proue deuout. Pa. What is that? Spi. Very thankfull.
Pa. A goode reward I like it not. Spi. Then scorne.
Pa. That's worst. Spi. Then endaungering your state
And fame, if they can reach it. Pa. What so briefe?
Spi. They doe not vse to dallie with their friends.
Pa. How oft they foes, that thus requite their friends?
Spi. Friends are held foes to them, that swarue in thought
From what they practise. Pa. Sure, they are diuine,
And merit adoration. Spi. Some beleiue
Their wordes as they were ghospell. Hi. God forbid.
Spi. Tut, I could instance Thonscot, Nodipol,
And diuers others sworne to be their slaues.
Hi. God rest their soules then. Spi. Why they are not dead.
Hi. To graue they seeme, that are not their owne men,
And haue forsworne their freedome, and good ~~yea~~ will
To serue the Clergie, and only trust in men.
Pa. What if we urge our labours as a debt,
And claime our due. Spi. Some one of them will saie,
Alas, we are Religious men you knowe
That liue in common, and call nothing ours;
Then he referres you to Superiours; they
To the Prouinciall, to the Generall hee;
And so

Should they withhold their influence, you'd shrink
And vanish into froth, while he may stand
Like an unshaken rock that splits the wrath
Of angry Neptune and outbraves the winds.
Spirius. Now to your other doubt, your want of means
And trusting to Bolnutus' words: I grant
They are but slender warrants; their rewards
Come always halting, after long expense
Of time and labor, and the least disgust
Cuts off all hope of payment but in coin
Will scarce prove current.
Pamoppus. What is that?
Spirius. Why, thanks.
Pamoppus. A poor reward, I like it not.
Spirius. Then scorn.
Pamoppus. That's worse.
Spirius. Then undermining your estate
And fame, if they can reach it.
Pamoppus. What, so brief?
Spirius. They do not use to dally with their friends.
Pamoppus. How use they foes, that thus requite their friends?
Spirius. Friends are held foes to them, that swerve in thought
From what they practice.
Pamoppus. Sure, they are divine
And covet adoration.
Spirius. Some believe
Their words as they were gospel.
Nicodimus. God forbid.
Spirius. Tut, I could instance Thonscot, Nodipol,
And diverse others sworn to die their slaves.
Nicodimus. God rest their souls then.
Spirius. Why, they are not dead.
Nicodimus. To grace they seem, that are not their own men,
And have forsworn their freedom and good will
To serve the church, and only trust in men.
Pamoppus. What if we urge our labors as a debt
And claim our due?
Spirius. Some one of them will say,
"Alas, we are religious men, you know,
That live in common and call nothing ours";
Then he refers you to superiors; they
To the provincial; to the general he;

And see to heaven, and there you must expect
What here they cannot spare, but for themselves.
Pa. What's that? Spi. Reward. Ne. This doctrine in effect
Denies good works, and merit in his life
To all but friends. Spi. 'Tis true, to other men
They place it in the next, and that's as good.
Pa. Not altogether, I would taste of both.
Ca. But neither will doctrine, I feare me. Ex. Feare,
And preach not Candle; you and I may mend.
Spi. But what an asse am I to argue thus
Against our friends, who (as the Proverb saies)
Sitt in one quill with us, and in these warres
Runn the same hazards; were the time soe, then
I could have railed against them by the clocke
Whole howres, and daies, as manie as I spend
Against the Bishopps now. Ca. Not at your Boarde
Or saying their prayers. Spi. But now we finde
They only knowe the policie to climbe,
Which they were minded not, but nowe admire
And faine would be their apes but knowe not howe:
Goe lett that passe, and thus in briefe to you,
If what my braine conceaves shall take effect,
And I become the sole Ruler of our Kingdoms,
As I have laid the plott, you neede not feare,
I will commend your meritt to our freinds,
Who are not conceited people, or precise,
But rather lavish of their wordes and meanes,
And liberall of preferment to their pouertie
And you shall rest contented in the end.
If other hopes should faile, meane time come in
And helpe us to consult. Ne. The dye is cast,
Lead on. Pa. The day is ours, the Bishopp falls.
Ex. Still hovering on your heads, I feare at last.
Ca. That they would hazard heaven, to winn the rest.

Grex.

And so to heaven, and there you must expect
What here they cannot spare but for themselves.
Pamoppus. What's that?
Spirius. Reward.
Nicodimus. This doctrine in effect
Denies good works and merit in this life
To all but friends.
Spirius. 'Tis true, to other men
They place it in the next, and that's as good.
Pamoppus. Not altogether; I would taste of both.
Candle. But neither will deserve, I fear me.
Erudius. Peace,
And preach not Candle; you and I may mend.
Spirius. But what an ass am I to argue thus
Against our friends, who (as the proverb says)
Piss in one quill with us, and in these wars
Run the same hazard; well, the time hath been
I could have railed against them, by the clock
Whole hours and days, as many as I spend
Against the bishop now.
Candle. Not at your beads
Or saying other prayers.
Spirius. But now we find
They only knew the policy to thrive,
Which then we minded not, but now admire
And fain would be their apes, but know not how—
So, let that pass—and thus in brief to you:
If what my brain conceives shall take effect,
And I become chief ruler of our knights,
As I have laid the plot, you need not fear;
I will commend your merit to our friends,
Who are not counted gripple or precise,
But rather lavish of their words and means
And liberal of performance to their power,
And you shall rest contented in the end.
If other hopes should fail, meantime come in
And help us to consult.
Nicodimus. The die is cast,
Lead on.
Pamoppus. The day is ours, the bishop falls.
Erudius. Full heavy on your heads, I fear at last.
Candle. Tut, they would hazard heav'n to win the cast. [*Exeunt.*]

Grex

Lucianus. Therulus

But when comes Largus dauncer to act his parte?
I longe to see the dunce kindly plaide;
Haue you read Fryer Rush, ther and Bacon.
Lu. He made fine sporte among the Fryers. The. As I
Hope Largus make anon amongst these knights,
Haue patience but a while, the musicke plaies

Actus quartus

Scena prima

Niuetta. Bitomattus

Thy seruant you can courte as well as praie.
Bi. Yes Madam; courtshipp is a prayre to saints.
Ni. What saints? Bi. the woemen Images of God.
Ni. You were Idolatrs. Bi. Mistake it not
Niuetta. Thus I make my sayings good
From outward beautie, that in woemen shines
And take a scantling of their mortall soules
Sets Gods likings; thence I finde a waie,
To courte the deitie, & make my praiers.
Ni. But doth not your deuotion light sticke,
And often stumble forward by the waie;
Bestowing more deuotion to the shape,
Then to the pictures substance? By. Say it doe
'Tis but a Peccadillo, or mistake.
Ni. But now resolue me, what mistake was that
Which humor cast upon you, when you made
To you a Ladies foote to tempt her stomache,
Which made her blush for anger? By. I was to trie
her constitution

Grex.

Lucianus, Therulus.

Lucianus. But when comes Jargus down to act his part?
I long to see the devil kindly played;
Have you read Friar Rush?
Therulus. And Bacon.
Lucianus. He made fine sport among the friars.
Therulus. As I
Will Jargus make anon among these knights,
Have patience but a while. The music plays.

Actus quartus

Scena prima

Nivetta, Bitomattus.

Nivetta. Then, servant, you can court as well as pray.
Bitomattus. Yes, madam; courtship is a prayer to saints.
Nivetta. What saints?
Bitomattus. To women, images of God.
Nivetta. You teach idolatry.
Bitomattus. Mistake it not,
Nivetta. Thus I make my saying good:
From outward beauty that in women shines,
I take a scantling of their molded souls
Into God's liking; thence I find a way
To court the Deity, so make my prayer.
Nivetta. But doth not your devotion light short
And often stumble, servant, by the way,
In giving more attention to the case
Than to the picture's substance?
Bitomattus. Say it do;
'Tis but a *peccadillo* or mistake.
Nivetta. But now resolve me: what mistake was that
Which rumor cast upon you, when you trod
Upon a lady's foot to tempt her strength,
Which made her blush for anger?
Bitomattus. 'Twas to try

Ther constitucion Madam; but I finde,
By her displeasure, she was chaste as snowe,
And like yourselfe. Ni. Those that are doctors feele
In wemens wrists to finde their sicknes; you
Steale from their eies the temp of their mindes.
By. Most true, for by their lookes is Symptomiz'd
The state of our affections. Ne. Lovers gods:
But is it lawfull servant, you should tempt
Our weaknes in this sort? Say wee should give
Allow you such trialls, would you not prove fire,
And worke upon the softnes of our sexe,
Thee to consume, and not preserve our fames
Of white, and chaste, and vertuous Madames: By. Yes,
Were you to judge me by my outward garb,
You'd sweare, I were a wanton, or a knight
Of most affected pantie; but looke
Within me further, Madame you shall see
Such colours of a mortified minde,
As few or none have ever knowne the like.
Ni. I would be loath to trie you Bitemattus,
Or looke so farre into you for a world
But to encrease my faith in that good part
That dwells within you, and so well you yeild
The smalle accompt, but in such toyes as these
Are wont to serve, to make the people laugh;
Tell me, why, are you so affected growne,
And in your speeches so prophane to such,
Unto a modest Ladie, that her breasts
(which then she would have covered) were not made
By nature to be stopped, or hidd;
But rather were laide open to invite
The curious eye, and feaste it with delight,
Words more befitting Aretine, then yor [illegible]
For this

Her constitution, madam; but I found,
By her displeasure, she was chaste as snow,
And like yourself.
Nivetta. So that as doctors feel
On women's wrists to find their sickness, you
Fetch from their toes the temper of their minds.
Bitomattus. Most true, for by their feet is symptomized
The pace of our affections.
Nivetta. Very good;
But is it lawful, servant, you should tempt
Our weakness in this sort? Say we should give
Upon such trials, would you not prove fire
And work upon the softness of our sex,
So to consume and not preserve our fames
Of cold, and chaste, and virtuous madames?
Bitomattus. Yes,
Were you to judge me by my outward garb
You'd swear I were a wanton or a knight
Of most affected vanity; but look
Within me further, madam, you shall see
Such tokens of a mortifièd mind,
As few or none have ever known the like.
Nivetta. I would be loath to try you, Bitomattus,
Or look so far into you for a world,
But to increase my faith in those good parts
That stalk within you, and of which you yield
So small accompt but in such toys as apes
Are wont to show to make the people laugh.
Tell me, why are you so affected grown,
And in your speeches so profane to say
Unto a modest lady that her breasts
(Which then she would have covered) were not made
By nature to be canopied or hid,
But rather were laid open to invite
The curious eye and feast it with delight,
Words more befitting Aretine than you?

Is this your holy courtshipp? By-Names he gaue
Of courtshipp Ladies, whose allusion
Did point at Eve's unmasked innocence;
Which gaue content to Adam, without shame.
Ni. This Servant, you may relate and scorne
And faire allusions from the very stewes,
That may seeme holy. Further I would knowe,
Why you are so officious in the Courte?
Not fawning on the great ones? so extreame
In visiting Ambassadors, as some
Doe call you troublesome, intruding, rude,
Importunate, nay impudent? And why
Amongst the Ladies are you such a barre,
Especially the rich ones, as you strike
At on[e] turne upon their Honors, and strive
To rule their Families? dispose their Almes?
Preferr them Officers, and Chamber-maides,
Appointing Priests to serve them, of [illegible] Tribe?
One order only, for all other Tribes,
Or orders, you speake contemptibly, as though
All goodnes were confined in your owne,
And at your birth the holy Ghost did breath
His guifts and favours, to the grounder
Of Church Authorities, and Bishops power,
While you traduce amongst your noble friends
Of State Impostures; and usurped Right
And thus you strive to blowe the coales of Schisme.
By detraction [illegible] Madam; still our vertues waite,
And Envie sticks on Honor like a moath;
A man is a Compendium of the world,
Natures Epitome, and Fortunes Summe;
And therefore in his actions should be cast
Like

Is this your holy courtship?
Bitomattus. 'Twas to pass
Off courtship, lady, whose allusion
Did point at Eve's unmaskèd innocence,
Which gave content to Adam without sin.
Nivetta. Thus, servant, you may whiten any speech
And force allusion from the very stews
That may seem holy. Further I would know
Why you are so officious in the court?
So fawning on the great ones? so extreme
In visiting ambassadors, as some
Do call you troublesome, intruding, rude,
Importunate, nay imprudent? And why
Amongst the ladies are you such a [burr],
Especially the rich ones, as you stick
At ev'ry turn upon their sleeves, and strive
To rule their families? dispose their alms?
Prefer them officers and chambermaids?
Appointing priests to shrive them, of one tribe,
One order only? For of other sirs
Or dons you speak contemptibly, as though
All goodness were confinèd in your choice,
And at your beck the Holy Ghost did breathe
His gifts and favors, to the prejudice
Of church authority and bishop's power,
Which you traduce among your nobler friends
Of flat imposture and usurpèd right?
And thus you seem to blow the coals of schism.
Bitomattus. Detraction, madam, still on virtue waits,
And envy sticks on honor like a moth;
A man is a compendium of the world,
Nature's epitome, and Fortune's sum,
And therefore in his actions should be vast,

Like heauen full of varietie and change;
Whose changes are but Mediums to one end,
Which bounds our actiue Spiritts, like the Sonne
Nay, to be all with euery man
And to communicate that goodnes lent
To vs by God, with others, and dispose
Our spiritts to man for their good;
Is this a crime? Ni. If with indifference
You should proceede; Is it not, but your all
In all is but a forme to lighten shine
Whom most you fauor, and cry downe the rest;
For though it be but iust to please our friends,
Yet too affectedly to speake their prayse,
And with neglect of others, or contempt,
Or which is worse, with slanders and wrongs,
These are not charitable Symptomes. By. See
You would inforce me partiall and vniust.
Ni. I would not but you said it, that knowe best.
By. But since I were religious, and constrain'd
By vowes obedience, to promote the cause
Of these supposed friends. Ni. You were too blame
To doe it in a fashion so absurd
Your pardon seruant, if the word offends;
(For I can make it good.) By. Sweete Mris doe,
I dare not call your beautie to accompt.
Ni. Yes hardly, and my iudgement if it erre;
You neede not feare, Ile kick you downe the staires,
But to the point; obedience you pretend
And vowed seruice to the best of knights
That share the counsell Floore, me thinks it fitt
You should resist the Bishopp in this cause,
Yea, and his power that made him, that's the Pope.
By. Saint Paule resisted Peter to his face,
And may not wee the Pope behinde his backe?
Ni. That's but a weakening consequent inforc'd;

And like

Like heaven full of variety and change;
Which changes are but *Mediums* to one end
Which bounds our active spirits like the sea.
Nay, to be all with every man
And to communicate that goodness lent
To us by God with others and dispense
Our charity to many for their good:
Is this a crime?
Nivetta. If with indifferency
You should proceed is it not, but your all
In all is but a form to lighten some
Whom most you fancy and cry down the rest:
For though it be but just to pleasure friends,
Yet too affectedly to speak their praise
And with neglect of others, or contempt,
Or which is worse, with prejudice and wrong,
These are no charitable symptoms.
Bitomattus. So
You would infer me partial and unjust.
Nivetta. I would not but you said it that know best.
Bitomattus. But say I were religious, and constrained
By vow's obedience to promote the cause
Of those supposèd friends.
Nivetta. You were to blame
To do it in a fashion so absurd.
Your pardon, servant, if the word offends,
For I can make it good.
Bitomattus. Sweet mistress, do;
I dare not call your beauty to accompt.
Nivetta. Yes, hardly, and my judgment if it err;
You need not fear I'll kick you down the stairs.
But to the point: obedience you pretend
And vowèd service to the best of knights
That share the golden fleece; he thinks it fit
You should resist the bishop in this cause,
Yea, and his power that made him, that's the pope.
Bitomattus. Saint Paul resisted Peter to his face,
And may not we the pope behind his back?
Nivetta. That's but a sneaking consequent inferred;

And like another daingerous speech of yours
Pronounc'd on like occasions, when you said,
You would not trust a terrifying Pope
For whose sake, but since St Paule withstood
St Peters private iudgment in a Truth;
May you not in another Truth aswell,
Withstand Superiors in the Popes behalfe,
That are more private, and subordinate?
By. Yes, if the truth were knowne, but this requires
A longer tyme to sift, and stronger proofes
Then the bare word, or Breve of the Pope
Which wee can muster yet to serve our turnes.
Ni. 'Tis well that faith must stand to Grammer Rules,
And every Critick censure must controule
The Text of Writers, and Canons, 'twas not so
Before Erasmus dayes, or these our tymes,
Thanks to your grave Example I should thinke
The barest word, or Breve of a Pope,
Affirming him our Pastor, wth his Flocke,
And you inferiors in the charge of Soules,
More to be credited then all your reasons,
Or any priviledge you can pretend,
To contradict it; 'Tis not heresie,
By. A womans reason must not be gainesaid,
Els I should it controule. Ni. Who shall iudge?
But he that can make Bishopps, and most worth
Who saies that he is one for, is ordain'd;
And for our good with ordinarie power?
By. A delegate with ordinary powre,
Is not an ordinary I suppose
But in a comely phrase, as those wee call,
A trifle of small worth, in comon speech,
An ordinarie thinge, and so is hee.
An ordinary Bishopp, and for forme

But not

And like another dangerous speech of yours
Pronounced on like occasions, when you said
You would not trust a versifying pope
For Urban's sake. But [say] Saint Paul withstood
Saint Peter's private judgment in a truth;
May you not in another truth as well
Withstand superiors in the pope's behalf,
That are more private and subordinate?
Bitomattus. Yes, if the truth were known, but this requires
A longer time to sift and stronger proofs
Than the bare word or breve of the pope,
Which we can conster yet to serve our turns.
Nivetta. 'Tis well that faith must stand to grammar rules,
And every critic censure must control
The text of briefs and canons; 'twas not so
Before Erasmus' days or these our times.
Thanks to your grave example I should think
The barest word or breve of a pope,
Affirming him our pastor, us his flock,
And you inferiors in the charge of souls,
More to be credited than all your nays,
Or any privilege you can pretend
To contradict it; 'tis no heresy.
Bitomattus. A woman's reason must not be gainsaid,
Else I should it control.
Nivetta. Who shall judge
But he that can make bishops and whose word
We have that he is one for us ordained,
And for our good with ordinary power?
Bitomattus. A delegate with ordinary power
Is not an ordinary, I suppose,
But in a homely sense, as when we call
A trifle of small worth in common speech
An ordinary thing, and so is he
An ordinary bishop, and for form,

But not a Bishop that is Ordinarie;
And for this cause some will not call him Lord,
But stile him but Doctor, though much worth.
Mr. [illegible]: they are Clownes, or fooles, or Puritane men;
And your conceipt of Ordinary power
Is more then senceless, and confutes itselfe;
You say that Popes doe iuggle in their Breefes,
And cozen us with wordes of doubtfull sence.
In making Ordinary those, a power
Of some Archpriest at first, in extent;
And since of Jurisdiction not so great;
For he had power you graunt to binde and loose,
In either cause, his Worshipp must have none:
And thus like Foxes you would steale the goose,
And stick us up a feather, you would meane.
The state we owe to Pastors to bestowe
It resolves on your dreames, and idle tales.
Where, though I be a woman and but weake,
I could convince, who knowes not it is weak,
If he be delegate, t'is from the Pope:
A Prince, and for two kingdomes yet his charge,
An universall, not a single care?
May iudge in the first Instance, arm'd with power
Of Ordinaries, and the rest of his owne:
For though it may at pleasure be recall'd,
This makes it not the lesse, but more enlarg'd
By priviledge, as in extent of place;
And thus you force us women to peruse
Both Breefes and Canons, to finde out your shifts,
That we may knowe our Pastors voice from yours.
By the [illegible] my Mistris lately is instruct
With Orbena, and Alcoma's stile
And like an other Sappho can instruct
The learned [illegible], with [illegible]

Mr. Naylor

But not a bishop that is ordinary;
And for this cause, some will not call him ''Lord,''
But style him ''Master Doctor'' at each word.
Nivetta. Sure, they are clowns, or fools, or frantic men;
And your conceit of ordinary power
Is more than senseless and confutes itself.
You teach that popes do juggle in their briefs
And cozen us with words of doubtful sense
In making ordinary power, a power
Of some archpriest at furthest in extent,
And force of jurisdiction not so great;
For he had power, you grant, to bind and loose
In either court, the bishop must have none:
And thus like foxes you would steal the goose
And stick us up a feather, you would mean
The faith we owe to pastors to bestow
It wholly on your dreams and idle tales;
Which, though I be a woman and but weak,
I could convince. Who knows not it is read,
If he be delegate, 'tis from the pope,
A prince, and for two kingdoms good his charge,
An universal, not a simple cure?
May judge in the first instance, armed with power
Of ordinaries, and the use of his own?
For though it may at pleasure be recalled,
This makes it not the less but more enlarged
By privilege, as in extent of place;
And thus you force us women to peruse
Both briefs and canons to find out your shifts,
That we may know our pastor's voice from yours.
Bitomattus. It seems my mistress lately is inspired
With Odoena and Falconia's style,
And like another Sappho can enchant
The hearer's sense with raptures of her wit.

Ni. Nay ist not: though I neuer could translate
St Augustins Confessions, or expresse
Some Troilus legend, to the readers teares;
And sett forth Bookes of Cabinetts and Caskets,
yet can I this, my Goode, bestowe the thing
And be as sensible of anie wronge:
Done to me in the Historie, as the best.
By. Well Mris here come Ladies to the rest
Els I should chide you for your want of faith,
And sharpnes of discourse. Ni. Who teaches you?
By. My friend Aggeus, or my second selfe
He wrote a Booke of affectation,
I keepe it in my bosome. Ni. Cast it out
Tis not such Iewell servant. By. What the Booke?
Ni. Noe affectation, it becomes you not.
By. Still bitter Mris. Ni. Better then to glose.
Madam Valeria, and Celia;
Sweete Ladies welcome.

Scena Secunda.

Valeria, Ninetta. Celia, Bitomattas, Aggeus.

Val. Faire Ninetta thankes,
Haue you and Bytomattus strucke a heate,
Your Cheekes so purple. Ni. Yes, he putts me to't
I thanke him. Val. To the worst he will not sure.
Ni. Nor shall he Madam. Cel. Is your cause so good?
By. Her weapons haue the vantage, and not her cause.
Cel. And what are those? By. Her beautie, and discourse;
But this to silence, still the other speakes.
Ni. Indeede the one is longe a womans fault,
The other is a fiction of his owne,
Or else the Booke, it cannot speake it selfe;
Much lesse

Nivetta. Nay, jest not. Though I never could translate
Saint Augustine's *Confessions*, or express
Count Troilus' legend to the reader's tears,
And set forth books of cabinets and knacks,
Yet can I say my creed, believe the church,
And be as sensible of any wrong
Done to her in her pastors as the best.
Bitomattus. Well, mistress, here come ladies to the close,
Else I should chide you for your want of faith
And sharpness of discourse.
Nivetta. Who ushers them?
Bitomattus. My friend Aggeus, or my friend-self.
He wrote a book of affectation,
I keep it in my bosom.
Nivetta. Cast it out,
'Tis no such jewel, servant.
Bitomattus. What, the book?
Nivetta. No, affectation; it becomes you not.
Bitomattus. Still bitter, mistress.
Nivetta. Better than to gloss.
[*Enter Valeria, Celia, Aggeus.*] Madam Valeria and Celia,
Sweet ladies, welcome.

Scena secunda

Valeria, Nivetta, Celia, Bitomattus, Aggeus.

Valeria. Fair Nivetta, thanks;
Have you and Bitomattus struck a heat?
Your cheek's so purple.
Nivetta. Yes, he puts me to 't,
I thank him.
Valeria. To the worst he will not, sure.
Nivetta. Nor shall he, madam.
Celia. Is your cause so good?
Bitomattus. Her weapons have the vantage and not her cause.
Celia. And which are those?
Bitomattus. Her beauty and discourse;
Put this to silence, still the other speaks.
Nivetta. Indeed, the one is long a woman's fault,
The other is a fiction of his own,
Or else so brief it cannot speak itself,

Much lesse in anie cause. Val. Come, lett that passe,
For so it will in time as it hath done
Alreadie in some Ladies that doe paint,
And to the purpose why wee came. Ni. Sitt downe,
Then, sir, your minde. By. Aggas and my selfe
Would crave you to your counsells for a time
If you can keepe them Ladies. Ni. If wee faile
You cannott keepe them for vs, keepe your ware.
Agg. Your servant Madam. Ni. That's an other Knight,
If I mistake not, of the holy Court.
Cel. He is a Gentleman, but not a Knight;
Was once imploy'd in busines of State,
And therefore during pleasure stil'd a Lord,
Which is your Bishopps case. Ni. But is the date
Of his commission out, and he recall'd?
Ce. It is. Ni. Soe, not the Bishopp, there's the knott,
Nor is it ever likely, while he lives.
Besides, in case it were, he cannott loose
The name of Bishopp, or the stile of Lord
[illegible] in your censure. Val. Come, thou art so quick,
Wee cannott fasten on thee for thy good,
I prithy tell me freely, to my last care
Dost thou commit the secrett of thy humor?
For I am somewhat curious in this point.
Ni. I briefly answere: See he be approv'd,
[illegible] can confesse to aime for a wooer,
Of discreete habits and, [illegible]
Both learned, and exemplar, and discreete.
Cel: But is there anie such, amongst the Guelfes?
Val. Noe question, Madam; what should make you doubt?
Cel. The reason of their factious conquest,
Which that of Ghibellines. Ni. Lett's leave the odds.
Cel. The one

Much less in any cause.
Valeria. Come, let that pass,
For so it will in time, as it hath done
Already in some ladies that do [paint],
And to the purpose why we came.
Nivetta. Sit down,
Then say your mind.
Bitomattus. Aggeus and myself
Will leave you to your counsels for a time,
If you can keep them, ladies.
Nivetta. If we fail,
You cannot keep them for us; keep your way.
Aggeus. Your servant, madam. [*Exit Bitomattus and Aggeus.*]
Nivetta. That's another knight,
If I mistake not, of the holy court.
Celia. He is a gentleman but not a knight,
Was once employed in business of state
And therefore during pleasure styled a lord,
Which is your bishop's case.
Nivetta. But is the date
Of his commission out, and he recalled?
Celia. It is.
Nivetta. So not the bishop's, there's the knot,
Nor is it ever likely while he lives.
Besides, in case it were, he cannot lose
The name of bishop or the style of lord,
As in your presence.
Valeria. Come, thou art so quick
We cannot fasten on thee for thy good;
I prithee tell me freely: to whose ear
Dost thou commit the secret of thy sins?
For I am somewhat curious in this point.
Nivetta. I briefly answer: so he be approved,
I can confess to any for a need;
Of custom but to one, whom I esteem
Both learnèd, and exemplar, and discreet.
Celia. But is there any such amongst the Guelfs?
Valeria. No question, madam, what should make you doubt?
Celia. The reason of their institute compared
With that of Ghibellines.
Nivetta. Let's hear the odds.

Cel. The one is comon, Secular of course;
The other chosen, Regular, exempt.
He. These are not contraries, that doe expell
Each other from the subiect of our faith,
Nor of good workes; But Madam, is it fitt
That those three Articles, I beleeue in God,
In Jesus Christ, and in the holy Ghost,
Should be compar'd, or brought into dispute,
When they concurr alike, and to oppose
Th'one with th'others, were to lose our faith?
Cel. It is not, I confesse. He. Nor is it iust
(If I may patterne great with lesser things)
You should compare two callings in the Church,
And both ordain'd by Christ, by diuers waies
To mediate their owne and others good,
To make them opposite. If comon things
Be counted base, why should we liue by aire?
Or vse the Elements? or honor God
That is the comon ffather of vs all?
Or why should we preferr a comon good
Before our priuate ends? Nor may the name
Of Secular in Guelfes, depresse their worth,
No more then in St. Paule, or in the rest
Of the Apostles, that were truly call'd
Doctores Saeculi, or Seculars.
As for your word of course, by which you meane
Some simple men, not graced with those parts
Or priviledge, which the world admires,
From which the Ghibellins doe some exempte,
Lett them be vertuous, though they knowe noe more
Then Pastorall dutie, and performe it well,
They neede not other priviledge to make
Their callings gratious in the sight of God.

Or espetially

Celia. The one is common, secular of course;
The other chosen, regular, exempt.
Nivetta. These are no contraries that do expel
Each other from the subject of our faith
Or of good works. But, madam, is it fit
That these three articles, I believe in God,
In Jesus Christ, and in the Holy Ghost,
Should be compared or brought into dispute,
When they concur alike, and to oppose
Th'one with th'others were to lose our faith?
Celia. It is not, I confess.
Nivetta. Nor is it just
(If I may pattern great with lesser things)
You should compare two callings in the church—
And both ordained by Christ, by diverse ways
To mediate their own and others' good—
To make them opposite. If common things
Be counted base, why should we live by air?
Or use the elements? or honor God,
That is the common Father of us all?
Or why should we prefer a common good
Before our private ends? Nor may the name
Of secular in Guelfs depress their worth,
No more than in Saint Paul or in the rest
Of the Apostles, that were truly called
Doctores Seculi or seculars.
As for your word of *course*, by which you mean
Some simple men, not gracèd with those parts
Or privileges which the world admires,
Of which the Ghibellines do seem to vaunt;
Let them be virtuous, though they know no more
Than pastoral duty and perform it well,
They need no other privilege to make
Their calling precious in the sight of God,

Or profittable for the soules of men,
Whose charge they take, upon Pastors may come short,
And misse the marke; Simplicitie in a Woman
Which takes not staine but Ignorance; and this
May neither be imputed to the Guelfes,
Nor Ghibellins in generall, howsoe're
Some passion more or lesse, may weaken sides,
And blinde the wills, and judgements of a parte;
Of wch the Common sence must judge, or voice
Of higher Courts; For women must submitt.
Val. Thou art not woman sure of Common straine,
But some Athenian Student, like Pope Joan,
Brought in by head and shoulders to the world
To countenance our moderne Scholars to these;
See how to crosse our women Ghibellins.
But tell me hath not Odorna's head
A friar in his skull? Ar. I must confesse
I owe to Odorna what I have
Of better'd understanding; but the will
To the offensive, not defensive skill,
Is farr from both our thoughts. Besides I have
Some better Cards to shew of grave Divines
To warrant what I said, in the behalfe
And right of Pastors; For to me the Guelfes
And Ghibellins, are in that nature one,
By priviledge, and charitie the last;
The first by right, and order of their place,
Yet both to be respected and belov'd
With equall state. But should they breake the bounds
Of charitie, and flowing into parties,
Enforce a breach of order in the Church,
Which should wee follow, but the safe Streame,

And that's

Or profitable for the souls of such
Whose charge they take, when boasters may come short
And miss the mark. Simplicity's a gem
Which takes no stain but ignorance, and this
May neither be imputed to the Guelfs
Nor Ghibellines in general, howsoe'er
Some passion more or less may weaken sides
And blind the wills and judgments of a part;
Of which the common sense must judge, or voice
Of higher courts, for women must submit.

Valeria. Thou art no woman, sure, of common strain,
But some Athenian student, like Pope Joan,
Brought in by head and shoulders to the world
To countenance our modern spleen to popes;
So thou to cross our women Ghibellines.
But tell me, hath not Odoena's head
A finger in this plot?

Nivetta. I must confess
I owe to Odoena what I have
Of bettered understanding, but the will
To use offensive, not defensive skill,
Is far from both our thoughts. Besides, I have
Some better cards to show of grave divines
To warrant what I say in the behalf
And right of pastors; for to me the Guelfs
And Ghibellines are in that nature one:
By privilege and charity the last,
The first by right and order of their place,
Yet both to be respected and beloved
With equal share. But should they break the bounds
Of charity, and, flowing into parts,
Enforce a breach of order in the church,
Which should we follow but the safe stream,

And that's the Hierarchie, or Bishopps Sea!
And leave the torrent of new fangled witts,
That would with Mists deceive our weaker sence,
And drawe us to their Bias, in the darke.
Cel. Therein, you are mistaken in the men:
They make a breach of order in the Church;
They are the only Proppes that holde it upp,
The Atlasses and Columnes that have stood
Against the rage of Heresies, and Stormes
Of heaven and Earth, whom Envious Clouds the more
They darken with detraction, still they rise
With more advantage both of fame and Worth.
The world had nowe bene ignorant but for them.
The Emulation of their abler parts
Hath bene a whetstone to the rest of witts
That have contriv'd to lift this later Age
In learning, to an universall height;
In wch respect, all former tymes give place,
And doe it homage: To drawe nerer home,
Within the compasse of this Isle, of late,
What Starrs have shin'd! what multitudes have left
The trade of Schisme by [illegible] meanes!
Who placed first those diamonds in our Ringe
And wrote such learned Bookes, as after times
Will glory in him. [illegible] death,
And [illegible], howe have they prevailed
Upon the world to entrance of beliefe!
In these our daies, who knowes not by report
Christus, and Suaris, Flurius,
[illegible], Fisherbottus, and the rest
That beate downe Pamphlets daily peeping forth
Of Doctor Featly, and Sr Humfrey Lind,
With other Giant writers of his land?
Fal. Now Celia hath set the Serpent forth,
Lett mee

And that's the hierarchy or bishop's [see]?
And leave the current of newfangled wits,
That would with mists deceive our weaker sense
And draw us to their bias in the dark.
Celia. How much you are mistaken in the men.
They make a breach of order in the church?
They are the only props that hold it up,
The Atlases and columns that have stood
Against the rage of heresies and storms
Of heaven and earth, whom envious clouds the more
They darken with detraction, still they rise
With more advantage both of fame and worth.
The world had now been ignorant but for them;
The emulation of their abler parts
Hath been a whetstone to the rest of wits
That have concurred to lift this later age
In learning to an universal height;
In which respect all former times give place
And do it homage. To draw near home,
Within the compass of this isle of late
What stars have shined? What multitudes have left
The road of schism by Perinosis' means?
Who placèd first these diamonds in our ring,
And wrote such learnèd books as aftertimes
Will glory in him. Pamicanus' death
And pithy reasons, how have they prevailed
Upon the world to bett'rance of belief?
In these our days who knows not by report
Sheriffus, and Suavis, Fluvius,
Rosimus, Sfirherbettus, and the rest
That beat down pamphlets daily peeping forth
Of Doctor Eatfly and Sir Humfrey Blind,
With other giant writers of this land?
Valeria. Now Celia hath set her pageant forth,

Lett me saie somethinge in my ffreinds behalfe,
The glorious Knights of Malta. To omitt
Precedent tymes, and the conversion
Of Kingdomes by them, puttinge ours in cheife,
And not to name the manie Kings and Popes,
And Emperors that haue bene glad to shroud
Their greatnes, in that habitt, and from thence
Were rais'd to rule the world; If stones could speake,
How would they witnes for them, that the Sunne
Ne're sawe more venerable men, or grac'd
More goodly buildings, with his polisht beames,
Then they were Masters of:. although wronge hands,
And ruder hearts haue levell'd them to dust,
And thrust the owners out with fire and sword;
Yet from their ashes, Phenix-like, haue sprunge
A race of learned and accomplisht men,
As Saperton, Laborus, with the graue
And wise Claudie, and a hundred more
Of skill'd and curious spiritts. Ni. True of those
haue writt against the Bishopp and the Popes,
And shewne a Masse of witt; but to what end?
I praie resolue me: ffor I would be gladd
To parallell thinstances with auncient tymes,
Were but this doubt remou'd. Val. Laborus writes
In favour of Exemptions made by Popes
Unto that Order, from the Bishopps power;
But Sapton, in the defence of Kinges,
And of the high Prerogatiue they hold
In case of deposition; and withall,
To disoblige more Austiouers that sought
This was a point of state. Ni. Indeede the case
Goes hard with Subiects, when two Soueraigne powers,
The spirituall and temporall, stand at oddes;

Andrewes

Let me say something in my friends' behalf,
The glorious Knights of Malta. To omit
Precedent times, and the conversion
Of kingdoms by them, putting ours in chief,
And not to name the many kings, and popes,
And emperors that have been glad to shroud
Their greatness in that habit, and from thence
Were raised to rule the world—if stones could speak,
How would they witness for them that the sun
Ne'er saw more venerable men, or graced
More goodly buildings with his polished beams
Than they were masters of? Although rough hands
And ruder hearts have leveled them to dust
And thrust the owners out with fire and sword,
Yet from their ashes, phoenixlike, have sprung
A race of learnèd and accomplished men,
As Saperton, Laborus, with the grave
And wise Elander, and a hundred more
Of culled and curious spirits.

Nivetta. Two of these
Have writ against the bishop and the pope,
And shown a mass of wit, but to what end?
I pray resolve me, for I would be glad
To parallel their fames with ancient times,
Were but this doubt removed.

Valeria. Laborus writes
In favor of exemptions made by popes
Unto that order from the bishop's power,
But Saperton in the defence of kings,
And of the high prerogative they hold
In case of deposition, and withal,
To disoblige men's consciences that thought
This was a point of faith.

Nivetta. Indeed the case
Goes hard with subjects when two sovereign powers,
The spiritual and temporal, stand at odds;

And wee, that for them both would spend our lives,
Are brought to that necessitie of choice:
That either we must lay our Bodies downe
To free our Soules, or runne a doubtfull hazard
With certaine danger (if the greater part
of writers erre not, with the voice of Ages)
To loose both soule and bodie, in the end
Through breach of Conscience, which is said to binde
Were it erroneous, being doubtfull, more,
But certaine, most of all. You here should wee
Avoide this terrible Dilemma? Or
Expresse our duties best, and not offend
the one or other more? the State hath lawes,
And strength, and Argument, and witt enough,
To punish us without the learned helpe
Of a Domestique Foe, that lies in waite
To urge, and aggravate a crime, he knowes
not to proceede from malice, but from feare
of greater ill, should we shunne the losse.
Val. Nay. thinke you, not commaunded by the State,
But of his owne accord, he writt this Booke?
Hi. It is suspected so. if not presum'd.
Val. Sure were it so, that for some other end,
Then for his former cause, and zeale of Truth,
He putt himselfe unbidden to this taske,
As upon spleene, or flattery, or pride
Or feare, or hope of gaine, or for reward,
I know not what to saie in his excuse,
Unlesse a Man were bound to shew his skill,
And make himselfe a partie in a cause
of purpose to betraie his friends, not call'd
To his officious Action by a Power,
That may exact it. Though having by some
To like

And we, that for them both would spend our lives,
Are brought to that necessity of choice,
That either we must lay our bodies down
To free our souls, or run a doubtful chance
With certain danger (if the greater sort
Of writers err not, with the voice of popes)
To lose both soul and body in the end
Through breach of conscience, which is said to bind
Were it erroneous, being doubtful more,
But certain, most of all. Then how should we
Avoid this terrible dilemma? or
Express our duties best, and not offend
The one or other power? The state had laws,
And strength, and arguments, and wit enough
To punish us without the learnèd help
Of a domestic foe, that lay in wait
To urge and aggravate a crime he knew
Not to proceed from malice but from fear
Of greater evil, should we shun the less.

Valeria. Why, think you, not commanded by the state,
But of his own accord he writ those books?

Nivetta. It is suspected so, if not presumed.

Valeria. Sure, were it so that for some other end
Than for his prince's cause and zeal of truth
He put himself unbidden to this task,
As upon spleen, or flattery, or pride,
Or fear, or hope of gain, or for reward,
I know not what to say in his excuse,
Unless a man were bound to show his skill
And make himself a party in a cause
Of purpose to betray his friend, not called
To his officious action by a power
That may exact it. Princes, though they seem

To like the consequence of such a fact;
Yet oftentimes the Princes displease,
As they may love the Treason, not the meanes,
Or men that acte it. It was wisely said
By a iudicious Counsellor of State
Within his Land, unto a forward Knight,
That offer'd basely to betraie his Sovraine,
For being Priest, unto the hands of Laie:
Prepar'd to be his hangman out of zeale,
He plaid the Tyrant, not a Flatterers part,
And shew'd himselfe a Subiect out of tyme;
Then bidd him take not care, but leave the charge
To see him punisht, when he should be found,
To him, and others, whom it did concerne:
But this I will not iudge to be the case
Of Caperton. Ne. Nor I; but by his grounds
Iustly feare it. For, his chiefest proofe,
Or his Achilles, as I am inform'd,
Is but a halfe fac'd definition
Of probable, the other halfe conceal'd,
Drawne out of Aristotles Topicks like
A man halfe shav'd out of the Barbers shoppe
To countenance and strike in a fray,
That leaves for haste the other halfe untrimm'd.
Val. Goe to, you are unhappie. Take next,
What saie you to Layorus workes? Ne. Not more
Then what is said alreadie by the Court
Of Inquisition, and the learned voice
Of Sorbonists. It is not currant coyne
But counterfeit, and well deserves the fire.
They might have sav'd the Suffrage, and handes
Of such abused Doctors as were drawne
This drift by subtletie and sleight.

Of a

To like the consequence of such a fact,
Yet oftentimes the premises displease:
As they may love the treason, not the means
Or men that act it. It was wisely said
By a judicious counselor of state
Within this land, unto a forward knight
That offered basely to betray his son,
For being priest, unto the hands of law:
Prepared to be his hangman out of zeal,
He played the tyrant, not a father's part,
And showed himself a subject out of time;
Then bid him take no care, but leave the charge
To see him punished, when he should be found,
To him and others whom it did concern.
But this I will not judge to be the case
Of Saperton.
Nivetta. Nor I; but by his grounds
Justly fear it. For his chiefest proof,
Or his Achilles, as I am informed,
Is but a half-faced definition
Of probable, the other half concealed,
Drawn out of Aristotle's *Topics*, like
A man half shaved out of the barber's shop
To countenance and stickle in a fray,
That leaves for haste the other half untrimmed.
Valeria. Go to, you are unhappy. To the next:
What say you to Laborus' work?
Nivetta. No more
Than what is said already by the court
Of Inquisition and the learnèd voice
Of Sorbonnists. It is no current coin,
But counterfeit, and well deserves the fire.
He might have saved the suffrages and hands
Of such abusèd doctors as were drawn
To this device by subtlety and slight

Of a dishonest rashe, and falsely past;
Yet not to wronge the Author (had not haste
And violence of passion, in this point
Borne him beyond the lymitts, and the trust,
And easie faith he gave to rash reporters
Of spirits, who first, they said, sett fier,
Like an Erostratus, unto this frame
Of our united mindes, and rais'd this smoake)
He might be rank't amongst those happie witts
That beautifie this Isle; although there want
Not some that place him farr above the Moone,
And all his fellowe Starrs, among the rest
Sr Errant Kemper Colonell is one,
A blower downe of Bishopps, with his breath,
And noyse of words. Cel. I knowe him passing well:
He sometyme was the onely ffreind of Guelfes;
But since he carried favour wth the knights
Of Colchos, hence he Leapt to Malta, there
He makes a stand. Val. He is not like to fall
That fixeth there his foote. Ni. Some broken reeds
Are found at Malta, as in other parts,
That are not to be lean'd to, over hard,
ffor feare in trusting those that cannot hold,
They fall themselves that venture on their heades.
I speake not this, Valeria, you should leave
Their ffreindshipp, or the confidence you have
In their great parts, as Celsa and I
In others that we favour and affect:
But to this end, we should suspend our thoughts
And strickt Judgements in discerning men,
And matters of importance. ffor we knowe
That flesh, and bloud, and passion over-rules
The greatest spiritts; and when Mountains fall,

Great ruyns

Of a disguisèd case and falsely put;
Yet not to wrong this author (had not haste
And violence of passion in this point
Borne him beyond the limits, and the trust
And easy faith he gave to rash reports
Of Spirius, who first, they say, set fire,
Like an Exostratus, unto this frame
Of our united minds and raised this smoke)
He might be ranked amongst those happy wits
That beautify this isle; although there want
Not some that place him far above the moon
And all his fellow stars; among the rest
Sir Errant Ramper Colonel is one,
A blower-down of bishops with his breath
And noise of words.

Celia. I know him passing well:
He sometime was the only friend of Guelfs;
But since he curried favor with the Knights
Of Colchos, thence he leaped to Malta, there
He makes a stand.

Valeria. He is not like to fall
That fixeth there his foot.

Nivetta. Some broken reeds
Are found at Malta, as in other parts,
That are not to be leaned to, over-hard,
For fear in trusting props that cannot hold.
They fall themselves, that venture, on their heads.
I speak not this, Valeria, you should leave
Their friendship or the confidence you have
In their great parts, as Celia and I
In others that we fancy and affect,
But to this end: we should suspect our thoughts
And secret judgments in discerning men
And matters of importance. For we know
That flesh, and blood, and passion overrules
The greatest spirits, and when mountains fall

Great numbers followe, and nowhere is left
But one, to flie the danger. Cel. Why is that?
To cleave to Bishopps. Ni. Yes, and leave our wills.
The Church in Bishopps hath one soveraigne starre
To guide and save us, wishing not other sort
Of men would dare challenge, and our Wills
Have ranged like Icarus against the Sunne,
That melting plunge us in a Sea of woes.
Cel. Good doctrine, would you followe it your selfe.
Ni. I will endeavour Madam. Cel. I observe,
Of all these Wits, Valeria and my selfe
Have workt on our side, excepting two,
You have noe quarrell to the rest. Ni. Not I,
Nor yet to them, this question set a part,
Which seemes to undermine the Churches State,
And Bishopps claime. And as those wch theyr rite
Deserve eternall prayse, so would I still
Th'had kept the selfe same tenor, and not chang'd
The subiect of their Actions into spleene,
And teeth against a Bishopp and his Power,
Of wch infection most of those you nam'd
Have lately taken tincture; and 'tis thought
That Perinosus, whom you so extoll,
Layde the first grounds, to shuffle Bishopps off,
And place a Monopoly there of Kingship
To Anarchie, and ruffle in his land,
That if they could not rule, would ruine Rules:
And his [illegible] was but a breathing forth
Of his impostum'd humor; And those Men
That followe it so closely, are but friends,
Or rather creatures tutor'd in his Schoole,
And from their tender age [illegible] in the trade;
And singular worshipp, were of [illegible]

Then all

Great ruins follow, and no way is left
But one to fly the danger.
Celia. Which is that?
To cleave to bishops?
Nivetta. Yes, and leave our wills.
The church in bishops hath a sovereign force
To guide and save us, which no other sort
Of men could ever challenge, and our wills
Have wings, like Icarus against the sun,
That melting plunge us in a sea of woes.
Celia. Good doctrine, could you follow it yourself.
Nivetta. I will endeavor, madam.
Celia. I observe,
Of all those wits Valeria and myself
Have reck'ned on our side, excepting two,
You have no quarrel to the rest.
Nivetta. Not I,
Nor yet to them, this question set apart,
Which seems to undermine the church's state
And bishop's claim. And as those which you cite
Deserve eternal praise, so would I still
T'had kept the self-same tenor, and not changed
The subject of their actions into spleen
And tooth against a bishop and his power,
Of which infection most of those you named
Have lately taken tincture. And 'tis thought
That Perinosus, whom you so extol,
Laid the first grounds to shuffle bishops off
And place a monopoly there of knights
To anarchize and ruffle in this land,
That if they could not rule, would ruin souls,
And this last act was but a breaking forth
Of this impostumed humor; and those men
That follow it so closely are but friends,
Or rather creatures tutored in his school,
And from their tender age possessed with pride
And singular conceit, more of themselves

Thou all the worlde besides; And hadst not thou
On this occasion fallne into these termes,
This totall drift had vanisht into ayre,
As theirs will into fier, with all their workes
And writinge of this subiect in the end,
As iustly may be fear'd. Cel. your doubt is such
I see alreadie. Ni. Doe it hitt the marke?
Noe matter though a foole deliuer it.
Val: Come, come, thou art noe foole, nor yet so wise
But thou maist be deceau'd. Ni. As others I,
But not so willingly I hope, as some.
Val. Thou meanist me, or Celia, or both.
Ni. I neither meane your selfe, nor Celia
Nor anie that I knowe; yet some are found,
Noe doubt, that willingly become themselues
And winke at their owne Errors. Val. Come, lett's in,
Till Bytomastus and Aggeas come;
That thou maist dresse thy selfe to goe with us.
Ni. Pray, whither? Val. To a meeting of the wisest
And gravest Ghibellins upon the point
Of knowledge from Bishops. Ni. Is there place
For women? Val. yes, for women of our ranke,
That promise secrecie, and will performe
As thou art one, I hope. Ni. A woman I?
Nor pleade I knowledge aboue my sexe,
And wish the Ghibellins would challenge none
Aboue their calling. Val. Tongue noe more that stringe
It strikes a discord. Ni. Discords haue a power
To sweeten musicke. Cel. This is harsh and sower.

Scena tertia.

Jargus, downe from the Chimney.

I see the coast is cleare, I am about
I feare me, by this Candle yet I gaine

me though,

Than all the world besides; and had not they
On this occasion fallen into these terms,
His total drift had vanished into air
As theirs will into fire, with all their works
And writings of this subject in the end,
As justly may be feared.

Celia. Your bolt is shot,
I see, already.

Nivetta. So it hit the mark
No matter though a fool deliver it.

Valeria. Come, come, thou art no fool, nor yet so wise
But thou mayst be deceived.

Nivetta. As others, I,
But not so willingly, I hope, as some.

Valeria. Thou meanest me, or Celia, or both.

Nivetta. I neither mean yourself, nor Celia,
Nor any that I know; yet some are found,
No doubt, that willingly deceive themselves
And wink at their own errors.

Valeria. Come, let's in
Till Bitomattus and Aggeus come,
That thou mayst dress thyself to go with us.

Nivetta. Pray whither?

Valeria. To a meeting of the choice
And gravest Ghibellines upon this point
Of privilege from bishops.

Nivetta. Is there place
For women?

Valeria. Yes, for women of our rank
That promise secrecy and will perform,
As thou art one, I hope.

Nivetta. A woman I,
Nor plead I privilege above my sex,
And wish the Ghibellines would challenge none
Above their calling.

Valeria. Touch no more that string,
It strikes a discord.

Nivetta. Discords have a power
To sweeten music.

Celia. This is harsh and sour. [*Exeunt.*]

(*text continued on following page*)

Me thought, some talke, and whispering in the roome,
It seemed not of [illegible]; but ffriends.
Well, if he haue bewitcht me in this sort,
And for his pleasure made me plaie the part
Of Robin-good-fellow, or Frier Rush;
To serue for signe here to the Divells bush,
Ile studie to requite him, if I liue.
ffor we can thinke of iniuries sometimes,
As well as doe them, and repaie them back
With treble Interest; yet hold our selues
Not loosers by the bargaine. In our bloud
The spirit of revenge can runn as smooth,
As deepest rivers, that with silence slide
Not vexed by wrangling pebbles. Here's the spight,
I cannot putt this Divells habit off
Without some helpe; tis fastned to my back
With a close lace, the knot whereof my hands
Cannot attaine to; that I must be forc'd
To staie for companie, or call for helpe.
Now, whether for a penny? If I call,
They'le thinke the substance of me like my cloake,
And flie my presence, and giue out, this house
Is haunted by the Divell. If I staie,
I can expect nothing but shame,
And scorne, and scoffing from my best of ffriends.
How will the Iustices insult, when they shall heare
Of my disgrace, that am their Bishopps scourge,
And call'd another Attila, or Rodd
Of Iustice and Hierarchie; here am I catch'd
Upon a suddaine; stopt in my careere;
And forc'd to begg this favour of my ffriends
And others, not to laugh outright, but smile
At my disaster: This will proue a Theme
For Comedies hereafter, and my Name
Will flie upon the stage, outliving spight,
Of others revenge, in [illegible],
Or els, the Polititians made, transform'd and
Caracteriz'd,

Scena tertia

Jargus, down from the Chimney.

Jargus. I see the coast is clear. I am abused,
I fear me, by this Candle. Yet I heard,

Methought, some talk and whispering in the room,
It seemèd not of pursuivants, but friends.
Well, if he have betricked me in this sort,
And for his pleasure made me play the part
Of Robin-good-fellow or Friar Rush
To serve for sign here to the Devil's Bush,
I'll study to requite him if I live.
For we can think of injuries sometimes,
As well as do them, and repay them back
With treble interest, yet hold ourselves
No losers by the bargain. In our bloods
The spirit of revenge can run as smooth
As deepest rivers, that with silence slide
Not checked by wrangling pebbles. Here's the spite:
I cannot put this devil's habit off
Without some help; 'tis fast'ned to my back
With a close lace, the knot whereof my hands
Cannot attain to, that I must be forced
To stay for company or call for help.
Now, whether for a penny? If I call,
They'll think the substance of me like my coat
And fly my presence, and give out this house
Is haunted by the devil. If I stay,
I can expect no other end [but] shame,
And scorn, and scoffing from my best of friends.
How will the Guelfs insult when they shall hear
Of my disgrace, that am their bishop's scourge
And called another Attila or rod
Of Guelfs and hierarchists? How am I calmed
Upon a sudden? stopped in my career?
And forced to beg this favor of my friends
And others, not to laugh outright, but smile
At my disaster? This will prove a theme
For comedies hereafter, and my name
Will fly upon the stage, entitling plays
Of church revenge in "Jargus' Chimney Plot,"
Or else, "The Politician Mewed, Transformed,

Caracteriz'd, Endossell'd, and such stuffe.
Well, patience protect me, I must hide
Myselfe till night, when I may speake unseene,
And call some friend to succour me. I'le stepp
Behinde this Arras, here I'le take a napp;
For I am wearie, sleepie, and opprest
With manie cares. Let Fortune worke the rest.

Scena quarta.

Davus. Onoplutus. Pamophus.

You are but children to me in this point
Of witt, and practise of the course of thinges;
Nor know you how to carry this my plott
With best advantage. Have not I convers'd
With Dukes and Cardinalls, and had as free
Accesse and regresse, to and from the Pope
As you may have from me, or to this [illegible]:
On. A strange example, not to be withstood.
Pa. I'me sure 'tis foolish, be it ne're so strange.
Da. Why sirra, know you what you said? Pa. I doe,
And sirra, leave your prating and your bragges
Of Popes and Cardinalls that I heard you talke.
They were full wearie of you, I'le be sworne,
If you can speake not wiser then you doe;
And to the point: Wee are not hither come
To heare your commendations, but to take
Directions for our businesse in hand.
Da. Forsu, confesse then, Am not I the man
From whom you are to take them? so confirm'd
By voice of three superiors? On. With these eares
I heard them said so. Pa. Are you such an Asse
To thinke they meant, that he should play the foole,
And when he should instruct us, praise himselfe?
Dio mene guardi. Is not this a point
Of Rhetorick, to purchase favour first,
And creepe into the hearers good conceit
Before wee come the matter. I dare you sure,

An Igno:

Characterized, Endevilled,'' and such stuff.
Well, patience protect me, I must hide
Myself till night, when I may speak unseen
And call some friend to succor me. I'll step
Behind this arras; there I'll take a nap;
For I am weary, sleepy, and oppressed
With many cares. Let Fortune work the rest. [*Exit*.]

Scena quarta

Davus, Onoplutus, Pamoppus.

Davus. You are but children to me in this point
Of wit, and practice of the course of things,
Nor know you how to carry this my plot
With best advantage. Have not I conversed
With dukes and cardinals, and had as free
Access and regress to and from the pope
As you may have from me or to this post?
Onoplutus. A strong example, not to be withstood.
Pamoppus. I'm sure 'tis foolish, be it ne'er so strong.
Davus. Why, sirrah, know you what you say?
Pamoppus. I do,
And, sirrah, leave your prating and your brags
Of popes and cardinals that heard you talk—
They were full weary of you, I'll be sworn,
If you can speak no wiser than you do—
And to the point. We are not hither come
To hear your commendations, but to take
Directions for our business in hand.
Davus. *Orsu*, confess them, am not I the man
From whom you are to take them? So confirmed
By voice of three superiors?
Onoplutus. With these ears
I heard them say so.
Pamoppus. Are you such an ass
To think they meant that he should play the fool,
And when he should instruct us, praise himself?
[*Davus.*] *Dio me ne guardi*! Is not this a point
Of rhetoric, to curry favor first
And creep into the hearer's good conceit
Before we touch the matter? Are you such

An Ignoramus? See illiterate?
En. It is a point of Oratorie here;
And I haue read it when I was a Boy,
In Cicero's Epistles, or else where.
Pa. Talke not to me of Rhetorick, or points
Of Oratorie; Logick is my Lawe.
Looke heere: with this I'le beate into your heads
That they are ffooles that loue not to be beate.
En. Staie, satisfie him Damus for his oune,
Els he will strike vs. Da. Che vergogna! eh.
You'le strike, and be irregular; you will;
And excommunicate; It is a case
Reseru'd from Bishopps heere: and which is more,
ffrom Regulars Confessors. Come, hold your hands,
And saue a voyage, els you must to Rome
ffor Absolution: When you come, I doubt
Whether the Pope will put the matter vp,
And grant a Pardon for you, when he knowes
To whom you offer'd violence. En. Were like.
Da. I'ad better strike the Bishopp heere, then me,
And sooner be acquitted. En. Thinke you soe?
I feare you oft haue call'd the Bishopp Asse,
And others knaues, or ffooles, that beare his part;
But neuer knew the reason of't till now.
It is the credit, sure, you haue with Popes
And Cardinalls, and other ffriends at Rome.
Da. Ma, che pensate? Is not his enough
To beate off flies that would molest me? Pa. Noe.
ffor, not long since, it had not power enough
To beate off doggs from tearing out your throate,
Had not some helpe come in. Da. It was but one,
A small flea-bite; heere's a scarre indeede;
But I beshrew the Surgeon, ffor this scratch
might haue bene cur'd without it; But all doggs
may take example by him here they bite
Anointed flesh againe. En. Why, was he hang'd?
Da. Basta,

An *Ignoramus?* so illiterate?
Onoplutus. It is a point of oratory sure,
And I have read it, when I was a boy,
In Cicero's *Epistles*, or elsewhere.
Pamoppus. Talk not to me of *rhetoric* or points
Of *oratory*; *logic* is my law.
Look here: with this I'll beat into your heads
That they are fools that love not to be brief.
Onoplutus. Stay, satisfy him, Davus, for this once,
Else he will strike us.
Davus. *Che vergogna? eh!*
You'll strike and be irregular, you will,
And excommunicate! It is a case
Reserved from bishops here, and which is more,
From regulars themselves. Come, hold your hands
And save a voyage, else you must to Rome
For absolution. When you come, I doubt
Whether the pope will put the matter up
And grant a pardon for you, when he knows
To whom you offered violence.
Onoplutus. Very like.
Davus. Y'ad better strike the bishop here than me,
And sooner be acquitted.
Onoplutus. Think you so?
I hear you oft have called the bishop ass,
And others knaves, or fools, that took his part,
But never knew the reason of't till now.
It is the credit, sure, you have with popes
And cardinals and other friends at Rome.
Davus. *Ma, che pensate?* Is not this enough
To beat off flies that would molest me?
Pamoppus. No.
For not long since it had not power enough
To beat off dogs from tearing out your throat,
Had not some help come in.
Davus. It was but one,
A very fleabite; here's a scar indeed,
But I beshrew the surgeon, for this scratch
Might have been cured without it; but all dogs
May take example by him how they bite
Anointed flesh again.
Onoplutus. Why, was he hanged?

Da. Basta. As good he had, he was conuaid
Invisibly out of the world, not knowne
The man or master, maide or Mris knowe
Unto his graue. On. A politick deuise:
Lett's heare the secrett. Da. Pardonate mi,
I am not triviall; my reuenge proceedes
Not on such slender sleights to make
The world acquainted, otherwise then that
I put vp wronges, when I take vengeance home.
Pa. A goodly peece of sleight indeede
To kill a dogg; whelp, but others can doe more;
They can kill calues and others like yourselfe.
Da. Sfacciato, che tu sei; Am I a man
Of likelyhood to giue or take the horne?
Pa. But you may blowe your owne. Da. You lye. On. O Lord!
I feare they'l fight, t'is time to hide myselfe.
Pa. Sirra, that lye doth blister on your tongue,
Which I must launce, to send it downe your throate.
Da. You see I haue not weapon but myselfe.
Pa. If that cannott defend you, take your tongue;
T'is longe and sharpe enough. Da. But not of steele.
Pa. T'is worse then Aspicks stinge, or Scorpions taile,
It kills at any distance. Da. Shall a word
Moue you to murder me? Pa. O Sr, your words
haue murdered many. Da. What the lye? Pa. Your lyes
haue sett debate amonge vnited friends,
And broake the heart of charitie and truth,
And I must now retort them in his kinde.
On. O Lord, the diuell Sr. Pa. What ailes this foole?
On. The diuell on my conscience. Pa. Spitt him out
And send thy praiers. On. The diuell. Pa. Where? On. Goe looke
Behinde the Arras, there. Da. His witts are strai'd,
On. else he comes to take Panoppus off,
And doe me this good turne. Say, Doue sta?
Where is he? che diauol? On. Take the paines
To seeke

Davus. *Basta*, as good he had; he was conveyed
Invisibly out of the world, nor know
The man or master, maid or mistress, how
Unto this hour.
Onoplutus. A politic device:
Let's hear the secret.
Davus. *Perdonate mi*,
I am not trivial; my revenge proceeds
Not on such slender policy to make
The world acquainted otherwise than that
I put up wrongs when I strike vengeance home.
Pamoppus. A goodly piece of policy indeed,
To kill a dog! Why, but others can do more:
They can kill calves and oxen like yourself.
Davus. *Sfacciato*, *che tu sei.* Am I a man
Of likelihood to give cr take the horn?
Pamoppus. But you may blow your own.
Davus. You lie.
Onoplutus. O Lord!
I fear they'll fight; 'tis time to hide myself. [*Exit behind the arras.*]
Pamoppus. Sirrah, that lie doth blister on your tongue,
Which I must lance to send it down your throat.
Davus. You see I have no weapon but myself.
Pamoppus. If that cannot defend you, take your tongue;
'Tis long and sharp enough.
Davus. But not of steel.
Pamoppus. 'Tis worse than aspic's sting or scorpion's tail:
It kills at any distance.
Davus. Shall a word
Move you to murder me?
Pamoppus. O sir, your words
Have murdered many.
Davus. What, the lie?
Pamoppus. Your lies
Have set debate among united friends
And broke the heart of charity and truth,
And I must now retort them in this kind. [*Enter Onoplutus.*]
Onoplutus. O Lord, the devil, sirs!
Pamoppus. What ails this fool?
Onoplutus. The devil, on my conscience!
Pamoppus. Spit him out
And say thy prayers.
Onoplutus. The devil!
Pamoppus. Where?

(*text continued on following page*)

Onoplutus. Go look
Behind the arras, there.
Davus. His wits are strayed,
Or else he comes to take Pamoppus off
And do me this good turn. Say, *dove sta?*
Where is he? *che diavol'?*
Onoplutus. Take the pains

To seeke him out yourselfe, as I have done;
For I have noe more heart then hath that Iester.
Pa. Noe, nor so much; for that is heart of Oake;
But sirr, what dost thou see? or where? or how?
On. I sawe the Divell, as I hidd myselfe,
Iust iust behind the hanging he appear'd,
In a most monstrous shape. Pa. Thy coward feare
hath plaide the Painter. Let us heare. On. The first
That mett me was his nose. Pa. A goodly where,
And first in sight. On. It lookt for all the world
Like to a mightie Gamon, newly drest,
But of the chimneys end, bestuck with cloves
As broade as oyster-shells, and stunck of secke
Abhominably. His eyes shott flames of fire,
Like two brasse kettles glowing in a hott
And furious fornace; And his mouth puft smoake
Like some Tobacco-shopps: But then his taile,
T'was horrible, and still it whirl'd about,
Much like a mustard-querne, and voided filth,
And ordure from his intrailes. Pa. Stop vp thy mouth,
I smell the rest. Da. T'is a stinking lye,
Or els thou wert afraide. On. I pray what were you
Whom for the lye you had beene brought but now,
Had not I shew'd you by this devise?
Thus much in merriment. But now I speake
In sober sadnes. As I crept beside
That Arras, groaping out my waie, I felt
Some ougly fashion'd Monster, like a Beare,
Which made me squeake, and hither runn for helpe.
Pa. A water Spaniell, or some shagg-haird curr.
Da. It may be some oxe-hide, the hornes and all.
Pa. Be it the Divell or his Dam, I'le see.
It is the Divell sure, who would come by
This monster els into this roome? I feele

My haire

To seek him out yourself as I have done;
For I have no more heart than hath that post.
Pamoppus. No, nor so much, for that is heart of oak;
But say, what dost thou see? or where? or how?
Onoplutus. I saw the devil as I hid myself,
And just behind the hanging he appeared
In a most monstrous shape.
Pamoppus. Thy coward fear
Hath played the painter. Let us hear.
Onoplutus. The first
That met me was his nose.
Pamoppus. A goodly piece,
And first in sight.
Onoplutus. It looked for all the world
Like to a mighty gammon newly dropped
Out of the chimney's end, bestuck with cloves
As broad as oyster shells, and stunk of soot
Abominably. His eyes shot flames of fire
Like two brass kettles glowing in a hot
And furious furnace, and his mouth puffed smoke
Like ten tobacco shops. But then his tail,
'Twas horrible, and still it whirled about
Much like a mustard quern, and voided filth
And ordure from his entrails.
Pamoppus. Stop thy mouth,
I smell the rest.
Davus. 'Tis a stinking lie,
Or else thou wert afraid.
Onoplutus. Pray, what were you,
When for the lie you had been broached but now,
Had not I rescued you by this device?
Thus much in merriment. But now I speak
In sober sadness. As I crept behind
That arras, groping out my way, I felt
Some ugly-fashioned monster like a bear,
Which made me squeal and hither run for help.
Pamoppus. A water spaniel or some shag-haired cur.
Davus. It may be some ox hide, the horns and all.
Pamoppus. Be it the devil or his dam, I'll see. [*Pulls back arras.*]
It is the devil sure, who could convey
This monster else into this room? I feel

My haire to bristle. Da. I have lost my heart,
T'is falne into my breeches. On. So is mine;
You would not creditt me. Pa. Nor can I yet;
Why sure the divell's dead, or fast a sleepe;
Ile trie his Spirit. Da. Stay, what neede you wake,
Or trouble him, before he trouble us?
For ought wee knowe, he is our freind and comes
To guarde this place from theifs that would disturbe
Our holy Synod. On. Then he comes from heaven.
Da. But you should not wake a sleeping dogg, much less
A sleeping Divell. Pa. Stand aside. On. not heare,
Said he should prove a divell of our deaths?
Pa. I am resolu'd to strike, and trie him.

Scena quinta.

Targus.

Spoile;
Pamoppus, Onoplatus; Danus. Sot,
They are affrighted all; and fledd, while I
Am left alone to play the divell still
Without redemption. Had I not awak'd
By chance, and overheard them, I had lost
My dearest parte of beeing, that's my life;
I will not saie my soule; For that, I hope,
Is warranted by fate, I should saie God,
And by superiors, with whose pride we move
More then our knowledge of our times of right.
It makes us fearelesse. Where were my care,
And huge circumference of witt? A snuffe,
A poore candle end, a brittle braine
Hath outslept me, that I must to schoole,
And learne the Politicians trade againe,
Before I can win quittance: lett me see;
Now could I moralize upon my selfe,

And shew

My hair to bristle.
Davus. I have lost my heart;
'Tis fallen into my breeches.
Onoplutus. So is mine;
You would not credit me.
Pamoppus. Nor can I yet;
Why sure the devil's dead, or fast asleep;
I'll try his spirit.
Davus. Stay, what need you wake
Or trouble him before he trouble us?
For aught we know, he is our friend and comes
To guard this place from Guelfs that would disturb
Our holy synod.
Onoplutus. Then he comes from heaven.
Davus. But you should not wake a sleeping dog, much less
A sleepy devil.
Pamoppus. Stand aside.
Onoplutus. Yet hear,
Say he should prove a devil of our coat?
Pamoppus. I am resolved to strike and try him.

Scena quinta

Jargus.

Jargus. Hold,
Pamoppus, Onoplutus, Davus! [*Exeunt Pamoppus, Onoplutus, Davus.*] So,
They are affrighted all and fled, while I
Am left alone to play the devil still
Without redemption. Had I not awaked
By chance and overheard them, I had lost
My dearest part of being, that's my life;
I will not say my soul, for that, I hope,
Is warranted by fate—I should say God—
And by superiors, with whose voice we move
More than on knowledge oftentimes of right;
It makes us fearless. Where is now my reach
And huge circumference of wit? A snuff,
A very candle end, a critic's brain
Hath [overleapt] me, that I must to school
And learn the politician's trade again
Before I can cry quittance. Let me see:
Now could I moralize upon myself,

And shew how God permitteth humane witts
To be outstript, and fall into those trapps
They make for others. I could raise my voice
Yet higher yet, and in a Tragick vaine
Describe Achitophel with all his plotts
Brought unto naught, and strangled with himselfe,
And talke of Ecebolius with his feares
And counterfeited zeale in Julians tyme,
And many another Proteus of State,
Here and abroade, that found but badd successe,
Or ruine for their paines. Nay, I could never
Repent my plott in stirring up the laie
Against their Bishopp, were it not for shame,
And that my fellow knights would cast me off,
Or I might gett a penaunce in the end,
Should I confesse, more then could be borne;
Yet still be had in jealousie amongst
My brethren, for being the first man
That asked pardon for a publique fault
In case of Scandall, Slaunder or the like,
Which never yet was knowne to come from us,
Nor ever shall; the reason as I guesse,
Is our Impeccabilitie or straight
That all we doe, can be but veniall sinnes,
And therefore pardonable of themselves,
Without all further circumstance: This point,
Although we dare not justifie abroade,
We practise it in private. But noe more,
I heare some coming hitherward: I must
Returne into the chimney; for it seemes
The rubbish's raised, and I shall straight be sought
By curious eyes, or kept with Exorcismes
By mine owne brethren; which to prevent
Ile creepe into the vault, till this be spent.

Scæna sexta.

And show how God permitteth human wits
To be outstripped and fall into those traps
They make for others. I could raise my voice
Up higher yet and in a tragic vein
Describe Achitophel with all his plots
Brought unto naught and strangled with himself,
And talk of Ecebolius with his fears
And counterfeited zeal in Julian's time,
And many another Proteus of state,
Here, and abroad, that found but bad success
Or ruin for their pains. Nay, I could now
Repent my plot in stirring up the lay
Against their bishop, were it not for shame
And that my fellow knights would cast me off,
Or I might get a penance in the end,
Should I confess, more than could be borne,
Yet still be had in jealousy among
My bretheren, for being the first man
That askèd pardon for a public fact
In case of scandal, slander, or the like,
Which never yet was seen to come from us,
Nor ever shall. The reason, as I guess,
Is our impeccability, or faith
That all we do can be but venial sins
And therefore pardonable of themselves
Without all further circumstance. This point,
Although we dare not justify abroad,
We practice it in private. But no more,
I hear some coming hitherward. I must
Return into this chimney, for it seems
The hubbub's raised, and I shall straight be sought
By curious eyes, or vexed with exorcisms
By mine own bretheren, which to prevent
I'll creep into this vault till day be spent. [*Exit.*]

Scena Sexta.

Spirius, in a Surplice, with a Stole & Booke.
Pamphagus, with a Crucifix.
Onoplutus, and Dauus } with wax Tapers.
A Seruant, with Holie watter.

A God's name forwards. Beare aloft your lights
Aduance the crucifix. your candles dropp,
Hold them sprightly, that the world may see
And iudge us by our workes, and diuells flye,
Our sight, and prayers. Ono. God grant our prayer's haue force
To fright this diuell where we haue in hand:
I am afraide our workes are somewhat darke,
Such is our frailtie. I would be deuout
Me thinks in earnest now. Pa. Why, canst thou iest
That seest the diuell here. On. Not I, but some
Doe make a iest of diuells, and of God.
Da. Andiamo, ch. Who puts into your heads
These Ghiribizzos, these Intrigis: Spi. Marry,
And be you readie when I call, to cast
The holie water. Seru. If my heart will serue,
I shall not faile for one. Spi. To come away,
I see by thy complexion thou art whiter
About the liuer. Pa. yet his nose is redd.
Seru. I; so is your's: and would be more,
Could you but keepe my diett. Pa. What is that?
Seru. A cupp of Aqua vitæ, next your heart
And all day-long, as much strong Ale, or Beere
As you can carry, yet hold up your head,
And sometimes Wine, our seruice now a dayes
Would freeze without these comforts. Da. Via, on.
Spi. I see noe diuell yet. On. Noe more did we,
Till wee touch'd him first; but then he rowz'd.

Da. He did

Scena sexta

Spirius in a surplice with a stole and book
Pamoppus with a crucifix
Onoplutus,
and } *with wax tapers*
Davus,
A Servant with holy water.

Spirius. 'A God's name, forwards! Bear aloft your lights.
Advance the crucifix. Your candles drop;
Hold them uprightly that the world may see
And judge us by our works, and devils fly
Our sight and prayers.
Onoplutus. God grant our pray'rs have force
To fright this devil hence we have in hand.
I am afraid our works are somewhat dark,
Such is our frailty. I could be devout,
Methinks, in earnest now.
Pamoppus. Why, canst thou jest
That saw the devil late?
Onoplutus. Not I, but some
Do make a jest of devils and of God.
Davus. *Andiamo*, eh. Who puts into your heads
These *ghiribizzos*, these *intrighis?*
Spirius. March,
And be you ready, when I call, to reach
The holy water.
Servant. If my heart will serve,
I shall not fail for one.
Spirius. To run away.
I see by thy complexion thou art white
About the liver.
Pamoppus. Yet his nose is red.
Servant. Aye, so is [yours], sir, and would be more
Could you but keep my diet.
Pamoppus. What is that?
Servant. A cup of aqua vitae next your heart,
And all day long as much strong ale or beer
As you can carry, yet hold up your head,
And sometimes wine; our service nowadays
Would freeze without these comforts.
Davus. *Via*, on.
Spirius. I see no devil yet.
Onoplutus. No more did we
Till we provoked him first, but then he roared.

Da. Hee did indeede, Pamophus was too rash,
He told him of't before. Pa. You told a lye,
He did not sweare. Da. He call'd us by our Names.
On. I, as familiarly as though he had
Beene sworne a brother to us, and cri'd, hollo.
Da. As much, to saie, he swore, I'le make it good.
Pa. You'le make the Divell good as soone. Spi. Forbeare,
This is no time to quarrell, or dispute,
Remember where you are, and whom before,
The Crowne weare this morninge. Pa. Now you can preach
Devoutly, Spirit, would you doe soe well.
Spi. As well as you, Pamophus. On. Marry alike
And so let's all agree. Da. Content, and take
My pro vi fallia, instead a haire to sleepe,
Wee're Bishops quellers all. Spi. Devoute, and one
Else you shall take that chardginge in our waie.
On. Not I, without a Warrant, or Commaunde
From the Provinciall. Da. Nor I, for feare
My Spectacles should fall, then I were gone,
How should I fight with Divells in the darke?
On. Peace with your tongues. Pa. That rather fights for them.
I durst doe ~~more then~~ this, and more, had I but time
To make a short Confession. Spi. Fye for shame,
Art thou growne scrupulous? Why, tis not Pride,
Or Drunkennes, or Lust, or Anger here
Should vex thy Conscience now. Pa. Not much, some spice
Of Sacriledge it may be, though. Spi. As how?
Hast thou stolen Church stuffe? Pa. No. Spi. Deflowr'd some Nunne?
Pa. Cut Nada. Spi. What a divell ayles thee then?
Pa. The Bishop is a Barr, that will not downe
Our safety, nor health; and, which is worse,
I told him innocent, yet have so railed
Upon him, and the Pope, that will not stand
For us against him; that I feele my minde is
much troubled

Davus. He did indeed. Pamoppus was too rash,
I told him of't before.
Pamoppus. You told a lie:
He did not roar.
Davus. He called us by our names.
Onoplutus. Aye, as familiarly as though he had
Been sworn a brother to us, and cried, "Hold!"
Davus. As much to say, he roared; I'll make it good.
Pamoppus. You'll make the devil good as soon.
Spirius. Forbear,
This is no time to quarrel or dispute;
Remember where you are and whom before;
You know what this imports.
Pamoppus. Now you can preach
Devoutly, Spirius, could you do so well.
Spirius. As well as you, Pamoppus.
Onoplutus. Much alike,
And so let's all agree.
Davus. Content, and take
My *pro vi faccia*, not a hair to choose;
We're bishop-quellers all.
Spirius. Proceed, and one
Of you pull back that hanging in our way.
Onoplutus. Not I, without a warrant or command
From the provincial.
Davus. Nor I, for fear
My spectacles should fall. Then I were gone;
How should I fight with devils in the dark?
Onoplutus. Why, with your tongue.
Pamoppus. That rather fights for them.
I durst do this and more, had I but time
To make a short confession.
Spirius. Fie, for shame!
Art thou grown scrupulous? Why, 'tis not pride,
Or drunkenness, or lust, or anger sure
Should vex thy conscience now.
Pamoppus. Not much; some spice
Of sacrilege it may be thought.
Spirius. As how?
Hast thou stolen church-stuff?
Pamoppus. No.
Spirius. Deflow'red some nuns?
Pamoppus. Tut, *nada*.
Spirius. What a devil ail'st thou then?
Pamoppus. The bishop is a burr that will not down
So easily, methinks; and, which is worse,
I hold him innocent, yet have so railed
Upon him and the pope, that will not stand
For us against him, that I feel my mind

Much trouble at it. Spi. Is this all? Pa. The same
Is cast in this. Spi. Goe on; be bold; you neede
Noe further assurance then my words;
That shall secure and warrant you. Pa. Enough;
Now I have shew'd the divell, and confest.
He followes next in order. Di. Speake Lady.
Pa. That thus I built the divell. Or. He is gone.
Spi. What solemne sophistry is this, to raise
A rumor thus of divells without cause!
Or. Speak Daniel in thy conscience, wist thou that
See much about thee; was not there a thing
Wee sawe to make a divell of? Da. There was,
Els I'ld forsweare my spectacles, might these
With them doe never faile. Or. I now can tell
What made the divell vanish. Spi. What was that?
Or. 'Tis evident. Spi. 'Twas holy water sure,
The divell loves it not. Pa. The exorcisme
It was more likely. Da. Noe, the hallowed light.
Or. 'Twas none of both; Pamphilus tooke a torch,
The divell hates that worse then any thing,
Or holie water, or the hallowed light.
It scar'd him quite. Spi. But doe so noe more,
Unles you meane to shame us, and marre
Our cause in hand. Pa. Pray pardon me this once,
I doe not willingly commit such fault.
Or. The divell was so neere his elbowe then
I blame him not, it might have bene my case.
Da. And mine. Spi. But none of mine; confesse a start
To preiudice our cause? 'Twas it were a thing.
Pa. Why, wouldst thou let the divell take thee first?
Spi. What care I for the divell in this case?
Take what he can, he takes not me to sure
In such a debate. Or. Hold thee there, brave Sparke.
Wee may admire, but hardly imitate.

They resolve.

Much troubled at it.
Spirius. Is this all?
Pamoppus. The sum
Is cast in this.
Spirius. Go on; be bold; you need
No further absolution than my word;
That shall secure and warrant you.
Pamoppus. Enough;
Now I have shunned the devil and confessed,
It follows next in order—
Davus. You be [hanged].
Pamoppus. That thus I bolt the devil. [*Pulls back arras.*]
Onoplutus. He is gone.
Spirius. What solemn foolery is this, to raise
A rumor thus of devils without cause?
Onoplutus. Speak, Davus, in thy conscience (if thou hast
So much about thee) was not there a thing
We saw to make a devil of?
Davus. There was,
Else I'll forswear my spectacles; mine eyes
With them do never fail.
Onoplutus. I now can tell
What made the devil vanish.
Spirius. What was that?
Onoplutus. 'Tis evident.
Spirius. 'Twas holy water sure;
The devil loves it not.
Pamoppus. The crucifix
It was, more likely.
Davus. No, the hallowed lights.
Onoplutus. 'Twas none of these: Pamoppus told a truth;
The devil hates that worse than crucifix,
Or holy water, or these hallowed lights.
It shamed him quite.
Spirius. But, sir, do so no more,
Unless you mean to shame us and mar
Our cause in hand.
Pamoppus. Pray pardon me this once,
I do not willingly commit such faults.
Onoplutus. The devil was so near his elbow then
I blame him not; it might have been my case.
Davus. And mine.
Spirius. But never mine. Confess a fact
To prejudice our cause? Say it were truth.
Pamoppus. Why, wouldst thou let the devil take thee first?
Spirius. What care I for the devil in this case?
Take what he can, he takes not me, be sure,
In such a dotage.
Onoplutus. Hold thee there, brave spark!
We may admire, but hardly imitate

Thy resolution. Lett vs now discusse
This night the divell went. Da. Goe thou be gone
What skills it? Che importa? Well I saie,
(Pray you he staid not yet in th' scene of vs.)
Me thought I felt a winde goe through me.
Sp. Goe, it went through, there is noe feare. But whist,
Noe word of what is past, least all the Towne
Hoote at vs, and the divell flie abroade
In every Tailors mouth, and Apple-Stall.
Or. Nay, nay, that's done already; ffor the same
A Basket woman caught the Rumor first,
And bore it o're the Kingsbench, where the
It fills the Towne. Da: Noe matter, wee'le out-face
It well enough againe. Sp. meane time lett's in;
ffor straight our holie Synod shall begin.

Grex

Lucianus. Therulus.

This busines followed well; I was afraide
The divell would be found, and so the sport
Should end. ffor I grew wearie of the Play,
And fell a sleepe before his coming downe:
But now I wish the latter Act would bee
As longe as all the rest. The. Sport and I.

Actus quintus.

Scena prima.

Egrudius. Candle.

What times are these! how are these later daies
Chang'd from their Predecessors! Ca. Nay be sure
These are the dogg-daies guiltie accounts
In the Platonick yeare, the world's turn'd round,
I can

Thy resolution. Let us now discuss
Which way the devil went.
Davus. So he be gone
What skills it? *che importa?* Well, I say,
Pray God he stay not yet with some of us.
Methought I felt a wind go through me.
Spirius. So it went through, there is no fear. But whilst,
No words of what is past, lest all the town
Hoot at us, and this devil fly abroad
In every tinker's mouth and apple stall.
Onoplutus. Nay, nay, that's done already. For by chance
A basket woman catched this rumor first
And bore it o'er the threshall, and by this
It fills the town.
Davus. No matter, we'll outface
It well enough again.
Spirius. Meantime let's in;
For straight our holy synod shall begin. [*Exeunt.*]

Grex.

Lucianus, Therulus.

Lucianus. This business cottons well; I was afraid
The devil would be found, and so the sport
Should end. For I grew weary of the play
And fell asleep before his coming down,
But now I wish this latter Act would be
As long as all the rest.
Therulus. Expect and see.

Actus quintus

Scena prima

Erudius, Candle.

Erudius. What times are here? How are these later days
Changed from their predecessors?
Candle. Nay, be sure,
These are the dog days pointed to attend
On the Platonic year.
Erudius. The world's turned round.

I can remember, yet I am not old,
More strife and zeale exprest, in bloudie times
By Roman Catholicks, then nowe I finde.
Ca. Such bloudie times must bring them back againe,
Or els farewell Religion, and the Pope
May whistle for his fflock, and longe enough,
Ere they will heare, or heareing will obey,
Soe manie Shepheards leade them, that agree
Like Sampsons-ffoxes, only by the tayles,
Their heads and tongues, and other parts drawe wide.
Ex. The more's the pittie, if it could be helpt.
Ca. Assure yourselfe, his holynes, whoe would heere
Frowne but an idle finger, and his vowe
Weare yeares, before he could reduce your heads
Into one minde; and I begin to doubt
Whether our [illegible] State, or some of them
Would more respect him, were he in their wayes;
For I have noted two or three decrees
Much slighted by the Ghibellins of late
By him enacted: Ex. Which are those? Ca. The one
A prohibition from erecting fformes
Of new Sodalities, and making Prayers
Besides the Common Course, as if the Church
Fail'd in this part, or Catholicks did needs
Their factionizing waies to helpe their Cause;
devotion the pretence; the middle Schisme;
The end wilde confusion. Ex. Stopp thy mouth,
It overflowes; and to the next. Ca. The next,
A publick Bull, printed, and proclaym'd
Confining Regulars unto the Lawe
Of Approbation by their Ordinaries,
All former ffreedomes in that case repeal'd:
Even by the power that gave them. but it falls
Just as the divell would, it is not kept.
Your [illegible] Pope is the beame, or block, they saie;
That Jupiter once cast amongst the frogges,

That slept

I can remember, yet I am not old,
More faith and zeal expressed in bloody times
By Roman Catholics than now I find.
Candle. Such bloody times must bring them back again
Or else farewell religion, and the pope
May whistle for his flock, and long enough,
Ere they will hear or hearing will obey;
So many shepherds lead them, that agree
Like Samson's foxes, only by the tails,
Their heads, and tongues, and other parts draw wide.
Erudius. The more's the pity, if it could be helped.
Candle. Assure yourself, this present pope would here
Prove but an idle cipher, and his voice
Wax hoarse before he could reduce your heads
Into one mind; and I begin to doubt
Whether our Bintrian state, or some of them,
Would more respect him were he in their reach;
For I have noted two or three decrees
Much slighted by the Ghibellines of late
By him enacted.
Erudius. Which are those?
Candle. The one
A prohibition from erecting forms
Of new sodalities and making prayers
Besides the common course, as if the church
Failed in this part, or Catholics did need
Such factionizing ways to help their cause:
Devotion the pretense; the middle schism;
The end will be confusion.
Erudius. Stop thy mouth,
It overflows; and to the next.
Candle. The next
A public breve, printed and proclaimed,
Confining regulars unto the law
Of approbation by their ordinaries;
All former freedoms in that case repealed
Even by the power that gave them. But it fails
Just as the devil would, it is not kept.
Your bishop is the beam, or block, they say,
That Jupiter once cast [amongst the] frogs,

That slipt about, and set him in place
His Ordinary Shipp but in the myre;
Which made his Subiects better fedd then taught,
And him confirm'd. But God may send a Storke
Will swallowe them for this, and pick them up
ffor Sallads in the end. Ex. But the pretence
He is not Ordinary, and his power
Not compatible with our State and times.
Ca. When hast thou they would saie it were; though State
And times were never so indulgent! Ex. Now.
Ca. That's never, never; as the instant passe'd
Can never be reclaim'd. Ex. Why sure the Now's,
Are not so metaphysicall; they grant
Some morall instants. Ca. Surely, more those
They cannott, lesse they will not part withall,
And so are Metaphisicks all in all;
And to none others morall but themselves.
Ex. But in their ffriends and ffavourites. Ca. They must out
Of course then Bishopize, or els growe colde
In the Gnathonian Art. Ex. What's that? Ca. To sooth
And humor every word they speake; for deedes,
They must not be misthought without a crime.
If gentlie toucht, tis scandall. Ex. Never King
Affected fflattery lesse, although that state
Is most exposed to such oylie Moaths.
But these are meere Hyperboles of time,
Or els some Satyr'd-up Rumors from the mouth
Of Heretickes, and Libertines. Ca. Fie on't,
Why should I seeke to slaunder them with lyes?
I never lived by it; I appeale to thee,
And all that stands for Rome, and Roman ffaith,
Whether among all orders in the Church,
Be but this partiall kinde of dealing nam'd,
If every common understanding [illegible]
[illegible] point out the man that is it must,

And almost

That skipped about and over him, and place
His ordinaryship but in the mire,
Which makes his subjects better fed than taught,
And him contemned. But God may send a stork
Will swallow them for this and pick them up
For salads in the end.

Erudius. But they pretend
He is no ordinary, and his power
Not compatible with our state and times.

Candle. When think'st thou they would say it were, though state
And times were never so indulgent?

Erudius. Now.

Candle. That's never, never; as the instant past
Can never be reclaimed.

Erudius. Why sure the now's
Are not so metaphorical; they grant
Some moral instants.

Candle. Surely, more than all
They cannot, less they will not part withal,
And so are metaphysics all in all,
And to none others moral but themselves.

Erudius. Put in their friends and favorites.

Candle. They must out
If once they bishopize, or else grow cold
In the Gnathonian art.

Erudius. What's that?

Candle. To soothe
And humor every word they speak; for deeds,
They must not be misthought without a sin.
If gently touched, 'tis scandal.

Erudius. Never kings
Affected flattery thus, although that state
Is most exposed to such oily [mouths].
But these are mere hyperboles of thine,
Or else some catched-up rumors from the mouth
Of heretics and libertines.

Candle. Pox on't,
Why should I seek to slander them with lies?
I never lived by't; I appeal to thee
And all that stand for Rome and Roman faith,
Whether among all orders in the church,
Be but this partial kind of dealing named,
If every common understanding wit
Cannot point out the men that use it most,

And almost quitt the rest, that give best signes
Of it to others. Ex. This is not denied
In some indeede. I neede not name them. Ca. No.
Their common practise teach them to report
And that to what may be expected shame;
Which makes me wonder how they found such gr
With other orders, that they should conspire
For such a publicke damnable affront.
Ex. O Sir, some broade sparks of those remaine
That are not [illegible] extinguished in the mindes
Of the religious; breeders of this plott.
I feare me Luther and his after-birth
had never suffered so against the Pope
had the Magistri nostri of those daies
Not stood, but taught the way of Christian Lo
With more humilitie; Nor had we tooke
Infection hence, had not the huge demeanes
Of our religious-howses, and their pride
Stood in the eye of Princes and great Men,
And dar'd them, for possession to exchange
Religion, conscience, the Pope and all.
Ca. T'was shrewdly guest. I see thou dost not m
To palliate abuses that have crept
Among the Romanists themselves. Ex. Not I.
And least I should seeme partiall in this point
I could endure a Cardinall of note
With many Prelates joyned with the throng
Of honor then, that lost, if not their faith,
Their consciences in those daies. Ca. yea, some their
Or life for't. Ex. Were it not I knowe the Ag
To be a thing sublimest in itselfe,
Yet sometymes to be with clowdes obscur'd,
My faith might oft miscarry in these mistes,
And tymes of dissolution; which these lighter
That should incourage us with every passe
That passion

And almost quit the rest that give less signs
Of it to others.
Erudius. This is not denied
In some indeed; I need not name them.
Candle. No.
Their common practice leaves them to report,
And that to what may be expected, shame;
Which makes me wonder how they found such grace
With other orders that they should conspire
In such a public damnable affront.
Erudius. O sir, some secret sparks of pride remain
That are not yet extinguished in the minds
Of the religious, seconds of this plot.
I fear me Luther and his afterbirth
Had never ruffled so against the pope,
Had the *magistri nostri* of those days
Not swelled but taught the way of Christian love
With more humility; nor had we took
Infection thence, had not the huge demesnes
Of our religious houses and their pride
Stood in the eye of princes and great men
And dared them for possession to exchange
Religion, conscience, the pope and all.
Candle. 'Twas shrewdly guessed. I see thou dost not mean
To palliate abuses that have crept
Among the Romanists themselves.
Erudius. Not I.
And lest I should seem partial in this point,
I could produce a cardinal of note,
With many prelates hurried with the swing
Of honor then, that lost, if not their faith,
Their conscience in those days.
Candle. Yea, some their souls
Or life for't.
Erudius. Were it not I know the church
To be a sun unblemished in itself,
Yet oftentimes to us with clouds obscured,
My faith might oft miscarry in those mists
And times of dissolution, [when] those lights
That should encourage us, with every puff

That Passion rather glimmer, or goe out,
And leave us in the darke to grope our way,
Were not that gratious helpe, that guide our soules
Unto Eternitie, our fixed Starr;
But wee that have done [illegible] all this while
ffor others Riotts, and had sought the cause
Of Gods iust Anger had bene now remov'd
With our humiliation, he inclin'd
To ease our sufferings with a pious hand,
And move the heart of him, that holds our lives
ffrom his high Throne in ffee, to lett the Lawe
ffall on our shoulders with a gentler poise,
In this laste Act to falter thus, and swarve
ffrom our owne doctrine, and the Churches forme,
That cannot with defect of Bishopps stand
In her full vigor long, and yet be held
Not alter'd from herselfe in ancient Light
Yea, some of us, to iustifie this Act
And strive to make it good upon pretence
Of State respect, which never yet they lov'd
Or tender'd from their hearts, as by their workes
May well be gather'd, witness'd to the world!
It makes me tremble when I thinke on't. Well,
ffor these and other scandalous escapes
Passt in this laste Edition of their lives,
Were it a Time to wish, about their neckes
Soe manie Milstones, as of them are found
Both of State and Bishopp haters in their hearts,
And all devour'd and swallow'd by the Sea!
Or may, rather not to wish, it were as Times
And not them, but all that beare [illegible]
Those are their Gracious Sister, and their needes
may seeme to be maintain'd with his Glosse;

It is agt

That passion raiseth glimmer, or go out,
And leave us in the dark to grope our way,
Were not that gracious help that guides our souls
Unto eternity, our fixèd star.
But we that have done penance all this while
For others' riots, and had thought the cause
Of God's just anger had been now removed
With our humiliation, He inclined
To ease our suff'rings with a pious hand
And move the heart of him that holds our lives
From this high grant in fee, to let the law
Fall on our shoulders with a gentler poise—
In this last act to falter thus and swerve
From our own doctrine and the church's form,
That cannot with defect of bishops stand
In her full vigor long, and yet be held
Not altered from herself in ancient times—
Yea, some of us to justify this act
And strive to make it good upon pretense
Of state respect, which never yet they loved
Or tendered from their hearts, as by their works
May well be gathered, witnessed to the world!
It makes me tremble when I think on't.

Candle. Well,
For these and other scandalous escapes
Past in this last edition of their lives,
Were it a sin to wish about their works
So many millstones as of them are found
Both state- and bishop-haters in their hearts,
And all devoured and swallowed by the sea?

Erudius. Nay, rather not to wish it were a sin,
And not them, but all that bear such minds,
How e'er their actions glister and their words
May seem to be enameled with this gloss,

It is against the lawe and State to yeild
Vnto a Bishopps power; when that same lawe
And State that made it, favoured nothing more
Then Bishopps then, but strangers they put back,
Though sent by Popes, the natiues still retain'd.
Nor must the lawe, intended to exclude
All Bishopps, not, nor euer, had they dreampt
The times that follow'd, would haue bred a dearth,
And though the present State admitt not power
That comes from Rome, but hinder it, they know
It lies not in our desire to doe the same,
And yet be Roman Catholicks. Our Staite
Cannot beare fire and water in one hand,
Or either well. Therefore not in a licence
Of doubts, we should wish our consciences, for
We hope to ... a iust and due regard.
Nor yet oppose they, we should not desire
A Bishopps powre, and such want for that end
Or hauing, should oppose it, when they pleas'd
To lett it runn some yeares without a checke,
Or publick notice taken, they haue halfe graunt
Had yet held out, had not the clamorous mou'd
The ... of some Ghibellins, that best
Can fish in troubled waters, to reverse
Their sleeping favours, and withall to take
This iust aduantage ~~from~~ of vs from our selues.
But where the fault remaines, iust God decide,
And to their wisdome we referre the rest.
Ca. ... said: 'Tis time our parley take an end,
~~Some~~ Strangers are coming. Ex. Lott's attend.

Scena Secunda.

Bytomattus. Aggaeus. Niuetta. Valeria. Celia.

Where Ladies ends our Iourney, this the house,
And here the roome, where our great Sage meete,
That must reforme this kingdome, and defend
The Subiects from the tyranny of Bishopps powre;
A worke

"It is against the law and state to yield
Unto a bishop's power"; when that same law
And state that made it, favored nothing more
Than bishops then, but strangers they put back,
Though sent by popes, the natives still retained.
Nor was the law intended to exclude
All bishops, no, nor any, had they dreamt
The times that followed would have bred a dearth;
And though the present state admit no power
That comes from Rome, but hinder it, they know
It lies not in our choice to do the same
And yet be Roman Catholics. Our faith
Cannot bear fire and water in one hand,
Or either well. They urge not as a breach
Of duty we should use our conscience, so
We keep to kings a just and due regard.
Nor yet expect they we should not desire
A bishop's power, and furth'rance for that end,
Or having, should oppose it, when they pleased
To let it run some years without a check
Or public notice taken, which half grant
Had yet held out, had not the clamors moved
The patience of some Ghibellines (that best
Can fish in troubled waters) to reverse
Their sleeping favors and withal to take
This just advantage of us from ourselves.
But where the fault remains, just God decide,
And to their wisdom we refer the rest.

Candle. Well said. 'Tis time our parley take an end;
Some synoders are coming.

Erudius. Let's attend. [*Exeunt*.]

Scena secunda

Bitomattus, Aggeus, Nivetta, Valeria, Celia.

Bitomattus. Here, ladies, ends our journey, this the house,
And here the room where our great sages meet
That must reform this kingdom and defend
The subjects from encroach of bishop's power,

A worke to please posteritie. Ni. With what?
With Elves (forsooth) placed in their bookes
Or else with Feathers? By. Well then what you will,
I would the world had knowne them sooner. Ni. Soft,
Unlesse they might be better trusted there,
That wish were vaine and idle. Manie thinke
Had they bene sooner knowne unto the land,
Posteritie should never rue those tymes
As now tis like they shall. Besides, much harme
Might then have bene prevented; and sure, those
Of yours had not bene drunke with their conceit.
By. I hope I have my witts about me. Ni. Yes,
But most ones, By. Somatus, by your leave:
Ni. Gods pretious, Madam, you'l discredit me,
Did I invite you hither to condemne,
And raile at reverend and vertuous Knights?
Or rather to be silent, and informe
Your understanding better of the men,
And of their rare example? Ni. rare indeede
And never seene before; that I admire
A thing should be so rare, and yet so grosse.
Ag. What saie you (Madame) to the Elephant
Or Beares, that some have seene, as bigg as Bulls,
Are they not rare, yet grosse. Ni. I would not have
You travaile further Sir, to make it good;
For I beleeve you. I did thinke it strange
Before, the Church was able to subsist
Without a Clergie (Secular I meane)
That without Bishopps, they without a Head.
Yet your discovery made in Countries, Sir,
Perswades to cleere this doubt; but makes us [illegible]
Our witts to credit you. Ag. They are not lost,
Your understanding only is troubled [illegible]
C. Faith, that Maisters Crafte [illegible]
[illegible]
[illegible]

Done to

A work to please posterity.
Nivetta. With what?
With elders, servant, placèd in their stead?
Or else with feathers?
Bitomattus. Call them what you will,
I would the world had known them sooner.
Nivetta. Soft,
Unless they might be better trusted here
That wish were vain and idle. Many think
Had they been sooner known unto this land,
Posterity should never rue these times
As now 'tis like they shall. Besides, much harm
Might then have been prevented, and such heads
As yours had not been drunk with their conceit.
Bitomattus. I hope I have my wits about me.
Nivetta. Yes,
But mad ones, Bitomattus, by your leave.
Valeria. God's precious, madam, you'll discredit me.
Did I invite you hither to contend
And rail at reverend and virtuous knights?
Or rather to be silent and inform
Your understanding better of the men
And of their rare example?
Nivetta. Rare indeed,
And never seen before, that I admire
A thing should be so rare, and yet so gross.
Aggeus. What say you, madam, to the elephants
Or bears that some have seen, as big as bulls;
Are they not rare, yet gross?
Nivetta. I would not have
You travail further, sir, to make it good,
For I believe you. I did think it strange
Before, the church was able to subsist
Without a clergy (secular I mean),
That without bishops, they without a head.
Yet your discovery made in twenty-six
Pretends to clear this doubt, but makes us lose
Our wits to credit you.
Aggeus. They are not lost;
Your understanding only is subdued
To faith, that masters reason as her slave.
Nivetta. And so she uses it, that dare not come
Into her presence to complain of wrongs

Due to the serious Affaires of the Soules;
She is above it much, against it more.
Ag. You are mistaken, Ladie, you must knowe
The Religious, whome thus you seeme to slight,
Are of the Clergie, yet the better part.
Ni. Leave Bishopps out, for those, it is true,
In state of life, and dignitie of place.
Better at home, then to converse abroade.
For contemplation, not to governe Soules.
For Cloysters, not the world, but for a neede,
And that with dispensation; otherwise
What more pretend they then inferior Clerke?
Can they administer the Sacraments
More efficaciously? with better forme?
With more advantage Christen, and absolve?
Annoile, and consecrate? impart more Grace?
Can they confirme? give Orders? Marry? play
The Curates better? take the Bishopps place
With greater right? Ag. Not so: they can instruct,
And catechise us with a better garb:
Give the spirituall Exercise, that ioynes
Our Soules in unitie with God. Ni. What's that,
If with our Neighbours we are still at warr,
As they with Bishopps? Ag. Rather he with them,
In urging they should aske to be approu'd.
Ni. A jealous quarrell. Ag. They denie it. Ni. See,
They may denie the Councells, Canons, Popes,
That warrant him to doe it. Ag. Nothing lesse.
Ni. He shewes his Breue. Ag. They interpret it.
Ni. Doth it containe some Errors? Ag. In some sort.
It was not plaine enough for curious witts,
Which then bold to conforme the Pope.
Ni. But did he move, and so confesse it? Ag. Noe.
Ni. Did he discountenance the Bishopps Champions?
And praise them for resisting him? Ag. Not yet.
Ni. And doe

Done to the very essence of the soul;
She is above it much, against it more.
Aggeus. You are mistaken, lady: you must know
The Ghibellines, whom thus you seem to slight,
Are of the clergy, yet the better part.
Nivetta. Leave bishops out, for others it is true;
In state of life and dignity of place;
Better at home, than to converse abroad;
For contemplation, not to govern souls;
In cloisters, not the world, but for a need,
And that with dispensation; otherwise
What more pretend they than inferior Guelfs?
Can they administer the sacraments
More efficaciously? with better form?
With more advantage christen and absolve?
Anneal and consecrate? impart more grace?
Can they confirm? give orders? marry? play
The curates better? take the bishop's place
With greater right?
Aggeus. Not so. They can instruct
And catechise us with a better garb;
Give the spiritual exercise, that joins
Our souls in unity with God.
Nivetta. What's that
If with our neighbors we are still at war,
As they with bishops?
Aggeus. Rather he with them
In urging they should ask to be approved.
Nivetta. A per'lous quarrel.
Aggeus. They deny it.
Nivetta. So
They may deny the councils, canons, popes
That warrant him to do it.
Aggeus. Nothing so.
Nivetta. He shows his breve.
Aggeus. They interpret it.
Nivetta. Doth it contain some errors?
Aggeus. In some sort.
It was not plain enough for curious wits,
Which them bold to reinform the pope.
Nivetta. But did he mend and so confess it?
Aggeus. No.
Nivetta. Did he discountenance the bishop's claim?
And praise them for resisting him?
Aggeus. Not yet.

Ni. And doe they excite the sale? Ag. They care not much.
The State takes notice of them now, and cleares
their actions in this point. Ni. But sure their cause
Should yet prove guilty to the Judge of such,
As well as actions? Breves from the Pope
By Roman Catholicks were allowed thought
The same that Proclamations from the Kinge,
Not to be question'd without high contempt:
And as the Kinge commaund or Bull directs
Not contradiction, cavill, or dispute;
Soe should not that of Popes, commaunding things
Not opposite, but helping to advaunce
The subjects duety to his God and Prince,
As this of Bishopps doth, is rightly waigh'd,
And without passion: Soe that, even the State,
Upon they appeale to, cannot chuse but finde
How much they straine their consciences in this point,
That rather then a Bishopp should take place
Will fight with their owne doctrine, and oppose
The words of Christ against the Popes intent;
The letter of the Lawe against the sence;
The Pope against the Kinge; the Bishopps power
Against the Magistrate; And last of all
Their owne fantastick dreames against the Church,
Soe holie are these fathers. Ce. Make an end;
You little thinke the divell, not longe since,
Was seene within his place. I feare these words
Of Blasphemie and slander will doe more
To bring him back againe, whom they with slaunders
Have banish't once. Ut. Come, thou shalt goe with me,
And be acquainted with my speciall friends,
Spirius and Sapertonus. Ce. Rather mine,
With Sargus and Dolhutus. Ja. I should first
T'is [illegible] they should goe with [illegible].

Ce. That's in

Nivetta. Do they expect he shall?
Aggeus. They care not much.
The state takes notice of him now and clears
Their actions in this point.
Nivetta. But say their cause
Should yet prove muddy to the judge of hearts
As well as actions? Breves from the pope
By Roman Catholics were always thought
The same that proclamations from the king:
Not to be questioned without high contempt.
And as the king's command or will admits
No contradiction, cavil, or excuse,
So should not that of popes, commanding things
Not opposite, but helping to advance
The subject's duty to his God and prince,
As this of bishops doth if rightly weighed
And without passion. So that even the state,
Whom they appeal to, cannot choose but find
How much they strain their conscience in this point,
That rather than a bishop should take place
Will fight with their own doctrine and oppose
The words of briefs against the pope's intent;
The letter of the law against the sense;
The pope against the king; the bishop's power
Against the magistrate; and last of all
Their own fantastic dreams against the truth.
So holy are these fathers.
Celia. Make an end;
You little think the devil not long since
Was seen within this place. I fear these words
Of blasphemy and slander will go near
To bring him back again, whom they with prayers
Have banished once.
Valeria. Come, thou shalt go with me
And be acquainted with my special friends,
Spirius and Sapertonus.
Celia. Rather mine,
With Jargus and Bolnutus.
Valeria. I spake first;
'Tis therefore reason she should go with me.

58

Ce. That's in the spirit. Since thus the monkes praise'd
Can with their presence edifie the more.
Then yours with all their learning and good workes.
Va. Some blame comparisons, none could decide
These hottly, for this. Ce. A touch's a truth,
And if you take it well, 'tis well, if not
My heart is shiver'd, and you are told.
Va. Well, if your ghostly fathers heare you thus,
I'le sweare they are Impostors. Ce. What are yours?
Va. Why, myne were Saints before your Breede was hatch'd.
Ce. That makes them now such sotts, all of the same.
Va. And yours such Drabons, fitt for dunghills. Hi. Hould.
My honor'd Ladies, how comes this to passe
Valeria and Celia should strive
About their Ghostly Fathers in this place?
Were, if the holy Synods were begun
This Language were enough to sett them all
Together by the eares. forbeare: And if
This quarrell be for me, I'le end the strife,
And travaile with you both, to both your Friends.
Va. Then Celia, your hand, our quarrell ends.
By. A faire conclusion, Ladies, wee'le expect
your short returne with others in this place.
Here come the valiant Champions of the bay;

Scena Tertia.

Polinodus, Bytomattus, Rudelbinus.
Corbus. Aggeus.

God save you Bytomattus, and your Friend.
By. The like salute returne wee to you three.
Wise Polinodus, learned Rudelbinus,
And my iudicious Corbus. you have lay'd
I heare, a good foundation for our Peare
And quiet heare there among the Sects,

That master

Celia. That's in her choice. I'm sure the men I named
Can with their presence edify her more
Than yours with all their learning and good works.
Valeria. Come, leave comparisons. Now could I chide
Thee heartily for this.
Celia. A truth's a truth,
And if you take it well, 'tis well, if not
My zeal is satisfied, and you are told.
Valeria. Well, if your ghostly fathers teach you thus,
I'll swear they are impostors.
Celia. What are yours?
Valeria. Why, mine were birds before your brood was hatched.
Celia. That makes them now such cocks, and of the game.
Valeria. And yours such cravens, fit for dunghills.
Nivetta. Hold!
My honored ladies, how comes this to pass,
Valeria and Celia should strive
About their ghostly fathers in this place?
Where, if the holy synod were begun,
This language were enough to set them all
Together by the ears. Forbear, and if
This quarrel be for me, I'll end the strife
And travel with you both to both your friends.
Valeria. Then Celia, your hand, our quarrel ends. [*Enter Bitomattus.*]
Bitomattus. A fair conclusion, ladies, we'll expect
Your short return with others in this place.
Here come the valiant champions of the lay. [*Exit Celia, Valeria, Nivetta.*]

Scena tertia

Polinodus, Bitomattus, Rudelbinus,
Corbus, Aggeus.

Polinodus. God save you, Bitomattus, and your friend.
Bitomattus. The like salute return we to you three,
Wise Polinodus, learnèd Rudelbinus,
And my judicious Corbus. You have laid,
I hear, a good foundation for our peace
And quiet usage here among the sects

81

That master-us, disabling such as urge
The Popes authoritie, and Bishopps power
Too much promoted by the Guelfe of late.
Ru. They are too little sett by, as it seemes,
Or not at all. I parted from a friend
But now, that much amaz'd me with his story
He said, when first the Ghibellins were sent
(Theabeliza raigning) to this land,
The charitable Guelfe (that vainely thought
Soe manie Angells dropt from Paradise
To helpe their labours) courteously receiv'd
And warm'd them in the houses where they liv'd;
Preferring them to all their friends, like fooles
(To use my Authors words) in every place;
And not content with this, oppos'd the State
In their behalfe; and suffer'd for their cause
The worst of Evills, [illegible] excepted, death;
Because they thought the end, for wch they came
Was comon to them both; the good of soules.
But what reward receiv'd they for this love,
And friendly charge? [illegible] a stinking one:
(If I use my Author still) Insteede of thanks
They thrust them shortly after from their house,
Supplanting them [illegible] credit, friends, and meanes,
With such a cheating holines, as men
And women madded, with the strange conceit
Of their perfections, wch in substance (some
Excepted, in these daies, that lived Saints
And died Martirs) like to rotten pears,
Were good for nothing but to poison wormes,
And harbor Waspes, and Earwiggs. Etc [illegible]
How could they be iniurious to their Goods
(Not having left before their Bodies free
From Wounds and Scarrs) as not to lett it runne
Into the monasteries, but upon [illegible]
And being iogn'd, to strive to cutt it off.
Upon their owne Mission, for defect [illegible]
[illegible]

Du[illegible] And that

That master us, disabling such as urge
The pope's authority and bishop's power,
Too much promoted by the Guelfs of late.
Rudelbinus. By us too little set by, as it seems,
Or not at all. I parted from a friend
But now that much amazed me with his speech.
He said, when first the Ghibellines were sent
(Theabeliza reigning) to this land,
The charitable Guelfs (that vainly thought
So many angels dropped from paradise
To help their labors) courteously received
And warmed them in the houses where they lived,
Preferring them to all their friends, like fools
(To use my author's words) in every place;
And not content with this, oppose the state
In their behalf; and suffered for their cause
The worst of evils, sin excepted, death,
Because they thought the end for which they came
Was common to them both, the good of souls.
But what reward received they for this love
And friendly usage? Faith, a stinking one
(I cite my author still): instead of thanks
They thrust them shortly after from their holds,
Supplanting them of credit, friends, and means,
With such a cheating holiness as men
And women madded with the strong conceit
Of their perfections, which in substance (some
Excepted in those days, that livèd saints
And dièd martyrs) like to rotten pears
Were good for nothing but to poison rooms
And harbor wasps and earwigs. Else (said he)
How could they be injurious to their head
(Not having left before their body free
From wounds and scars) as not to let it join
Unto the members but upon constraint,
And being joined, to strive to cut it off?
When their own mission for defect of that
Proved troublesome, yea hurtful to our cause,

And that most necessarie for the peace
Of Catholikes; which they had oft disturb'd
With Innovations, throwing in their way
ffalse baite, and goulden Apples of debate
To make them stepp aside, and loose the Goale,
Procuring from the Pope (that little dreampt
Of their designes) the new extorted power
Of an Arch-Priest, to sett them more at odds.
Without their voice or knowledge he was sent,
And therefore longe resisted, till the Pope
Appeas'd the Storme, which they of purpose rais'd
To put off Bishopps: had the Ghibellins
Not therefore bene ungratefull to their friends,
How could such discords growe amongst ourselves,
Not heard or seene before: such secret spleene,
Suspition, Jealousie, detraction, hate,
Such strangenes, and distinction, those of Guelfe,
And those of Ghibellins, as if one roofe
Could not containe them, whom the selfe-same charity
Had twinn'd in faith, and doctrine to one end!
By. A pretty metaphor, yet by his leave
They came not of one father. Rud. See he saide,
The Guelfe derive their clayme from Peters chaire,
The Ghibellins, he saith, [illegible] are yet to seeke,
Because the Saints that owne them, stand aloofe,
Nor take they notice of them by their workes,
That name thinks them changlinge. By. They were nurs'd
I'me sure, as well or better then the Guelfe,
And came to be their Masters in the ende,
And rule their Colledge. Rud. There lyes a tale
That made them proud; ffor Pride drew Ambition on,
Ambition Envie; Envie caused Strife;
Strife Partialitie; and that selfe-love;
Then consequentlie the divell came at last,
And sett some Jesuits a foote against the State,
As factors on those Maisters of the Guelfes:
The Appellants resting [illegible] free

ffrom all

And that most necessary for the peace
Of Catholics, which they had oft disturbed
With innovations, throwing in their way
False baits and golden apples of debate
To make them step aside and lose the goal—
Procuring from the pope (that little dreamt
Of their designs) the new extorted power
Of an archpriest to set them more at odds.
Without their voice or knowledge he was sent,
And therefore long resisted, till the pope
Appeased the storm which they of purpose raised
To put off bishops. Had the Ghibellines
Not therefore been ungrateful to their friends,
How could such discords grow amongst ourselves,
Not heard or seen before? such secret spleen,
Suspicion, jealousy, detraction, hate,
Such strangeness and distinction, here of Guelfs,
And there of Ghibellines, as if one roof
Could not contain them whom the selfsame church
Had twinned in faith and doctrine to one end?

Bitomattus. A pretty metaphor, yet by his leave
They came not of one father.

Rudelbinus. So he said.
The Guelfs derive their claim from Peter's chair;
The Ghibellines, he saith, are yet to choose,
Because the saints that own them stand aloof,
Nor take they notice of them by their works,
That many think them changelings.

Bitomattus. They were nursed,
I'm sure, as well or better than the Guelfs,
And came to be their masters in the end
And rule their colleges.

Rudelbinus. There lies a tale
That made them proud; pride drew ambition on,
Ambition envy; envy causèd strife;
Strife partiality; and that self-love;
Then covetousness the devil came at last
And set some plots afoot against the state,
All fathered on these masters of the Guelfs,
The scholars resting innocent and free

[Here the sixth quire ends. The
seventh quire is missing.]

Sa. Then we are free, and then the Pope will feare,
Nor stirre in hast to sett an [illegible];
Nor will the State be wanting to resist.
Hil. In the meane tyme, what refuge for the Soules
Of those that shall confesse, and crave your helpe,
To be assoil'd. Va. Madam, quite them leave
To end this scorne; they'le answere that anon.
Hil. And why not now Valeria, since it falls
Most fitly to the purpose; this agree'd,
The Synod may goe on with better speede:
Besides, I mov'd the question in your right,
That are their Penitents; and not myne owne,
That seeke not to them, nor have cause to doubt
Of Absolution, as my Spirit falls out.
Cel. Pray Madam keepe your Spirit, and leave [illegible],
Our Soules are warranted as well as yours;
T'is that I seeke to knowe, with such desire.
Can. Sure, should the Lady Longue, she dies for't. Er. Why?
Can. How can she knowe a thing, they cannott tell?
Pol. Your silence Lady, would become you better,
More then such questions. Corb. Women should not speake
In open Synods. Rud. Why should stopp their mouthes,
When once they are admitted? Va. T'was my fault
That first invited them. Ce. Yes sure, and myne,
Pray God we be not answerable both
For their transgression. Rud. Ladies, may I crave
The leave, to aske you who invited you?
[illegible]. O Lord Sr. there's not question for the one,
The Ladie Celia had my selfe conduct.
Ag. And myne Valeria. Rud. Then the Ladies, myne.
Is that be all with priviledge to speake,
Till shee be satisfi'd in her demaund.
Spi. Soft Rudelbinus you intrude, and want
The priviledge your selfe, you would bestowe
Upon

Sapertonus. Then we are free, and then the pope will fear
New stirs in case he set another up;
Nor will the state be wanting to resist.
Nivetta. In the meantime, what refuge for the souls
Of those that shall confess and crave your help
To be assoiled?
Valeria. Madam, give him leave
To end his speech; he'll answer that anon.
Nivetta. And why not now, Valeria, since it falls
Most fitly to the purpose? This agreed,
The synod may go on with better speed.
Besides, I moved the question in your right
That are their penitents, and not mine own,
That seek not to them, nor have cause to doubt
Of absolution as my choice falls out.
Celia. Pray, madam, keep your choice and leave us ours;
Our souls are warranted as well as yours.
[*Nivetta.*] 'Tis that I seek to know with such desire.
Candle. Sure, should the lady long, she dies for't.
Erudius. Why?
Candle. How can she know a thing they cannot tell?
Polinodus. Your silence, lady, would become you here,
More than such questions.
Corbus. Women should not speak
In open synods.
Rudelbinus. Who should stop their mouths
When once they are admitted?
Valeria. 'Twas my fault
That first invited her.
Celia. Yes, sure, and mine;
Pray God we be not answerable both
For her transgression.
Rudelbinus. Ladies, may I crave
The leave to ask you who invited you?
Bitomattus. O lord, sir, there's no question for the one:
The lady Celia had my self conduct.
Aggeus. And mine Valeria.
Rudelbinus. So this lady mine,
If that be all, with privilege to speak
Till she be satisfied in her demand.
Spirius. Soft, Rudelbinus, you intrude, and want
The privilege yourself you would bestow

As you are Sir. Rud. What is that? Spi. To speake
Concerning Men, or matters of the Church,
you being but a lay man. Rud. you that are
Chiefe President of this Synodicall
And grand Assembly, dare you stand to this?
Spi. I dare. Rud. Then with what foreheade durst you move,
And others rank'd with you, in this place,
My selfe, and other lay-men here to speake,
And write against a Prelate of the Church,
And in a cause so neere concerning Soules;
Had not hypocrisie possest your heart
And tongue, you double? May not I aswell
Speake here, explaine, and wrestle for the right
Of him, as you against him? Who dares call
Me subiect here? Now I have slipt the yoake
Of Bishopps from my neck with your instinct,
You making them Commaunders over Soules;
You but Assistants, Secondary helpers,
Yea, beggars without title to a haire,
But what we give you freely; that is strange
Your Worship should so outswell these Banks,
That you should snatch at honors here on earth,
Which you have once abiur'd; but you have taught
An easie waie, to make yourselves Condemn'd
By bringing thus your Betters in contempt.
Ah! you are wilfull blinde, and will not see,
How many Curses, you have brought, of Soules,
That shalbe damn'd upon, for this deede;
Unlesse you soone retract it, and wrongs [illegible];
The day shines not so cleere, as doth this truth,
You have not Iurisdiction to Absolve
(The Regulars I meane not but the lay)
Abstracting from this present Bishopps leave
Which is it you speake against, and so commit
A mortall

Upon another.
Rudelbinus. What is that?
Spirius. To speak
Concerning men or matters of the church,
You being but a layman.
Rudelbinus. You that are
Chief president of this synodical
And grave assembly, dare you stand to this?
Spirius. I dare.
Rudelbinus. Then with what forehead durst you move—
And others ranked with you—in this place,
Myself and other laymen here to speak
And write against a prelate of the church,
And in a cause so near concerning souls,
Had not hypocrisy possessed your heart
And tongue, you double? May not I as well
Speak here, exclaim, and wrestle for the right
Of him, as you against him? Who dares call
Me subject here? Now I have slipped the yoke
Of bishops from my neck with your instinct,
God making them commanders over souls,
You but assistants, secondary helps,
Yea, beggars without title to a hair
But what we give you freely; that is strange
Your poverty should so outswell her banks
That you should snatch at honors here on earth
Which you have once abjured; but you have taught
An easy way to make yourselves contemned
By bringing thus your betters in contempt.
Oh! you are willful, blind, and will not see
How many curses you have heaped of souls
That shall be damned upon for this deed,
Unless you soon retract it and cry creak.
The day shines not so clear as doth this truth:
You have no jurisdiction to absolve
(The regulars I mean not, but the lay)
Abstracting from this present bishop's leave,
Which is it you spurn against, and so commit

A mortall wronge to charitie of soules,
That are not left secure by your pretence;
To haue their deadly sinnes by Christ releas'd,
You being strictly bound in their behalfe,
To leaue a doubtfull, take the surest way:
Authoritie but probable's a toy;
A Power unquestionable, must be had,
Which onely on the Bishopps Graunt depends.
Sa. What had wee, when a Bishopp was not found,
Or knowne within the land? What should wee haue
Doone and at the point of death in neede
Of our Assistance? Rad. Neede requires, which
The Masters lawe, makes Absolution firme;
Not yours alone, but of the meanest Priest,
As Baptisme's valid, from the meanest hand:
An obligation is there not, where want
Of meanes to keepe the Lawe, excuseth it,
Which to impossibles was never tyde.
But now a Bishopp wanteth not, to putt
The case of Lawe in practice, and approue;
Impediments are filed off; not all
Your Penitents lye gasping, though some doe;
Some others may recover, in which case:
What is your Absolution but a meere
Conditionall Acquittance, with a Bond,
Upon recovery, to confesse againe
Unto a lawfull and approved Priest:
For more securitie, the Counsells, Popes,
And Doctors are so strict in the behalfe
Of Power Episcopall, nor can the Lawe
Giue place to anie Custome, out of minde,
Or be prescrib'd against, for want of use,
Which takes it not awaie, nor can the Pope
Graunt anie priuiledge, in generall termes,
To derogate

A mortal wrong to charity of souls,
That are not left secure by your pretense
To have their deadly sins by Christ released,
You being strictly bound in their behalf
To leave a doubtful, take the surest way;
Authority but probable's a toy;
A power unquestionable must be had,
Which only on the bishop's grant depends.

Sapertonus. What had we when a bishop was not found
Or known within the land? What should we have
Stood any at the point of death in need
Of our assistance?

Rudelbinus. Need requireth wings;
It masters law, makes absolution firm—
Not yours alone, but of the meanest priest—
As baptism's valid from the meanest hand.
An obligation riseth not where want
Of means to keep the law excuseth will,
Which to impossibles was never tied.
But now a bishop wanteth not to put
The case of law in practice and approve;
Impediments are filed off; not all
Your penitents lie gasping, though some die;
Some others may recover, in which case
What is your absolution but a mere
Conditional acquittance, with a bond
Upon recovery to confess again
Unto a lawful and approvèd priest
For more security, the councils, popes,
And doctors are so strict in the behalf
Of power episcopal? Nor can this law
Give peace to any custom out of mind,
Or be prescribed against for want of use,
Which takes it not away; nor can the pope
Grant any privilege in general terms

To derogate this lawe is not exprest
By word, or writing, or some other Act,
More then consent that's tacit, and abstract;
Soe that to pleade your Mission will not serve,
Or your not reference to tyme or men;
Much lesse that you are Delegates, and sent
By your Superiors there, which have noe right
To give you Jurisdiction over the least
Of Subiects, where a Bishopp beareth sway,
Unlesse he re-approve you: Thus, defect
Of Pastorall, and regular Commaund
Makes this divorce betwixt you heere, and Soules,
Not to be reconcil'd, without recourse
Made to the Bishopp, for whose peace of minde
In charge of Soules, he compells this grounde,
As for your utmost refuge where you saie
The Trentine Councell is not yet receiv'd,
Nor bindeth heere, before a Bishopp came,
And Jurisdiction over us was given;
I graunt it could not practically binde
A legall Person wanting to propose,
And publish it sufficiently, in poynts
(For great consideration was requir'd)
Of neede, and not offensive to the State;
As this of Approbation is proclaim'd.
What hurt to them, were Ghibellines approv'd,
But rather more secured from feares?
But now that barr and obstacle is quite
Remov'd, and you must yeild of force to right.
Thus Madam, I have urged to the height
Your iust demaund. Now, for which, my humble thanks,
Shall waite like Servants on you; I will add
This Corolarie only to adorne,
Though superficially, your honour's spouse.
Tho: Dorbine

To derogate this law, if not expressed
By word, or writing, or some other act,
More than consent that's tacit and obscure.
So that to plead your mission will not serve,
Or your not reference to time or men;
Much less that you are delegates and sent
By your superiors' choice, who have no right
To give you jurisdiction o'er the least
Of subjects where a bishop beareth sway,
Unless he re-approve you. Thus, defect
Of pastoral and regular command
Makes this divorce betwixt you here, and souls,
Not to be reconciled without recourse
Made to the bishop, for whose peace of mind
In charge of souls the councils thus provide.
As for your utmost refuge where you say
The Trentine council is not yet received,
Nor bindeth here before a bishop came
And jurisdiction over us was given:
I grant it could not practically bind
A legal person wanting to propose
And publish it sufficiently, in points
(For great consideration was required)
Of need, and not offensive to the state,
As this of approbation is presumed.
What hurt to them were Ghibellines approved,
But rather more security from fears?
But now that bar and obstacle is quite
Removed, and you must yield of force to right.
Thus, madam, I have urgèd to the height
Your just demand.

Nivetta. For which my humble thanks
Shall wait like servants on you; I will add
This corollary only to adorn,
Though superficially, your honored speech:

This doctrine thus infragably true,
And such Iniustice likely to ensue
By contradicting it, and harme to soules,
And Approbation of itselfe, a point
Of noe dishonor, iniury, or wronge,
On the Demaunded, or Demaunders side;
Nor hurtfull to the State; but were like
To prove most necessary for their Ends,
The Subiects good, and dutie to their Prince,
With helpe of Bishopps likely to improve;
Without it, ever subiect to revolt.
All this consider'ed, had it not beene faire,
And charitable dealing att the first,
The Bishopp hauing shewed them his Breefe,
The Ghibelins had yeilded in this point?
Att least when they referr'd it to the Pope,
They had with noyse, and clamors not provok't
The laytie to resist him, and denie
Their spirituall obedience, with fals crye
He was noe friend to Caesar, that the State
Might countenance their quarrell; but in case
The Breve had beene doubtfull, and his claime
Of ordinary power, as it was found,
And free from all Attaint, had they concurr'd
To gett his title cleered from the Pope,
Mou'd thereunto by Conscience, and the care
That good security were had for soules,
Whom they had first begott in him, whose name
They beare imprinted on their Colledge doores,
And should doe in their hearts, and for respect
Of temporall gaine, or profitt to themselves
Where they

This doctrine thus irrefragably true,
And such injustice likely to ensue
By contradicting it, and harm to souls;
And approbation of itself, a point
Of no dishonor, injury, or wrong
On the demanded or demander's side
Nor hurtful to the state, but very like
To prove most necessary for their ends
(The subjects' good and duty to their prince,
With help of bishops likely to improve,
Without it ever subject to revolts)—
All this consid'red, had it not been fair
And charitable dealing at the first,
The bishop having showèd them his brief,
The Ghibellines had yielded in this point?
At least when they referred it to the pope
They had with noise and clamors not provoked
The laity to resist him and deny
Their spiritual obedience, with full cry
He was no friend to Caesar, that the state
Might countenance their quarrel? But in case
The breve had been doubtful, and his claim
Of ordinary power (as it was sound
And free from all attaint), had they concurred
To get his title cleared from the pope,
Moved thereunto by conscience and the care
That good security were had for souls,
Whom they had first begot in him whose name
They bear imprinted on their college doors,
And should do in their hearts, and for respect
Of temporal gain, or profit to themselves,

Which they long since haue cast awaie, or should
By their profession; would not this haue great,
And gain'd them an immortalle renowne! Rad. It would
Noe doubt. Spi. What noyse without there? Dauus see.
Ono. He cannott finde his spectacles. Bol. See you.
Nic. See you Lamoppus with him. Can. They are iust
Beloued; the chiefe I heare a built this way,
Of Merchants. Ex. They are so: we must all
To prison then. Can. The best is they doe hunt
For Purses more then Prisons, and are call'd
By some, the chiefe obseruants of the time;
Nor want they great imployments. They may say,
Stand, and deliuer, in the open Streete,
Howse, and high way, and not be punisht for't,
As other fellowes that doe robbe for neede.
These, and Informers, are the Diuells band,
They studie how they may incense the State
Still more against them; and for hope of gaine
Accuse any man that beares an honest face
For Traytors, Seminaries, and the like;
Who are condemn'd to prison, or releas'd
As they giue Euidence; which falls out hard
Or fauourable, as they finde the tyde,
Of the delinquents purse to ebbe or flowe.
Those wretches must pay for't that are found so poore,
They cannott pay for't; that is, they must pay
They forfeit of their liberties, for want
Of meanes to liue. Dr. A miserable case.
Yet dare we not complaine, for feare the lawe
Proue more seuere, which drownes both rich and poore
In the same current. Can. You must make a shift
Heere to conceale your selfe, whilst I descend,
That mingled with the crowde, I may gett out;

My braine

Which they long since have cast away, or should
By their profession—would not this have graced
And gained them an immortal crown?
Rudelbinus. It would,
No doubt.
Spirius. What noise without there? Davus, see.
Onoplutus. He cannot find his spectacles.
Bolnutus. Go you.
Nicodimus. Go you, Pamoppus, with him. [*Exit Onoplutus and Pamoppus.*]
Candle. They are hushed
Below; methinks I hear a bruit this way
Of pursuivants.
Erudius. They are so; we must all
To prison then.
Candle. The best is, they do hunt
For purses more than persons, and are called
By some the purse-observants of the time;
Nor want they great employments. They may say,
''Stand and deliver,'' in the open street,
House, and highway, and not be punished for't,
As other felons that do rob for need.
These and informers are the Papists' bane:
They study how they may incense the state
Still more against them, and for hope of prey
Accuse each man that bears an honest face
For traitors, seminaries, and the like,
Who are condemned to prisons or released
As they give evidence, which falls out hard
Or favorable as they find the tide
Of the delinquent's purse to ebb or flow.
Those priests must pay for't that are found so poor
They cannot pay for't; that is, they must pay
[The] forfeit of their liberties for want
Of means to live.
Erudius. A miserable case.
Yet dare we not complain for fear the law
Prove more severe, which drowns both rich and poor
In the same torrent.
Candle. You must make a shift
Here to conceal yourself whilst I descend,
That mingled with the crowd I may get out;

My braine conceaves a plott, wch (if it take)
Shall free them all. Ex. Make hast. Cro. Wee are betraide;
The Pursevants are come, and have besett
The howse with Officers. Rud. Wee are undone.
Corb. A money matter, feare not. Spi. Let them shew
Their warrant first, ere you sett ope the dore.
Nic. They enter. Pam. On your perill, stand and shew
your Warrant quickly.

Scena quinta

Roc. Milston; with Constable and officers to them.

Sr: my name is Roc.
Mil. And Milston myne. Cro. Sweete morsells to digest.
Pa. Stand back here. Roc and Milstone, you must knowe,
Unlesse you shew Commission, wee must use
you heere like stones, that's, cast you out of dores,
your fittest place. Cro. For Gods sake, speake him faire,
Wee shall hardly compound else, or gett off;
For love or money. Pam. You have both alike.
Cro. Yes, at your service. Pa. How! Cro. I meane, my love.
Da. But not his money. Pa. See I thought, nor shall
My shoes, Sr be at yours, stand back I saie.
Roc. dare you oppose the State? Pa. Not; you I dare.
Roc. I am their Messenger. Pa. For what! lett's see.
Roc. Behould my Badge. Pa. Badge belong to knaves,
And wee are free men. Roc. you'le answere this?
Pa. I will. Mil. Neighbour Pumpkin, shew your selfe.
Con. Sr: I am Constable. Pa. Then may you be
The simplest there I see in all the Burrough;
And yet the honestest for ought I knowe.
Con. I represent the Kings owne person heere.
Pa. What fault hath he committed. Mil. Represent
the meanes. Pa. He does see; but not to the life.

Though wee

My brain conceives a plot which (if it take)
Shall free them all.
Erudius. Make haste. [*Exit Candle. Enter Onoplutus and Pamoppus.*]
Onoplutus. We are betrayed!
The pursuivants are come and have beset
The house with officers.
Rudelbinus. We are undone.
Corbus. A money matter, fear not.
Spirius. Let them show
Their warrant first, ere you set ope the door.
Nicodimus. They enter.
Pamoppus. On your peril, stand and show
Your warrant quickly.

Scena quinta

Rocs, Milston, with Constable and Officers to them.

Rocs. Sir, my name is Rocs.
Milston. And Milston mine.
Onoplutus. Sweet morsels to digest.
Pamoppus. Stand back there. Rocs and Milston, you must know,
Unless you show commission we must use
You here like stones: that's, cast you out of doors,
Your fittest place.
Onoplutus. For God's sake, speak him fair.
We shall hardly compound else or get off
For love or money.
Pamoppus. You have both belike.
Onoplutus. Yes, at your service.
Pamoppus. How?
Onoplutus. I mean my love.
Davus. But not his money.
Pamoppus. So I thought, nor shall
My speech, sir, be at yours. Stand back I say.
Rocs. Dare you oppose the state?
Pamoppus. No; you I dare.
Rocs. I am their messenger.
Pamoppus. For what? Let's see.
Rocs. Behold my badge.
Pamoppus. Badges belong to knaves,
And we are free men.
Rocs. You'll answer this?
Pamoppus. I will.
Milston. Neighbor Pumpkin, show yourself.

(*text continued on following page*)

Constable. Sir, I am constable.
Pamoppus. Then may you be
The simplest card I see in all the bunch,
And yet the honestest for aught I know.
Constable. I reprehend the king's own person here.
Pamoppus. What fault hath he committed?
Milston. Represent
He means.
Pamoppus. He does so, but not to the life,

Though very naturally for his part;
And so doe you for yours. Mil. Why, are wee fooles?
Pa. I said not soe. Roc. Noe Sr, but wee are knaves,
If you remember well. Mil. That's true indeede.
Con. A certaine truth, I'le be depos'd upon it.
Pa. Then it is confest you are; what would you more?
Roc. What are wee? Pam. knaves indeede, and so depos'd
By mr Constable for fell of ffriends;
Come breefely, shew your warrant, or be gone.
Roc. See, heere it is, nowe reade it to your cost.
Pa. Enough, heere Spirus peruse it. Con. Nay
Good mr Roc, and Millstone be more soft,
Wee knowe you can undoe us. Roc. Before God,
You knowe not well your selves, that knowe not me.
Pa. What are you I praie? Roc. What am I not?
The only ffavorite of Judges Clerkes,
And Justice. Con. Nay then you may doe much,
That's questionlesse. Roc. A Preist cannot peepe forth,
Or passe the Streete, but I have hounds to hunt,
And dogg him to his lodging, that I may
Besett the house next morning, where I take
Him napping, or at Masse; then in his robes,
His Vestment, Stoale, and Manuple, his Albe,
Amias, I conduct him through the Streete,
In solempne shape, to make the people laugh;
Disrobed in the Jayle, I leade him straight
Before a Justice, he committs him safe.
Next must, he is arraign'd, condemn'd, and hang'd;
First being drawne, then quartered: O the tymes
Wherein my power was absolute; they sure
Were full of Justice, nowe our zeale is lost;
My selfe abridg'd of more then halfe my gaines:
Wee fall into barratours nowe for Money,
Aswell as Lawyers; and our comming in,

Will starve

Though very naturally for his part,
And so do you for yours.
Milston. Why, are we fools?
Pamoppus. I say not so.
Rocs. No, sir, but we are knaves,
If you remember well.
Milston. That's true indeed.
Constable. A certain truth, I'll be deposed upon it.
Pamoppus. Then 'tis confessed you are; what would ye more?
Rocs. What are we?
Pamoppus. Knaves indeed, and so deposed
By Master Constable for fail of friends;
Come, briefly show your warrant or be gone.
Rocs. See, here it is; now read it to your cost.
Pamoppus. Enough. Here, Spirius, peruse it.
Onoplutus. Nay,
Good Master Rocs, and Milston, be more soft;
We know you can undo us.
Rocs. Before God,
You know not well yourselves that know not me.
Pamoppus. What are you, I pray?
Rocs. What am I not?
The only favorite of judge's clerks
And justices.
Onoplutus. Nay, then you may do much,
That's questionless.
Rocs. A priest cannot peep forth
Or pass the street but I have hounds to scent
And dog him to his lodging, that I may
Beset the house next morning, where I take
Him napping or at mass; then in his robes—
As vestment, stole, and maniple, his alb,
Amias—I conduct him through the street
In solemn pomp to make the people laugh;
Disrobèd in the jail, I lead him straight
Before a justice; he commits him safe.
Next [nuse] he is arraigned, condemned, and hanged,
First being drawn, then quartered. O the times
Wherein my power was absolute! They sure
Were full of justice, now our zeal is lost;
Myself abridged of more than half my gains.
We fall into vacations now for months
As well as lawyers; and our comings in

Will starve, maintaine our poorer sort of Stabbers
From being lowsie; that I am inforst,
To feede the Castalls, either for their wives
Acquaintaunce, or some other such respect;
Commissions come for dropping to their hands;
And straight expire, that they are forst to faine
Some newe, or furbish old ones, and insert
Newe dates unto them (though they venter
Limbe or life for't) to supply their present want,
The Papist, though abuz'd, will rather parte
With reasonable somes, then run the hazard
To question them, for feare of worse successe.
Spi. your warrant heere is limitted to Staines,
For one Themisus Bishopp to the State;
held dangerous; it is withall to take
Suspected persons to be Romish Preists.
Bol. Theere are none such. Or. Noe simple ones he meanes;
For we are mixt, or double, not contain'd
In odious names. Bol. Nor is Themisus heere.
Da. Wee would not hide him you, if he were,
Be sure of that. Ro. Gentlemen be content,
I knowe you, and I knowe you not; suspect,
And not suspect you, as you prove in faulte.
Avoide the roome my Maisters, Milston saide,
And Mr Constable be you without,
To keepe good order; Gentlemen you see,
Were I dispos'd, I could suspect you all;
Were it that knight, this gentleman, that Esquire,
You knowe the Lawe runns thus; your estate
And goods are forfeited: I have a soule
The lord be thanked which I hope to save;
And a most tender conscience, still inclin'd
To works of mercie, chiefly to myselfe
Next to my greatefull friends; and last of all,
To all

Will scarce maintain our poorer sort of scabs
From being lousy, that I am enforced
To feed the rascals, either for their wives'
Acquaintance or some other such respect;
Commissions come so dropping to their hands
And straight expire, that they are forced to feign
Some new, or furbish old ones and insert
New dates unto them (though they venter
Limb or life for't) to supply their present want.
The Papist, though abused, will rather part
With reasonable sums than run the chance
To question them, for fear of worse success.

Spirius. Your warrant here is limited to search
For one Themisus, bishop to the state,
Held dangerous; it is withal to take
Suspected persons to be Romish priests.

Bolnutus. Here are none such.

Onoplutus. No simple ones he means;
For we are mixed, or double, not contained
In odious names.

Bolnutus. Nor is Themisus here.

Davus. We would not hide him [from] you if he were,
Be sure of that.

Rocs. Gentlemen, be content.
I know you, and I know you not; suspect,
And not suspect you, as you prove in hand.
[*To officers.*] Avoid the room, my masters; Milston, stay;
And Master Constable be you without
To keep good order. Gentlemen, you see,
Were I disposed I could suspect you all,
Were it that knight, this gentleman, that squire
You know the law runs riot; your estates
And goods are forfeited. I have a soul,
The Lord be thanked, which I hope to save;
And a most tender conscience, still inclined
To works of mercy, chiefly to myself,
Next to my grateful friends, and last of all

100*

To all good subiects, that can cleere my doubts
By Arguments of waight, for in my hand
The Scales are put; a trifle swayes them downe,
Some tenn, or twenty, forty, three score graines,
An hundred sometimes, more as hopes, and meanes
Diminish, or encrease. Mil. He meanes pounds,
Doe not mistake him. Roc. You know my minde,
Consider well amongst your selves, the way,
How I may pleasure you, and save my State,
That is; be saved harmelesse from the lawe;
Withall, you must acknowledge what a grace,
And favour I have done you, not to search
your pockets, when the Constable was here;
Nor take awaie your weapons, I have lost
God knowes how manie watches, purses, rings,
And other duties by't. Mil. It is suppos'd
Wee deale with knights, and Gentlemen that knowe
How to accept, and to requite good turnes.
Sa. First Mr Roc, you know I am a peere
Above your reach, a Prisoner to the State,
And under their Command. Roc. I know it well.
Sa. Next, that our meeting was in their behalfe,
And to his disadvantage whom you seeke.
Di. He meanes the Bishopp. Roc. Pardon me for that
Good mr Saperton, wee are not bred
In Schooles, nor knowe we to distinguish more
Then what our warrant leads vs by the nose,
And pointes vs to; let it suffice, your selfe
May freely take your way, and passe our Wardes;
As for your friends, they light into the handes
Of such as have a feeling of their case.
Dr. He meanes our money, and he must be dealt.
Wee are noe Puritans, that seeke for blood
More then t'is fitt the bodie should forgoe
To save the whole Estate. Dr. Thy physick againe,
And that

To all good subjects that can clear my doubts
By arguments of weight, for in my hand
The scales are put; a trifle sways them down—
Some ten, or twenty, forty, threescore grains,
An hundred sometimes, more as hopes and means
Diminish or increase.
Milston. He meaneth pounds,
Do not mistake him.
Rocs. No, they know my mind.
Consider well amongst yourselves the way
How I may pleasure you and save my stake,
That is, be saved harmless from the law.
Withal, you must acknowledge what a grace
And favor I have done you, not to search
Your pockets when the constable was here,
Nor take away your weapons; I have lost
God knows how many watches, purses, rings,
And other duties by't.
Milston. It is supposed
We deal with knights and gentlemen that know
How to accept and to requite good turns.
Sapertonus. First, Master Rocs, you know I am a prey
Above your reach, a prisoner to the state
And under their command.
Rocs. I know it well.
Sapertonus. Next, that our meeting was in their behalf,
And to his disadvantage whom you seek.
Davus. He means the bishop.
Rocs. Pardon me for that,
Good Master Saperton; we are not bred
In schools, nor know we to distinguish more
Than what our warrant leads us by the nose
And points us to; let it suffice, yourself
May freely take your way and pass our ward;
As for your friends, they light into the hands
Of such as have a feeling of their case.
Onoplutus. He means our money, and the purse the case.
[*Rocs.*] We are no Puritans, that seek for blood
More than 'tis fit the body should forgo
To save the whole estate.
Onoplutus. The purse again,

And that must take a charge to saue the angels.
Roc. This only, if you haue acquaintance can bring
Some ready cash, to sett them off, in hast
They haue not summes about them, send them straight
Before more notice taken, they will
To pleasure them; you know they all or most
Doe want not meanes, or credit to repaie.
Sa. It shall be done. Roc. Now Gentlemen you may
Stepp to an inner roome, and there consult
Of your affaires, I will be with you straight.
Mil. Amos, and ffinger, bring another prey.

Scena Sexta.

Amos, Finger, with Erudius, Roes, Milston.

As wee were ransacking the roomes above
Wee lighted on this   who had crept
Under a bedd, in hope to scape our hands.
Fin. I spy'd his heeles, and drag'd him out, he saies
he is a Gentleman, but very poore.
Mil. Pox on him, then you should haue lett him goe.
Wee gett not by such bargaines. Roc. Hold your peace,
You know not what you saie, wee gett enough,
In that he goes to prison for the rest
That can come fairely off; wee keepe withall
Our Reputation currant with the State,
That would support us, had wee not such tales
To draw opinion on, of our worth,
And double diligence. Mil. Troth in deede
ffor I haue knowne some Justices o'the peace
Inspir'd with zeale, among the rest a Knight
Doe quarrell in searching of an house,
And forward to undoe the Parish Constable,
He doe the Kings best seruice, he more sleepe
In paying

And that must take a purge to save the whole.
Rocs. This only: if you have a friend can bring
Some ready cash to set them off, in case
They have no sums about them, send them straight
Before more notice taken, stop   will
To pleasure them; you know they all, or most,
Do want no means or credit to repay.
Sapertonus. It shall be done.
Rocs. Now, gentlemen, you may
Step to an inner room and there consult
Of your affairs; I will be with you straight. [*Exeunt Gentlemen.*]
Milston. Amoy and Finger bring [another] prey.

Scena sexta

Amoy, Finger with Erudius, Rocs, Milston.

Amoy. As we were ransacking the rooms above
We lighted on this   who had crept
Under a bed in hope to 'scape our hands.
Finger. I spied his heels and dragged him out; he says
He is a gentleman but very poor.
Milston. Pox on him, then you should have let him go;
We get not by such bargains.
Rocs. Hold your peace,
You know not what you say. We get enough
In that he goes to prison for the rest
That can come fairly off; we keep withal
Our reputation current with the state,
That would suspect us had we not such stales
To draw opinion on of our precise
And double diligence.
Milston. Precise indeed.
For I have known some justices of the peace
Inspired with zeal; among the rest a knight
So punctual in searching of an house,
And forward to undo the Papists (though
He do the king less service, be more slow

102x

In paying double Subsidies, and Loanes,
And freely giving Almes unto the poore
Enriching of the Countrie and State,
Yet saies, nor Statute, Acts, nor sundry Armes)
That he hath brought in Engineers by Arte
With Mathematicks, and Instruments to sound
The depth, the breadth, and length of ev'ry Roome,
To see what close conveyance may be found,
Or secret place, that might conceale a Priest,
There to imploy his Manhood, but it chanc'd
Unhappily one day, as he survey'd,
With other Justices, a certaine walle,
And somewhat over-curiously peer'd
Each cranny, from a pidgion hole above
He starr'd an Owle, that flying dropt a pearle,
By Chimicall Extraction it dissolv'd,
Upon his worshipps Costard; and his one,
Had that daies service. Rol. Justices there are
That stole my place, but hange them they are voide
Of his inventive facultie, in which
I have outstript them all, that went before,
Or shall come after me: Mil. Not Justice Deyon
Filpott, and Tolson. Rol. They had larger scope,
Yet I surpasse them farr for if I list,
You cannot hide a needle from my sight,
But I will sift it out, much less a Priest,
Or anie secret place: though I confesse,
My sight is now impair'd. Mil. you have bene thought
To practise by the divill and a dogge.
Rol. T'is true, I have bee surely, had I liv'd
In Nero's tyme, I should have borne the Bell
For ferretting of [illegible] from their holes,
Besides a Masse of wealth, I should have gott,
Now am I like a Grey-hound in a leash,

That though

In paying double subsidies and loans,
And freely giving alms unto the poor,
Enriching of the country any way,
Yet pays no statute, fees, nor sundry fines)
That he hath brought in engineers by art,
With mathematic and instruments to sound
The depth, the breadth, and length of ev'ry room,
To see what close conveyance may be found,
Or secret place that might conceal a priest,
There to employ his manhood; but it chanced
Unhappily one day as he surveyed,
With other justices, a certain wall,
And somewhat over-curiously perused
Each cranny, from a pigeon hole above
He scared an owl that flying dropped a pearl;
By chemical extraction it dissolved
Upon his worship's costard, and this end
Had that day's service.
Rocs. Justices there are
That seek my place, but hang them! they are void
Of this inventive faculty; in which
I have outstripped them all that went before
Or shall come after me.
Milston. Not Justice Guyon,
Filpott, and Telfon.
Rocs. They had larger scope,
Yet I surpass them far; for if I list
You cannot hide a needle from my sight,
But I will spy it out, much less a priest
Or any secret place; though I confess
My sight is now impaired.
Milston. You have been thought
To practice by the devil and a dog.
Rocs. 'Tis true, I have so surely. Had I lived
In Nero's time, I should have borne the bell
For ferreting of Christians from their holes,
Besides a mass of wealth I should have reaped;
Now am I like a greyhound in a leash,

That though I slipp my collar, cannot runn
At myne owne pleasure, but am watch'd in;
With-held, beware of Christians, with a Pox;
Are Papists now held Christians? For am I
And Milstone, you, yo^u Ffinger, and Almo,
And others of our Ranke, that would not stirre
(Turne but the weather-cock) to ply your Saylers
On any Quarter, following winde and tyde.
Mil. I promise you, I doubt your Consciences.
Er. This consequence you would say. Mil. That's all one
Amongst us officers. Er. Or rather, none.
Rob. Know for your more Instruction, I have spent
A world of money, in corrupting Maides,
And other houshold servants to betraie
The secrett places, and the Vaults that hee,
And come to ev'ry church, that hardly one
Can scape my quick intelligence; which whom
I dally oftentymes for Monthes, and yeares,
Before I take them; which is never done
Without some great advantage, and respect
Of Vicarage that may grease my fist
With goulden oyntment; But the Pensions, Fees,
And yearely Tributes, I receave from such,
As are desirous to redeeme with gould
Their owne repaires, purchasing by guifts,
My secrett favour, I should never end,
Should I begin to reckon: they are gladd
They have it for me; for which we to Rome
They have their Estats, and many times, their lives,
Els forfeited to the devouring lawe,
And suffred by the Romans; yet t'is strange,
That all these incomes have not made me rich,
But I am yet a beggar, to begin
My trade againe; if I would purchase land.
Ffinger wee're in the same predicament all.
Er. Hee'd say, predicament, I cannot guesse.

though

That though I slip my collar, cannot run
At mine own pleasure, but am rated in,
"Withhold, beware of Christians," with a pox!
Are Papists now held Christians? So am I,
And Milston you, you Finger, and Amoy,
And others of our rank that would not stick
(Turn but the weathercock) to ply your sails
On any quarter, following wind and tide.

Milston. I promise you, I doubt your conscience.
Erudius. His consequence, you would say.
Milston. That's all one
Among us officers.
Erudius. Or rather none.
Rocs. Know for your more instructions, I have spent
A world of money in corrupting maids
And other household servants to betray
The secret places and the priests that go
And come to ev'ry house, that hardly one
Can 'scape my quick intelligence; with whom
I dally oftentimes for months and years
Before I take them, which is never done
Without some great advantage and resort
Of personages that may grease my fist
With golden ointment; but the pensions, fees,
And yearly tributes I receive from such
As are desirous to redeem with gold
Their own vexation, purchasing by gifts
My secret favor, I should never end
Should I begin to reckon. They are glad
They have it for me, for with me to friend
They have their states and, many times, their lives,
Else forfeited to the devouring law,
And thirsted by the Commons; yet 'tis strange
That all these incomes have not made me rich,
But I am yet a beggar, to begin
My trade again, if I would purchase land.
[*Finger.*] We're in the same pedicularment all.
Erudius. He'd say predicament; I cannot choose,

164r

Though were imprisonment, but smile to heare
Their madd discourse. Roc. Well maisters, guard him well,
Whilst I goe drive my bargaine with the rest.

Scena Septima.

Candle like a Scrivener; with many bagges
and bondes readie written vnder his arme;
Milston, Finger, Amo, Crudius.

The night drawes on, the time doth suite my plott,
I see my friend is taken; I me inform'd
By Saperton vpon what termes they stand;
I gott an honest Scrivener my friend,
To lend me his apparell, and these sommes,
Should my advice miscarrie, they are safe;
And shalbe soone repaid, if it holde
Their libertie is purchas'd without losse,
And these come flowing back into his handes,
That lent them forth; I have dispos'd the rest
Of circumstance to make vp the sport;
I pray God it proue so, yet my minde foretells
It cannot happen otherwise. God-den, ~~my good friends~~
My good friends. Mil. What are you? Ca. I am sent,
To ransome certaine Gentlemen, and Knights,
Late taken by the Enemie. Fin. The devil,
We are not Dunkerkes. Ca. What can I tell?
You should be some land-Pirats by your lookes.
Stay is not this your Prisoner? Am. What of that?
Ca. I come to fetch him off. Mil. your labour's lost,
For he is poore; and Scriveners will not trust
Without assurance. Ca. You are learned here
In Misteries belonging to our Trades
Were it not good you should expresse his Arts
Vnto your nicer prisoners, that the streame
Of their Benevolence may beare his chin
Vp with [illegible], and sett him on the shore?
Mil. It were a charitable deede, I graunt,
But who's so madd will doe it, in these daies?
Ca. At least conduct him in, and see. Mil. Alonge,
We may make somthing [illegible] of inquiring. Ca. Doe.
The roome hath voided here. I laid the ground

Of my

Though near imprisonment, but smile to hear
Their mad discourse.
Rocs. Well, masters, guard him well,
While I go drive my bargain with the rest. [*Exit Rocs.*]

Scena septima

Candle like a Scrivener, with many bags
and bonds ready written under his arm;
Milston, Finger, Amoy, Erudius.

Candle. [*Aside.*] The night draws on, the time doth suit my plot,
I see my friend is taken; I'm informed
By Saperton upon what terms they stand.
I got an honest scrivener, my friend,
To lend me his apparel, and these sums;
Should my advice miscarry they are safe
And shall be soon repaid; if it hold,
Their liberty is purchased without loss,
And these come flowing back into his hands
That lent them forth. I have disposed the rest
Of circumstances to make up the sport;
I pray God it prove so, yet my mind foretells
It cannot happen otherwise. God-den,
My good friends.
Milston. What are you?
Candle. I am sent
To ransom certain gentlemen and knights.
Late taken by the enemy.
Finger. He dotes;
We are no dunkirkers.
Candle. What can I tell?
You should be some land-pirates by your looks.
Pray, is not this your prisoner?
Amoy. What of that?
Candle. I come to fetch him off.
Milston. Your labor's lost,
For he is poor, and scriveners will not trust
Without assurance.
Candle. You are learnèd sure
In mysteries belonging to our trade;
Were it not good you should propose his case
Unto your richer prisoners, that the stream
Of their benevolence may bear his chin
Up with themselves and set him on the shore?
(*text continued on following page*)

Milston. It were a charitable deed, I grant,
But who's so mad will do it in these days?
Candle. At least conduct him in and see.
Milston. Along,
We may make something, sirs, of nothing. [*Exeunt Milston, Amoy, Erudius.*]
Candle. So,
The room thus voided, here I lay the ground

Of my invention, and the Thome must the
Within this chimney, if it take, wee'le laugh,
And have a merry fitt; if not, wee live
And knowe the worst. Bring Candles, here they come
There be my severall baggs of divers somes
Allready told: And here are bonds prepar'd
To be subscrib'd, and seal'd, and all is done.

Scena octaua.

Roc. With the rest of Pursevants and Prisoners to him.

I will not bate a farthing for your ffyne;
Ne're talke on't. It's an hundred pound so much,
For three such Ladies, with a Knight and Squire!
Byt. Wee are not dangerous persons, that the Lawe
Can take advantage of. Roc. How knowe I that?
It is enough, I tooke you in the Roome,
Where dangerous persons were; of whom the State
Takes speciall notice. Ag. Come, wee must not stand,
T'is tyme wee were gott off. Byt. Are you the man
That can befriend us with an hundred pounds?
Ca. I; here t'is ready told; subscribe your Name,
And straight Command it; lett but Mr Rocs,
And Mileton be a witness. Byt. There t'is done.
Roc. And there's my Name. Mil. And mine. Roc. You may be gon.
Amoy conduct them out. Bol. What is your will
With us now Mr Rocs? Roc. You know my minde,
Three landed men, and hold of great Estate
That may aspire to Baronets, I aske
But ordinary ffees, such as the State
Allowes me duely, for each head I take
In company of Preists; that's fiftie pounds
A man; some aske thousands, but you see
A righteous conscience guides me. Rut. Come, dispatch,
I stand on thornes. Corb. And I on burning stooles,
Till I be out of doores. Pol. Have you a Bond
Of fiftie, and an hundred pound writt out?
Ca. I have it: here's the money. Pol. Ther's my hand
Roc. I witness it. Mil. And I. Roc. The ffinger make

Their

Of my invention, and the scene must lie
Within this chimney. If it take we'll laugh
And have a merry fit; if not, we live
And know the worst. Bring candles. There they come.
Here be my several bags of diverse sums
Already told; and here are bonds prepared
To be subscribed, and sealed, and all is done.

Scena octava

Rocs, with the rest of Pursuivants and Prisoners to him.

Rocs. I will not bate a farthing for your fine,
Ne'er talk on't. Is an hundred pound so much
For three such ladies, with a knight and squire?
Bitomattus. We are no dangerous persons that the law
Can take advantage of.
Rocs. How know I that?
It is enough I took you in the room
Where dangerous persons were, of whom the state
Takes special notice.
Aggeus. Come, we must not stand;
'Tis time we were got off.
Bitomattus. Are you the man
That can befriend us with an hundred pounds?
Candle. Sir, here 'tis ready told; subscribe your name
And straight command it; let but Master Rocs
And Milston be a witness.
Bitomattus. Here, 'tis done.
Rocs. And here's my name.
Milston. And mine.
Rocs. You may be gone.
Amoy, conduct them out. [*Exeunt Amoy*, *Bitomattus*, *Aggeus*, *Ladies*.]
Bolnutus. What is your will
With us now, Master Rocs?
Rocs. You know my mind.
Three landed men, and held of great estates
That may aspire to baronies—I ask
But ordinary fees, such as the state
Allows me duly for each head I take
In company of priests—that's fifty pounds
A man. Some ask thousands, but you see
A righteous conscience guides me.
(*text continued on following page*)

Rudelbinus. Come, dispatch.
I stand on thorns.
Corbus. And I on burning steel
Till I be out of doors.
Polinodus. Have you a bond
Of fifty and an hundred pound writ out?
Candle. I have it; here's the money.
Polinodus. There's my hand.
Rocs. I witness it.
Milston. And I.
Rocs. Go, Finger, make

Their passage free, you knowe how wee agreed;
My maisters that are left, I will not bate
A doyt of six-score pounds to free this paire
Of goulden Knights. You Spirits wth your Mates
Must lay me downe as much, to buy me malt,
Or rather Sack and Claret, you that pleade
Some povertie, shall pay me forty pounds; —
But you must to the Jayle for being poore,
And having noe good talents you can shewe
More then your faculties, wch may be call'd
~~Meere difficulties [illegible]~~
Meere difficulties heere. Ex. They may, what helpe?
The end wee ayme at, cannot be obtain'd
Without such difficulties. Roc. If you meane
The Gallowes, to wch end I haue convay'd
By meditation, many of your coate,
T'is now become a point of difficultie
That fewe or none attaine to (though before
It came with ease) noe mercie of the lawe,
Or Lawyers, Judge, Justice, or Clerks.
Ca. Or Justice because I take it &c. Roc. Most true
My honest Commoner. Ex. To the living lawe
That mercie &c is dead, the rest you nam'd
Are dead Interpreters, that with it moue
And haue noe force without it. Roc. Haue you done,
The money tould, and all your Bonds subscrib'd?
Ca. Heere want but your two Bonds, and all is done.
Roc. Milston, conduct them hence, while I subscribe;
Licence the Constable; and straight returne
With ffinger and Amory, to write your name,
And helpe me to consult, what houses next
Wee shall beleaguer, for who knowes how longe
Or short a tyme may this Commission laste.
Now lett me see, an hundred, two, three, foure,
Five hundred thirtie pound, a prettie Some,
Gain'd in an instant: Sure, wee Lawyers see

That's under

Their passage free, you know how we agreed. [*Exeunt Finger, Rudelbinus, Corbus, Polinodus.*]
My masters that are left, I will not bate
A doit of six-score pounds to free this pair
Of golden knights. You, Spirius, with your mates,
Must lay me down as much, to buy me malt,
Or rather sack and claret. [*To Pamoppus and Nicodimus*]. You that plead
Some poverty shall pay me forty pounds.
[*To Erudius.*] But you must to the jail for being poor
And having no good talents you can show
More than your faculties, which may be called
Mere difficulties here.

Erudius. They may, what help?
The end we aim at cannot be obtained
Without such difficulties.

Rocs. If you mean
The gallows, to which end I have conveyed
By [mediation] many of your coat,
'Tis now become a point of difficulty
That few or none attain to (though before
It came with ease)—no mercy of the law,
Or lawyers, judges, justices, or clerks—

Candle. Or pursuivants, I take it, sir.

Rocs. Most true,
My honest scrivener.

Erudius. To the living law
That mercy, sir, is due; the rest you named
Are dead interpreters, that with it move
And have no force without it.

Rocs. Have you done,
The money told, and all your bonds subscribed?

Candle. Here want but your two bonds, and all is done.

Rocs. Milston, conduct them hence while I subscribe;
License the constable; and straight return
With Finger and Amoy to write your name
And help me to consult what houses next
We shall beleaguer, for who knows how long
Or short a time may this commission last. [*Exeunt Milston and Knights.*]
Now let me see, an hundred, two, three, four,
Five hundred thirty pound, a pretty sum
Gained in an instant. Sure, no lawyer's fee,

That's under an Attorney, for the Kinge
And such an one, I hope, that cook'd himselfe
A huge Estate, can equalize this prize,
Gott without sweat, and labour of the tongue,
For theirs are commonly with both. Ca. Your browes
Doe sweat for't often tymes aswell as theirs,
And then your tongue you knowe lyes not farr off,
There's but a space to put your Nose betweene.
Roc. And is that nothing thinke you? Ca. Noe such thing.
To be admired, though it may be fear'd.
Roc. For what? Ca. Least if your eyes were matches Sr
your face might take a fire. Roc. That iest comes stale,
Out of a Stationers shopp, where it hath layne
In Brokage many yeares. Ca. T'is nowe burnt out
And turned into Ashes, with your looke:
Now Sr, I must demaund of you my Fees.
Roc. What Fees? Ca. You would be ignorant it seemes;
But Sr it will not serue: Some light on knaves
Of Scriveners, as cunning as themselues,
Though I be counted honest, and doe aske
Most conscionably, in respect of some
Whose stepps I dare not followe else, because
I see they thriue not, but goe downe the winde
And fall sometymes in the Infernall depth,
Of being keepers of a Jayle, or soe;
That torture men aliue, and being dead
Make proffitt of their bones, vnlesse their crowne
Dropp downe, and not before, as I haue seene
Ingrossers of new Prisons at this howre
Of likelyhood to doe. Roc. I prithee speake,
What busines would'st thou come to by thy talke?
Ca. Marie, to a matter of some Twenty pounds
To be defalk'd out of the totall some,
Of Thirty and fiue hundred you haue gott;
A poore

That's under an attorney for the king
And such an one—Hook, that *Cooked* himself
A huge estate—can equalize this prize,
Got without sweat and labor of the tongue,
For theirs are commonly with both.
Candle. Your brows
Do sweat for't oftentimes as well as theirs,
And then your tongue, you know, lies not far off:
There's but a space to put your nose between.
Rocs. And is that nothing, think you?
Candle. No such thing
To be admired, though it may be feared.
Rocs. For what?
Candle. Lest if your eyes were matches, sir,
Your face might take a fire.
Rocs. That jest comes stale
Out of a scrivener's shop, where it hath lain
In brokage many years.
Candle. 'Tis now burnt out
And turnèd into ashes with your look.
Now, sir, I must demand of you my fees.
Rocs. What fees?
Candle. You would be ignorant, it seems,
But, sir, it will not serve. Some light on knaves
Of scriveners as cunning as themselves—
Though I be counted honest, and do ask
Most conscionably in respect of some
Whose steps I dare not follow close, because
I see they thrive not but go down the wind
And fall sometimes in the infernal depth
Of being keepers of a jail or so—
That torture men alive, and being dead
Make profit of their bones, unless their own
Drop down, and not before, as I have seen
Engrossers of new prisons at this hour
Of likelihood to do—
Rocs. I prithee speak:
What business wouldst thou come to [by] thy talk?
Candle. Faith, to a matter of some twenty pounds
To be defalked out of the total sum
Of thirty and five hundred you have got;

A poore requitall for my paines to write
Soe many Bonds, and furnish them wth Names,
Whereof the profitt only flowes to you.
Roc. Lett them be Answerable. Ca. They are gone,
And you must answere me, or stand to lawe,
That will award me more, if I informe
The Judge of your proceedinge. Mil. Lett him ha't,
ffore God we are vndone els. Fin. Let him ha't.
Roc. ffaith what doe lesse. Ca. I will not bate an haire
Of Twenty pounds, which either pay me downe,
Or free that Gentleman you haue in houlde,
Who owing me a debt of Twenty pounds,
Shall gett his libertie, I knowe his ffreinds,
And easily can recouer it, if he faile:
Are you content? Roc. Fye on't, how shall we foole
The world then in this Business, and saue
Our Creditt by't? Ca. your Creditt? what is that?
Twas neuer yet esteemed worth a Rush.
Fin. Nor myne to speake of, since my darling lasse;
And nor yours, since both your eares were cropt.
Ca. Resolue, for speedily I must be gone.
Roc. Why sure thou art noe Scrivener, but some ffoole
Vpstart vp of Charity; where wert thou borne?
Ca: As farre as Cornewall. Roc. Soe I thought, except
Thy selfe; a Scrivener of this kinde of stampe
Liues not betwixt the Mount, and vs. Art sure
Thou art noe Papist? Answere me. Ca. As sure
As thou art noe Christian. Roc. Can it bee?
A Scrivener and noe Papist, that should haue
The Conscience to cast away an Almes,
As thou dost on this ffugitiue? Ca. Why not?
Doe not your best of Protestants the same?
Roc. Tis true they spoyle our markett I confesse,
more Precise and Papists fly vnto this sort
Of Conscionable dealers, in distresse,
ffor succor,

A poor requital for my pains to write
So many bonds and furnish them with sums,
Whereof the profit only flows to you.
Rocs. Let them be answerable.
Candle. They are gone,
And you must answer me or stand to law,
That will award me more if I inform
The judge of your proceedings.
Milston. Let him ha't;
'Fore God we are undone else.
Finger. Let him ha't.
Rocs. Faith! What, go less.
Candle. I will not bate an hair
Of twenty pounds, which either pay me down
Or free that gentleman you have in hold,
Who sealing me a debt of twenty pounds
Shall get his liberty; I know his friends
And easily can recover it if he fail.
Are you content?
Rocs. Pox on't, how shall we fool
The world then in this business and save
Our credit by't?
Candle. Your credit? What is that?
'Twas never yet esteemèd worth a rush.
Finger. Nor mine to speak of, since my carting last;
Amoy nor yours, since both your ears were cropped.
Candle. Resolve, for speedily I must be gone.
Rocs. Why, sure thou art no scrivener, but some fool
Patched up of charity; where wert thou born?
Candle. As far as Cornwall.
Rocs. So I thought; except
Thyself, a scrivener of this kind of stamp
Lives not betwixt the Mount and us. Art sure
Thou art no Papist? Answer me.
Candle. As sure
As thou art no Christian.
Rocs. Can it be?
A scrivener and no Papist that should have
The conscience to cast away an alms,
As thou dost on this fugitive?
Candle. Why not?
Do not your best of Protestants the same?
Rocs. 'Tis true they spoil our market, I confess:
More priests and Papists fly unto this sort
Of conscionable dealers in distress,

ffor shelter, then in auntient times, they fledd
To Sanctuaries; how the world is chang'd!
When I haue knowne the times that had some freind
Spoke in a Preists behalfe, he should haue dy'd;
Yea, one was hang'd de facto, that was found
To make but restitution for his freind.
The very word gaue scandall, to restore,
Which made him straight suspected, and it prou'd
He was a Preist indeede, that had condemn'd
His Penitent to doe it, while himselfe
Was bould to act it; but he lost his life.
Ca. Sure, not for restitution. Roc. yes sure,
ffor some such paltrie doctrine. Mil. Aye vpon't.
Roc. Well, for this once your freind shalbe discharg'd,
But looke I finde him not so poore againe.
Ca. Subscribe, and take your way; Tis done; my thanks.
Ro. I neede not wish, the divell be his guide,
He has a badd tormentor. Ca. What is that?
Roc. Why Pouerty, [Ca.] that often comes from God.
Roc. The divell it does; I'ime sure it comes as oft
To Papists by our meanes, as other waies.
Ca. Nay, you are of the divells kinde in that,
Whom God gaue leaue to punish Job with scratches;
Set you to stick on Papists for a time;
But you not question, may fall off at laste.
Roc. Not from the Gallowes sure. Ca. ffaith some such thinge,
Should you attempt to come againe. Roc. Noe more.
Can. Nay, I haue done. Roc. The money. Can. Lett me stuffe
The Lights that you may, tell it if you please;
See now the sport begins. Roc. What noyse is that?
Mil. Tis Thunder. Fin. yes, and lightning too, me thinks.
Amor. The divell tis; see he comes tumbling downe
The chimney. Roc. I am damn'd then. Mil. Soe am I.
Fin. I hope not to be sau'd. Am. I cannot holde
my guts, like Judas, now from breaking forth.
me thinks

For shelter, than in ancient times they fled
To sanctuaries; how the world is changed!
Why I have known the time that had some friend
Spoke in a priest's behalf, he should have died;
Yea, one was hanged *de facto* that was found
To make but restitution for his friend.
The very word gave scandal, to restore,
Which made him straight suspected, and it proved
He was a priest indeed that had condemned
His penitent to do it, while himself
Was bold to act it; but he lost his life.

Candle. Sure, not for restitution.

Rocs. Yes, sure,
For some such paltry doctrine.

Milston. Fie upon't.

Rocs. Well, for this once your friend shall be discharged,
But look I find him not so poor again.

Candle. Subscribe, and take your way; 'tis done; my thanks. [*Exit Erudius.*]

Rocs. I need not wish the devil be his guide;
He has a bad tormentor.

Candle. What is that?

Rocs. Why, poverty.

Candle. That often comes from God.

Rocs. The devil it does! I'm sure it comes as oft
To Papists by our means as other ways.

Candle. Nay, you are of the devil's kind in that,
Whom God gave leave to punish Job with scabs;
So you to stick on Papists for a time;
But you, no question, may fall off at last.

Rocs. Not from the gallows, sure.

Candle. Faith, some such thing,
Should you attempt to come again.

Rocs. No more.

Candle. Nay, I have done.

Rocs. The money.

Candle. Let me snuff
The lights that you may tell it if you please.
[*Aside.*] So, now the sport begins.

Rocs. What noise is that?

Milston. 'Tis thunder.

Finger. Yes, and lightning [too], methinks.

Amoy. The devil 'tis; see he comes tumbling down
The chimney.

Rocs. I am damned then.

Milston. So am I.

Finger. I hope not to be saved.

Amoy. I cannot hold
My guts, like Judas, now from breaking forth;

111^x^

the Gibbet I feare then trouble. Ca. now play your p
these are the Instruments.

Scena nona.

Targus. Roc. Finger. Amoy. Candle.
Milston.

All this is myne.
Roc. Pray God the money may prosper us; oh!
My conscience pricks me; first for coming; next
For cosening: but most for seeking blood,
Then drunkennes, and whoredome. Fin. Oh my wife
Me thinks I see her ghost, the purse too
I brought her to the prison, where she looks
Like a most resolute bawde, that might be call'd
An other Cleopatra, while I stay'd
With a triumphant carting, where I star'd
And never blusht for't. Am. A carriage alas
comes to my minde, for which I lost myne eares;
Then turning hypocrite, and spye, betray'd
An hundred theives, and others to the stake;
In Treachery, who undoe himselfe then I,
Must needes goe farre. Mil. I have gone over seas
And brooks too, I confesse. Ca. Confesse noe more,
The Divell never can absolve your sinnes;
Followe my counsells, that you may escape;
But looke you stirre not yet, I have some skill
In conjuring, most Conjurers have the like,
That deale with curious spiritts; watch your tyme,
Whilst I conjure some spiritts of great power;
And when I give the watch word, out begon,
And then an other, till the spell be past.
Roc. But shall we loose the money? Ca. Is't not well
you can escape hence, hange it, t'is but trash,
If you respect your safetie, not a thought
[illegible] covetousnes I charge you; least you loose
your money, and your lives, you must repent.

All. wee

Methinks I feel them crack.
Candle. [*To Jargus.*] Now play your part;
These are the pursuivants.

Scena nona

Jargus, Rocs, Finger, Amoy, Candle, Milston.

Jargus. All this is mine! [*Takes the money.*]
Rocs. Pray God the money may excuse us. Oh!
My conscience pricks me; first for coming; next
For coveting; but most for seeking blood,
Then drunkenness and whoredom.
Finger. O my wife!
Methinks I see her ghost, the poison [too]
I brought her to the prison, which she took
Like a most resolute bawd, that might be called
Another Cleopatra, while I 'scaped
With a triumphant carting, where I stared
And never blushed for't.
Amoy. Perjuries, alas,
Comes to my mind, for which I lost mine ears;
Then turning hypocrite and spy betrayed
An hundred priests and others to the stake;
In treachery who wadeth worse than I
Must needs go far.
Milston. I have gone over shoes
And boots [too], I confess.
Candle. Confess no more:
The devil never can absolve your sins;
Follow my counsel that you may escape,
But look you stir not yet. I have some skill
In conjuring—most scriveners have the like,
That deal with covetous spirits—watch your time
Whilst I pronounce some speeches of great power;
And when I give the watchword, one begone,
And then another, till the spell be past.
Rocs. But shall we lose the money?
Candle. Is't not well
You can escape so? Hang it, 'tis but trash!
If you respect your safety not a thought
Of covetousness, I charge you, lest you lose
Your money and your lives. You must repent.

All. Wee doe, wee doe. Ca. But ti's from your hearts:
Thee how the diuell eyes you: To my taske,
I knowe not what to saie, unlesse I rite
Some verses out of Virgill; they shall serue.
First, thus I make my ~~circle~~ circle; I coniure
Thee Mammon, or what els, thou stirr not hence;
But stand and heare thy charge. Jar. What holds me back?
Ca. Dii quibus Imperium est Animarum, umbraeque silentes
Away Rogues. Chaos et Phlegethon loca nocte silentia late
Milston, fly. Sit mihi fas audita loqui, sit numine vestro
Finger, begon. Pandere res alta terra, et caligine mersas.
Banish Amor. Wee must be breefe for feare
They should reflect upon it, and returne;
Your diuells habitt off; make haste away,
Commend me to your ffreinds, that haue subscrib'd
Two seuerall bills, and bidd them ~~to~~ beare their bandes.
Tut, be not discontented, for a neede
To play the diuell, doth expresse the deede:
Lesse harme can diuells doe, in wageing warr
With Bishopps, then your [illegible] farr.
Jar. Well, I forgiue you, could I soe forgett,
How I was taken in the diuells nett;
ffarewell. Ca. Make haste; off goes my [illegible] beard;
Our Author thus saluts you: you haue heard
Of Scandall taken, is not giuen he saies,
By some we call religious in these daies:
Would they were soe in substance, not in name;
Or both religion should not suffer blame
ffor the persons that abuse it; but wee finde
Moste men are turned Satire in this kinde;
Some fooles that measure faith by length of haire,
As though there were a Church, wherein noe Art
Of scandall might be found; which could they knowe,
They might say somthing more, then make a showe.
Lett it suffice, our Author doth not adorne

The faults

All. We do, we do.
Candle. But 'tis from your hearts?
See how the devil eyes you. To my task.
[*Aside.*] I know not what to say unless I cite
Some verses out of Virgil—they shall serve.
First, thus I make my circle; I conjure
Thee, Mammon, or what else, thou stir not hence
But stand and hear thy charge.
Jargus. What holds me back?
Candle. *Dii quibus imperium est animarum umbraeque silentes*
(Away Rocs). [*Exit Rocs.*] *Chaos et* [*Phlegethon*] *loca nocte silentia late*
(Milston, fly). [*Exit Milston.*] *Sit mihi fas audita loqui, sit numine vestro*
(Finger, begone). [*Exit Finger.*] *Pandere res alta terra, et calignis mersus*
(Vanish, Amoy). [*Exit Amoy.*] We must be brief for fear
They should reflect upon it and return;
Your devil's habit off, make haste away;
Commend me to your friends, that have subscribed
Two several debts, and bid them tear their bonds.
Tut, be not discontented, for a need
To play the devil doth excuse the deed.
Less harm can devils do in waging war
With bishops than your antibishop far.
Jargus. Well, I forgive you, could I so forget
How I was taken in the devil's net;
Farewell.
Candle. Make haste. [*Exit Jargus.*] Off goes my scrivener's beard.
Our author thus salutes you: you have heard
Of scandal taken, if not given, he says,
By some we call religious in these days—
Would they were so in substance, not in name,
Or both: religion should not suffer blame
For persons that abuse it; but we find
Most men are turned caters in this kind—
Some fools that measure faith by things of fact—
As though there were a church wherein no act
Of scandal might be found; which could they know,
They might say something more than make a show.
Let it suffice our author doth not doom

The faults of all Religions, but of some,
And such as vex against the Common sence,
And practice of the Church; a sorrie offence.
Christ placeing Bishopps over humane things,
Of Soules Commanders, as of Bodies Kings;
Dividing those two powers, as day and night
Into the greater, and the lesser light.
As for particulars he doth referre
Their cause to him, whose Judgement cannot erre.
All the reward he lookes for, all he gaines
Is, if he may prove a Liar for his paines;
Yet bidds you not mistake, lest Envie storme,
His Muse may slipp in matter, not in forme.

Grex.

Therulus. Lucianus.

What think'st thou Lucian, of the Bishopps cause?
Lu. I thinke for certaine, that the Papall Lawe,
Condemn'd the Ghibellins, that seem'd to fight
With visible Decrees, against all Right.
Though wee that have invisible our Church,
May without blame, lay Bishopps in the Lurch,
Yet may not they. The. The same my Genius sings,
And soe good night. Lu. The Lord direct your wings.

Laus Deo. Finis.

The faults of all religious, but of some,
And such as go against the common sense
And practice of the church, a foul offence,
Christ placing bishops over human things,
Of souls commanders, as of bodies kings;
Dividing these two powers, as day and night,
Into the greater and the lesser light.
As for particulars, he doth refer
Their cause to Him whose judgment cannot err.
All the reward he looks for, all the gains
Is, if he may prove a liar for his pains;
Yet bids you not mistake, let envy storm,
His pen may slip in matter, not in form. [*Exit.*]

Grex.

Therulus, Lucianus.

Therulus. What think'st thou, Lucian, of the bishop's cause?
Lucianus. I think for certain that the papal law
Condemned the Ghibellines, that seemed to fight
With visible decrees against all right.
Though we that have invisible our church
May without blame lay bishops in the lurch,
So may not they.
Therulus. The same my genius says,
And so good night.
Lucianus. The Lord direct your ways.

Laus Deo. *Finis.*

TEXTUAL NOTES

5 *a*]The flourish that ends this line, as well as lines 7, 9, 40, 60, 80, and 82, is here an error for *a*.

174 *slight*] MS *flight*.

412 *Christ's*] MS *Christ*.

430 *gaming*] MS *gemeing*.

447 This is mislined in MS, which has *Jargus. Not well* as a separate line.

448-49 Mislined in MS, where *not* concludes l. 448. A sign of the scribe's confusion is his forgetting the speech prefix *Jargus* in l. 448, which he then interlined.

515 *human*] MS *humane*.

569 *To job him off*] *sic*; O.E.D. Job, v², 9, gives only nineteenth-century examples of this expression meaning "to put off by artifice"; cf. *fob off*.

593 *to*] MS *toe*.

599 *Note*] MS *Not*.

658 *o'er*] MS *are*.

697 *your*] MS *our*.

699 *Holy*] MS *h*.

715 *Nay*] MS *May*.

748 *Polinodus*] MS *Rud*., by anticipation of l. 750; Polinodus is leading the discussion.

762 *gagged*] MS *gog'd*.

775 *Tye thinks to overwrites us*] *sic*. The *o* in *overwrites* might be *e*, but that would not clarify the infinitive. Could *Tye* have been a nickname for Thomas Brudenell (Rudelbinus) and *to* an error for *he*?

797 *whither*] MS *whether*.

1061 *not*] ? error for *once*.

1067 *women*] MS *woen*.
goggle] MS *gogdle*.

1082 *daw*] *sic*; = *daunt*.

1104 *thing*] MS *things*.

1120 possibly *are* is omitted after *But*.

1154 *sponge*] MS *sprunge*.

1199 *Jargus*.] omitted.

1241 *Act*] MS *Arte*.

1256 *'tis*] MS *this*.

1285 *MS* line begins with redundant *And stand*, carried over from 1284.

1310 *woo*] MS *woe*.

1529 *Bolnutus*.] MS *Pol*.

1701 *warlocks*] MS *warlicks*.

1709 *Spirius*] Candle has interrupted, but 11. 1709-17 can only be spoken by Spirius, who is a knight (a Benedictine), which Candle is not.

1737 *Bolnutus.*] ?Bolnutus left the stage at l. 1559 and is not indicated for this scene. ll. 1738-42 suggest that he may be eavesdropping.
1738 *a*] necessary to rhythm and improves the sense. It may have fallen out, for MS is folded between *caught* and *knock*.
1891 *burr*] MS *barre*; cf. *stick*, l. 1892.
1919 *is it not*] *sic*; read *it is not*.
1949 *say*] MS *saies*.
2047 *paint*] MS *point*.
2142 *see*] MS *sea*, possibly a pun.
2171 *Rosimus*] *sic*. Though probably an anagram for *Norris*, there are three minims for the *m*.
2397 *but*] MS *by*.
2443 *Davus.*] ll. 2443-47 must be Davus's, not Pamoppus's. Davus has all the Italian tags, and at l. 2451 Pamoppus replies to the mention of rhetoric in l. 2444.
2581 *overleapt*] MS *ouerlopt*.
2644 *yours*] MS *your*.
2682 *burr*] *u* blotted, could be *barr*.
2692 *hanged*] MS *han'g*.
2726 *whilst*] *sic*; ? read *whist*.
2786 *amongst the*] MS *amongsthe*.
2811 *mouths*] MS *Moathes*.
2855 *when*] MS *whose*.
2993 *bold*] *sic;* ? a verb (Cf. *King Lear* 5. i. 26), or ?*made* omitted before *bold*.
2997 *Do*] *And* canceled before *Do*.
3087 *of*] *sic*; appears canceled because of ink blot from verso.
3138-3139 These lines are not continuous. l. 3138 ends quire 6; 3139 is preceded by 8, indicating the beginning of the eighth quire. The seventh quire is missing. See Introduction.
3155 *Nivetta.*] It is Nivetta who wants to know whether the souls of Celia and Valeria are "warranted" if their confessors have not received the bishop's approbation.
3332 *The*] MS *They*.
3399 *nuse*] ? the word begins with four minims and appears to be the name of a court sitting, like assize, unless it is a pun on *noose*.
3425 *from*] omitted.
3472 *Rocs.*] the line is indented and a speech prefix, which must be either *Rocs.* or, less probably, *Milston.* is omitted.
3479 *stop* *will*] spaces are left for missing words between *stop* and *will*, and after *will;* ? read *stop we will a while* (though this is hypermetric).
3485 *another*] MS *and other*.
3490 *this* *who*] space left between *this* and *who* for an omitted word (like *fellow*).
3576 *Finger.*] not abbreviated or italicized as speech prefixes usually are, but logically this is spoken by Finger to corroborate Roc's statement.
3668 *mediation*] MS *meditation*.
3719 *by*] MS *be* over *by*.
3788 *too*] MS *toe*.
3803 *too*] MS *toe*.
3814 *too*] MS *toe*.
3836 *Phlegethon*] MS *Plegethon*.
3857 *caters*] MS *Cators*; the buyer of provisions for a large household (O.E.D.). They may have had a name for dishonesty: cf. "Th'impatient fist of the false Cater" (Quarles, *Argalus and Parthenia*, 1621).

HISTORICAL NOTES

(Numbers refer to lines of the play)

4 *comic satire*] Ben Jonson applied the term *Comicall Satyre* to *Every Man Out of His Humour* in 1599. For a discussion of parallels between *Hierarchomachia* and *Every Man Out*, see Introduction.

65-66 *Pictoribus...potestas*] Horace, *Ars Poetica*, 11. 9-10.

98 *Bolnutus...Fleece*] Richard Blount, provincial of the Jesuits.

99 *Jargus, his second*] Laurence Anderton, S.J., alias Grey or Scroop, the Jesuit deputy provincial.

100 *Onoplutus, his procurator*] Thomas Poulton, S.J.

101 *Coredurus...Malta*] Mark Crowder, Benedictine provincial for the south.

102 *Spirius, his second*] Dom William Benedict Price, O.S.B.

103 *Sapertonus...order*] Dom Thomas Preston, O.S.B.

104 *Davus*] Dom David Codner, O.S.B.

105 *Nicodimus...James*] Thomas Middleton, O.P.; the anagram is of Dominicus.

106 *Pamoppus*] George Popham, O.P.

107 *Polinodus, alias Nodipol*] Mr. Francis Plowden.

108 *Corbus*] Sir Basil Brooke.

109 *Rudelbinus*] Sir Thomas Brudenell.

110 *Bitomattus, a concealed Ghibelline*] Sir Tobie Matthew, a secret Jesuit.

111 *Aggeus, his politic friend*] Mr. George Gage, who had served King James in negotiations with the papacy toward the Spanish match. See Introduction.

116 *Rocs*] Humphrey Cross.

117 *Milston*] Richard Tomlins.

118 *Finger*] John Griffin.

119 *Amoy*] Thomas Mayo.

125 Bintriana] Britain.

154 A bishop for their head] William Bishop, first bishop of Chalcedon, was appointed March 15, 1623; Richard Smith, second bishop of Chalcedon, was appointed at the end of 1624.

166-68 To rule...compare] By comparing the extent of the bishop's powers with that of other bishops and archbishops, the author avoids stating whether the bishop is an ordinary, which was a point of contention.

169-71 three general councils...approve] In lines 909-13 Polinodus says that Smith cites "Two general councils, Lateran and Trent,/ That also of Vienna....To show his full commission to approve/ With bulls of other popes to back his claim." This refers to the Fifth Lateran Council, which took place from 1512-17 and dealt, among other issues, with the suppression of certain privileges of the regulars; to the Counter-Reformation Council of Trent, 1545-63, the most recent one before the time of the play; and presumably to the Council of Vienne (France) of 1311-12. There was no Council of Vienna. Smith, however, in his "Letter to the Lay-Catholicks of England," says: "the Councell of Trent and Florence declare absolution cannot be given without jurisdiction" (C.R.S., 22: 150). The Council of Basel-Ferrara-Florence took place from 1431-47. There seems to be vagueness about bulls and briefs. The most relevant bull was Pius V's *Romani Pontificis Providentia* (1570), which stated that confessions made to regulars not approved by the ordinary were invalid. Gregory XV issued a bull, *Apostolatus Officium* (March 15, 1623), which consecrated William Bishop as bishop of Chalcedon: Urban VIII issued a bull of institution creating Richard Smith bishop of Chalcedon on November 29, 1624. Two briefs, *Ecclesia Romana* (March 23, 1623) and *Ecclesia Romana* (February 4, 1625) appointed respectively William Bishop and Richard Smith as bishops for England. (Cf.P. Gauchat, *Hierarchia Catholica Medii et Recentioris Aevi* [Regensberg, 1935], 4:147.

190 other captains] The other religious orders in England were Franciscans, Carmelites, and Minims.

213-17 the general council...not published] Behind the more immediate quarrels in the Chalcedon controversy lay the theoretical question of "whether the English Catholic community should be governed according to the disciplinary decrees of the Council of Trent or not" (John Bossy, *The English Catholic Community 1570-1850* [London, 1975], p. 53). The bishop's position depended partly on his claim to be carrying out the Trentine reforms. But there must have been some uncertainty or misrepresentation of his attitude at first, as on August 6, 1628, Viscount Montague, the bishop's supporter, wrote to the General of the Jesuits that it was "falsehood" that the "Bishop acknowledgeth the Council of Trent does not bind in England..." (C.R.S., 22:165). According to "An Apologetical answer to the viscount Montague," dated October 30, 1628, Crowder, Popham, and Anderton delivered to the bishop's vicar-general a letter containing many "passages against the acceptation of the council of Trent" (Godfrey Anstruther, *A Hundred Homeless Years: English Dominicans 1558-1658* [London, 1958], p. 132.

231-33 a public writing...power] "The 3 Laye Gentlemens Letter to My Lord Bishop" (1627) is signed "your Lordships obedient Lay Catholics of England" (reprinted C.R.S., 22: 156-57). In his reply the bishop notes that it is "a letter without date or name but delivered by three gentlemen" (C.R.S., 22: 157).

244-45 The bishop's part/ Inclines again] This implies that Smith was still in England, that is, before August 1631. His "part" began to decline once the question of his faculties was transferred from the Office of Propaganda to the Holy Office, in 1627, but all decrees and information took months to reach England; some, in fact, were never received. Consequently, those in England may not have known just where the matter stood until it was concluded.

253-55 Two several proclamations...not found] John Southcot's notebook gives the dates of these as December 11, 1628 and March 24, 1629 (C.R.S., 1: 105). But Southcot noted in a letter that when "matters were in hoatest treaty, the state was certainly informed where the Bishop was, and could haue then apprehended him if they had meant it really..." (AAW, A, 22: 154).

261-73 The pope...stands doubtful....matters are suspended] I.e., before the brief *Britannia* of May 9, 1631, which declared that approbation was not necessary for regulars. In "The Bishop's Answer to the 3 Gentlemen" of December 2, 1627, he says that he has offered "to the superiors of Regulars that I will approve them and all their subjects if they will but ask my approbation as a charitie done to their penitents and not as a thing done to me till his Holiness decide otherwise..." (C.R.S., 22: 158).

265 ordinary power over the lay] "If any object that neverthelesse my power or jurisdiction is not ordinarie but deligat I answer that to this purpose it importeth little whither my authoritie be ordinarie or deligat soe longe as it is as ample as the authoritie of ordinaries...." "The Bishop of Chalcedon's Letter to the Lay-Catholicks of England" (C.R.S., 22: 150). Allison shows that Smith knew his faculties to be more limited than he claimed ("Richard Smith, Richelieu and the French Marriage," pp. 189-90).

437 seculars and regulars] Parish priests, usually subject to a bishop, are called seculars, and priests subject to a rule (*regulus*), that is, in one of the orders like the Benedictine or Jesuit, are called regulars.

472-73 For by the breve...diocese] "As for the authoritie wherewith I demaunded it, that is as great as any ordinarie hath or can have to demaund the same of regulars in his cittie or diocesse for his holines in expresse tearmes by his Breve giveth me in England all and everie facultie which ordinaries have or can have in theyr citties and diocesses." "The Bishop of Chalcedon's Letter to the Lay-Catholicks of England" (C.R.S., 22: 150). Smith's powers are discussed in M. A. Tierney's edition of Charles Dodd's *Church History of England* (London, 1839-43), 4: cclxxvii-cclxxx, and 5: 93, n.1, and in Allison, "Richard Smith, Richelieu...," pp. 189-90.

479 We never could endure them, nor they us] The Benedictines were "traditional allies" of the seculars. They had made a pact with the first bishop of Chalcedon, William Bishop, who had then tried to interest the Jesuits in ratifying it. Once William Bishop died, "if the Jesuits ever liked [the pact], they soon conceived a hearty dislike." Furthermore, it was suspected that the pact was "designed to detach the monks from the Jesuits" (Maurus Lunn, O.S.B., "Benedictine Opposition to Bishop Richard Smith (1625-1629)," *Recusant History* 11 [1971]: 2-3).

481-86 From Sluxber...places] Sluxber is Brussels. The quarrels in the Abbey of the Glorious Assumption of Our Lady at Brussels echoed the dispute between the seculars and the regulars. Though ostensibly the Abbey was a Benedictine cloister, the nuns had a secular confessor. A few nuns were permitted to have an English Jesuit as director, and in 1624 four nuns broke off from the Abbey to found a convent at Ghent with a Jesuit confessor. This did not end the internal dissension in the Abbey. On September 23, 1628, the archbishop of Mechlin appointed Dr Anthony Champney, a leading secular and prominent anti-Jesuit since 1596, as the new confessor to the Abbey in Brussels (Peter Guilday, *The English Catholic Refugees on the Continent 1558-1795* [London, 1914], pp. 257-61).

490 three above the rest] Guilday says, "Out of the fifty-five nuns in the house, nineteen were rebels to [the Abbess's] authority, and they wanted a Jesuit as Confessor, and had refused to receive Holy Communion from Champney or to attend his Mass" (p. 261, n.2).

494-97 the men...spot them with aspersions] Various charges were brought against Champney, particularly that he had signed the Protestation of loyalty to Queen Elizabeth in 1603, but when the question was sent to the University of Louvain it was decided that his opinion, though false, was not contrary to the faith (Guilday, *English Catholic Refugees*, 261-63).

499-505 Some man...stratagem about] "A Jesuit, Fr. Richard Vavasour...directed the quarrel..." (Guilday, *English Catholic Refugees*, p. 262, n.2).

510 *Coredurus*. Spirius, my word is passed] Crowder first agreed to ask for approbation in April 1627, and then changed his mind at the urging of William Benedict Price (Spirius), "the person named by the seculars as being wholly responsible for this change..." (Lunn, "Benedictine Opposition," p. 7).

521-25 we are made his peers...popes] On January 31, 1628/9, G. Case, notary public, attested that a gentleman said in his hearing that "Mr. Price a benedictine monke" boasted that "he had as great faculties as were contayned in the bishop's breue, and greater" (AAW,A, 22: 12).

543-45 The council...this land] Again the argument of the bishop's enemies denying the relevance of the reforms of the Council of Trent; as Montague put it, they claim that "the Council of Trent...is not here received nor hath force to bind in this kingdom" because it was not promulgated in parish churches (C.R.S., 22: 164).

574-75 We have invented many...Rome] "Smith left Rome in September, 1610, convinced that Fr. Persons [the leading English Jesuit] had prejudiced the Pope and the cardinals against him" (Allison, "Richard Smith, Richelieu...," p. 167).

577 He was made bishop in despite of us] According to Allison, Jesuit opposition to the appointment of Smith, Richelieu's protégé, was "strong," though admittedly most of the evidence comes from "hostile sources" (Allison, "Richard Smith, Richelieu...," pp. 183-84).

590 *Lialga*] Gallia, i.e., France.

595-96 he'll strike me....Good captain on] Price was known for his fiery temper: "Interea praecipuus huius author tumultus...est...Benedictinus quidam monachus...dictus Gulielmus Pricius aliàs Benedictus Iones atque a morum rudi compositione et militari liberoque agendi modo vulgò Capitaneus Pricius, quem Comes de Gundomar iucunde vocitabat *El Segnor*

Alfier Maior. Hic Homo...ingenij turbulentissimi est....'' From a copy of a letter to Pope Urban VIII endorsed ''for Mr. Blackelo'' and asking that Price be recalled from the English mission (AAW, A, 23: 55).

596-600 the bishop came...from Lialga....graced too/ By the chief favorite there] Smith was in France from 1610 to 1624; he was a member of Richelieu's household for thirteen years (Allison, ''Richard Smith, Richelieu....,'' pp. 167-68).

693-94 *Polinodus*. You need not spur...packhorse] A description of Plowden, probably written for Panzani in 1635, says, ''Vir Saturnici ac proterui aspectûs, sed materno eloquio potens ad persuadendum. Ingenij turbulentissimi ac litium amantissimi. propriae opinionis ac voluntatis tenacissimus, assiduus sectator fori contentiosi, et in eius modi causis, ob experientiam panè quotidianam, bene versatus et hinc, quam plurimi Catholici eius operâ et consilio antehac vti consueverunt in plerisque suis negotijs temporalibus, atque ab eisdem habitus est vir prudens in rebus gerendis: Sed postquam à Tobia Matheo ac Jesuitis...actus est ad oppugnandum Episcopum eoque in negotio intemperantissimè se gessisse deprehensus, desijt à plerisque. Sapiens haberi, quin potius pro temerario et ridiculo passim denotatur à Catholicis, qualis ad viuum depingitur in comoedia, qua dicitur Antiepiscopus...'' (AAW, A, 28: 58).

727 Devil's Bush] Elizabethan taverns were identified by such signs and names; this one anticipates the plot.

750 *Rudelbinus*. A bishop mine. *Corbus*. And mine a bishop] The informant continues, ''Basilius Brook...Vir procerus ac decorus aspectu. praecipitis ingenij ac naturae facilis. ex assiduo commercio quod à plurimis annis habet cum Ploydeno (cuius diri solet vmbra) totus immersus est negotijs secularibus et contentiosis....Ex se magis propendet in Clerum Secularem quam in Regulares, et amicissimum se exhibuit tum priori Episcopo (qui in eius aedibus propè Londinum, quae communiter vocantur Aula Episcopi, diem suum obijt tum etiam moderno, ante incæptam controuersiam de approbatione Regularium), sed postea à Ploydeno tractus est in partes opponentium Episcopum, vnà cum Thoma Brudenello, qui modo est Baro...et contra propriam inclinationem, nullo alio magis motiuo, quâm amicitiae erga Ploydenum, vel certè aurae cuiusdam popularis, cui mirè deditus est quia opponentes Episcopum se ostentabant pro Sapientioribus et praecipuis Angliae Catholicis. postquam verò immersit se huic oppositioni, nullus fuit illo violentior aut acerbior contra Episcopum'' (AAW, A, 28: 58). Bossy writes: ''if any layman may be said to have led the movement which defeated the secular clergy's programme in the 1620s, it was Brudenell'' (*The English Catholic Community,* p. 52).

802 My wife solicits me to be a lord] Thomas paid 6,000 pounds, plus 600 to Buckingham, to become Lord Brudenell of Stonton on February 26, 1628 (Joan Wake, *The Brudenells of Deene* [London, 1953], p. 112.

847-48 I'll burn my library....fair one] The Brudenell library was famous, and Thomas was ''by nature a scholar...'' (Wake, *Brudenells*, p. 106).

859-60 A novelty...ten to that] ''The local episcopate ceased to be effective in the *Ecclesia Anglicana* from the moment when, in 1559, the civil authority which had deprived the bishops of their legal standing, took away their liberty also. The last survivors of Pole's hierarchy were the bishops of Lincoln (Thomas Watson) and St. Asaph (Thomas Goldwell). Watson died in 1584 and Goldwell in 1585'' (Philip Hughes, *Rome and the Counter-Reformation in England* [London, 1942], p. 292.

875 The powder treason] The Gunpowder Plot, 1605.

896-98 And this in answer....lay Catholics] ''A True Copie of the Bishop of Chalcedon's Letter to the Lay-Catholicks of England (16 Oct. 1627)'' (C.R.S., 22: 148-56).

908-9 the words that give/ Him ordinary power] ''his holines in expresse tearmes by his Breve giveth me in England all and everie facultie which ordinaries have or can have in theyr citties and diocesses'' (C.R.S., 22: 150).

910-11 Two general councils...Vienna] see note to lines 169-71.

928 In answering this letter] The answer, ''The 3 Laye Gentlemens Letter to My Lord Bishop'' (1627) emphasizes what the laity feared from the bishop's exercise of temporal power (C.R.S., 22: 156-58). Cf. Bossy, *The English Catholic Community*, pp. 54-59.

937-39 he may erect tribunals...prove faulty] "The extent of this assumed authoritye concerning the laitie wee shall humblie crave leve to lay open to your Lordship. First an ordinarye hath power of questioninge and provinge of wills. 2° of grantinge of administrations, 3° of decidinge of controversies of Tythes, 4° of contracts marriages divorses alimonie bastardye And fiftlye of slaunders and many others" (C.R.S., 22: 156).
963-64 let that be the word,/ *Recede*] "And we desire that itt may be made knowne both here and abrode for which wee cannot receed for the reasons formerlie expressed" (C.R.S., 22: 157).
979-80 Let it go....lay] The letter is signed, "Resting your Lordships obedient Lay Catholics of England" and the bishop in his answer notes that he had "receaved a letter without date or name but delivered by three gentlemen..." (C.R.S. 22: 157).
1075 bishop, vicar-general, and the like] William Bishop reestablished a system of church administration when he came to England in 1624. He had no authority from the Holy See to do so, and the chapter's position was anomalous at his death (Allison, "Richard Smith, Richelieu...," pp. 150-53).
1148 Byturne] Tyburne, location of the gallows.
1166 to the Indies] The Jesuit Francis Xavier first embarked for India in 1541.
1206 *ad majorem Dei gloriam*] The Jesuit motto.
1210 The case is altered here, so Ploydon says] Seventeenth-century historian Thomas Fuller explains the origin of this proverb in an anecdote about Elizabethan jurist Edmund Plowden (1518-85): "Plowden being of the Romish persuasion, some setters trepanned him...to hear mass. But afterwards Plowden understanding that the pretender to officiate was no priest, but a mere layman—on design to make a discovering—'Oh! the case is altered,' quoth Plowden, 'no priest, no mass' " (Thomas Fuller, *The Worthies of England*, ed. John Freeman [London, 1952], p. 476). The Polinodus of *Hierarchomachia* is Edmund Plowden's son Francis Plowden.
1314 Sakers] Small cannon.
1415 Were Bellarmine alive, or Lessius here] St. Robert Bellarmine, 1542-1621, entered the Society of Jesus in 1560; a leading controversialist. Leonard Lessius, 1554-1623, Jesuit theologian.
1425 Mine arm...kind] An anonymous letter to Urban VIII about Price says, "Olim (vti affirmant qui norunt) ludum aperuit in quo velut alter planè Vrbilius immoderato ferulae et virgarum usu suis pueris tyrannicè imperitabat" (AAW, A, 23: 55).
1443 As in my writings...proved] Sapertonus, Thomas Preston, O.S.B., was one of the most active in writing against the bishop (Lunn, "Benedictine Opposition," pp. 8-11). The works referred to here, limiting the pope's power, were probably those which appeared under the name of Roger Widdrington. Cf W. K. L. Webb, S. J., "Thomas Preston O.S.B., alias Roger Widdrington (1567-1640)," *Biographical Studies* 2 (1954): 216-68.
1476 Is general procurator for the knights] Thomas Poulton, S.J., was the procurator of the English Jesuit Province until December 12, 1630, when he was (temporarily) dismissed from the Society of Jesus. See Introduction, section 3.
1499-1512 The other two...first in place] Pamoppus is George Popham; Nicodimus is Thomas Middleton, appointed vicar-general of the Dominicans in England in 1622. The Dominicans at first accepted the bishop. A letter to Propaganda dated April 28, 1627, states that "the religious of St Dominic...have sought and obtained [the bishop's] approbation." But by later that year Popham was in opposition to the bishop and had joined Crowder and Anderton in writing the letter of the three regulars (Anstruther, *A Hundred Homeless Years*, pp. 125-33).
1539-40 your purse...friends] Middleton was accused of being in the pay of the Jesuits, or alternatively of the Benedictines, and the charge was repeated by Panzani, the papal envoy. Middleton himself, in a letter of November 7, 1632, strongly denied the charge (Anstruther, *A Hundred Homeless Years*, pp. 135-7).
1576-77 one of your order...predecessor up] This alludes to Diego de la Fuente, confessor to Count Gondomar, the Spanish ambassador. On April 27, 1621, archpriest Harrison and his

assistants petitioned Rome that de la Fuente, a Spanish Dominican, be made superior of the English clergy (Anstruther, *A Hundred Homeless Years*, p. 111). De la Fuente refused, but helped the English to obtain a bishop. There is a full discussion in idem, chap. 5, and letters from the clergy to de la Fuente and from de la Fuente to Edward Bennett are found in Tierney's *Church History of England*, 5: ccclxvi-ccclxvii.

1619 We are but few] Panzani reported in 1635 that there were seven Dominicans. Middleton had told Panzani twelve, but Anstruther suggests that the discrepancy occurred because Middleton included foreign Dominicans at embassies (Anstruther, *A Hundred Homeless Years*, pp. 148-50).

1634 *Pamoppus*. We are Ghibellines] "Popham, unlike Middleton, took an active part in resisting the claims of bishop Smith" (Anstruther, *A Hundred Homeless Years*, p. 132). Panzani asserts that Middleton was won over to the Jesuit side "by various promises" (idem, p. 150).

1660-62 You have taught schools...under-sheriff] "A man equally at home in sacred and secular circles, courts and pubs..." (Lunn, "Benedictine Opposition," p. 8). For the schools, see above, note to line 1425.

1709-17 [*Spirius*.] Besides...can you] These lines, which must be spoken by Spirius, refer to the pact between William Bishop and the Benedictines. See note to l. 479, and Lunn, "Benedictine Opposition," pp. 2-3.

1724 Chalcedon] Chalcedon is in Asia Minor.

1771 Thonscot, Nodipol] Nodipol is apparently another name for Plowden: in the list of speakers is "*Polinodus, alias Nodipol*" (l. 107). Thonscot is an anagram of Southcote, and probably the person referred to is Mr. John Southcote (son of the Elizabethan judge Sir John Southcote). The Jesuit Henry Floyd lived with Mr. Southcote for nineteen years (Henry Foley, S.J., *Records of the English Province of the Society of Jesus* [London, 1877-83], 1: 505).

1805-6 And I become...plot] "Ipse Pricius qui Prouincialem studuit se creare..." (AAW, A, 23: 55, undated letter to Urban VIII about the controversy). Apparently Price succeeded; a letter from Mr. Lovell (Southcot) to Mr. Hope of July 28, 1629, says "this good notion you make of compounding with the monkes...is a thing I alwaies desired, but I feare the monkes will beare of on their part, especially now that Price is chosen their Superiour, who neuer was much inclined to that course..." (AAW, A, 23: 125).

1821 Have you read Friar Rush? *Therulus*. And Bacon] *The Historie of Frier Rvsh: how he came to a house of Religion to seeke seruice, and being entertained by the Priour, was first made vnder Cooke*...(London, 1620). Friar Rush was a devil. Therulus may have read Bacon's *The Mirror of Alchimy*, published in London in 1597, but many legends accumulated around the historical Roger Bacon (1214?-94) that confuse his early scientific interests with magic. Robert Greene's play, *Friar Bacon and Friar Bungay* (ca. 1589) was widely known.

1828 *Nivetta*. Then, servant, you can court] Many sources attest to the courtly behavior of Sir Tobie Matthew. A letter from William Morgan (Case) to the bishop, May 9, 1632, describes one such scene: "One day he conducted my Patron into the chamber of a most gallant Lady and a principall courtier: as soone as he had espied the Lady a farr of, he falls into a wonderfull admiration, crying out and turning towards my Patron, *was there euer such a creature seene? behold my lord this admirable bewtie etc*. (my Lord tould mee it was in such an extrauagant manner that hee thought hee would haue *bawded* for him)..." (AAW, A, 26: 69).

1885 ff. I would know...] Compare with Nivetta's characterization this from the description probably prepared for Panzani: "Tobias Matheus...vir ingenij viuacissimi et concitatissimi, sed indicij haud solidi....Totus est in superlatiuis....Vbique est....Hispanorum mores mirifice affectat....Est praecipuum Jesuitarum instrumentum in hac curia et vrbe....Vulgò et verè creditur Sacerdos et Jesuita....magna illi intercessit controuersia cum Episcopo Chalcedonensi...et hinc est quod modis vibus impedire conatus sit Episcopi promotionem, et post promotionem, author fuerit, alijs vt eum impugnarent, arreptâ occasione ab approbatione Regularium, quare praecipuus incendij huius author a prerisque meritò reputatur" (AAW, A, 28: 58).

1929 But say I were religious] Matthew was ordained June 1, 1614, and was almost certainly a Jesuit by 1619 (John P. Feil, ''Sir Tobie Matthew and His *Collection of Letters*,'' Ph. D. diss., University of Chicago, 1962, p. 79).

1948-49 a versifying pope/ For Urban's sake] Obscure; Pope Urban VIII (1623-44) was known as a poet.

1974-75 A delegate...not an ordinary] This is the heart of the argument over the nature of Smith's powers. See Allison, ''Richard Smith, Richelieu...,'' pp. 189-190, and P. Hughes, *Rome*, pp. 343, 353-56, 396-97.

1988-89 a power/ Of some archpriest at furthest] English Catholics had three archpriests from 1598 to 1621. Their powers were severely limited: they had no authority over the laity, and for the most part their faculties were those any priest in a missionary country would need to have (P. Hughes, *Rome*, pp. 296-97).

2011 Odoena and Falconia's style] Odoena unidentified. Falconia may be Elizabeth Carey, Lady Falkland, 1585-1639. See Introduction, section 2.

2015-17 Saint Augustine's *Confessions*...Count Troilus' legend...books of cabinets] Nivetta is alluding to Matthew's activities as a writer and translator. In 1620 he brought out a translation from the Spanish, Juan de Avila's *The Audi Filia, or a Rich Cabinet full of Spirituall Jewels*, and also *The confessions of the incomparable doctour S. Augustine* (Feil, ''Sir Tobie Matthew,'' pp. 137-38). I find no reference to Matthew's having written a version of the Troilus legend.

2053-57 That's another knight....a lord] Godfrey Anstruther, O.P., *The Seminary Priests II: Early Stuarts 1603-1659*, pp. 120-21, describes George Gage as a secular priest, not a regular. See Introduction, section 2. The ladies' uncertainty was typical: in a contemporary list of Catholics Gage is described as: ''Reputatur inter Armigeros ex gratia et ex eo quod missus fuerit aliquando ad Principes Italiae, à Jacobo Rege tamquam Agent....Totus est à partibus hispanorum. Iesuitarum cultor eximius, quorum res, vnà cum Matheo, omni arte et industriâ promouere curat, et à diuersis reputatur esse Sacerdos et Iesuita...'' (AAW, A, 28: 58).

2069 So he be approved] The Council of Trent said that a regular priest needed the approbation of the bishop of the diocese before he could hear confessions and give absolution. Approbation was a central issue between Smith and the regulars. See P. Hughes, *Rome*, pp. 347 ff.

2124 women Ghibellines] Refers to Mary Ward's Institute of the Blessed Virgin, whose members were commonly called the Jesuitesses. See Guilday, *English Catholic Refugees*, pp. 163-214.

2163 Perinosus] Robert Persons, S.J.

2166 Pamicanus] Edmund Campion, S.J.

2170 Sheriffus, and Suavus, Fluvius] John Fisher, S.J.; John Sweet, S.J.; John Floyd, S.J. (alias Daniel à Jesu).

2171 Rosimus, Sfirherbettus] Murtagh gives Norris for Rosimus, though the manuscript clearly has an *m* (Cyril Murtagh, ''Hierarchomachia or The Anti-Bishop,'' *The Venerabile* 17 (1955): 166, n.1). Sylvester Norris, S.J., 1572-1630, wrote several controversial works (Foley, *Records*, 7: 552). Sfirherbettus is Thomas Fitzherbert, S.J.

2173 Doctor Eatfly and Sir Humfrey Blind] Daniel Featley (1582-1645) and Sir Humphrey Lynde (1579-1636) were both engaged in controversy with the Jesuits. Cf. Daniel Featley, *The Fisher Catched in His Owne Net* (*The occasion and issue of the late conference had between Dr. White...and Dr. Featley, with Mr. Fisher and Mr. Sweet, Jesuites*...), London, 1623. Humphrey Lynde wrote *Via Tuta* (1628) and *Via Devia* (1630) to prove that the Anglican church was the true and ancient Catholic faith. This was replied to by I.R. (John Floyd, S.J.) in *A paire of Spectacles for Sir Humphrey Linde*, 1631; after Lynde's death Featley published Lynde's response, *A Case for the Spectacles or a defence of Via Tuta*, 1638. Renaming Lynde ''Blind'' in *Hierarchomachia* in 1629/30 may indicate previous knowledge of these titles. Featley had debated Richard Smith on the doctrine of the Real Presence in Paris in September 1612 before an audience which included Ben Jonson; the report of this disputation, with Jonson's attestation of its accuracy, was published in 1630.

2192-93 Saperton, Laborus,...Elander] Benedictines Thomas Preston, Rudesind Barlow, and Leander Jones.

2194-95 Two of these...pope] In September 1627, Leander Jones and Rudesind Barlow brought out a joint manifesto against Smith's claim to be ordinary, and Lunn attributes the so-called "Letter of the three regulars" of November or December 1627, which was "vulnerable to accusations of minimising papal authority," to Preston ("Benedictine Opposition," pp. 9-10). All of Preston's works as Roger Widdrington are open to the same charge.
2199-2201 Laborus writes...bishop's power] Barlow's *Mandatum*, dated October 1, 1627, and published 1628, included "the astonishing claim that the whole province of Canterbury really belonged to the Benedictines, and, far from the monks being under Smith's jurisdiction, the seculars in the metropolitan area were subject to his (that is, Barlow's) orders" Lunn, "Benedictine Opposition," p. 12).
2202-4 Saperton in the defence of kings...deposition] this clearly shows that Preston was known to be the author of the Roger Widdrington books, which defend the Oath of Allegiance and deny the pope's power to depose kings (Webb, "Thomas Preston," passim).
2228 commanded by the state] There is evidence that Widdrington's books were printed by government order (Webb, "Thomas Preston," p. 229).
2260-61 a half-faced definition/ Of probable] In Widdrington's *Apologia Cardinalis Bellarmini pro Jure Principum* (1611), he claimed that the "doctrine of the deposing power was nothing more than a probable opinion" (Webb, "Thomas Preston," p. 230).
2267-70 Laborus' work....Sorbonnists] Barlow's *Mandatum* was reported to the Holy Office (the Inquisition), and "the Sorbonne repudiated the title 'Doctors of Paris' included among those who had approved the book" (Lunn, "Benedictine Oposition," pp. 12-14).
2280 Spirius, who first...set fire] See note to 11. 595-96.
2330-32 Perinosus...knights] Persons was influential in convincing his superiors that Jesuits should be sent to England. He and Campion were the first. When he arrived Persons noted the "immense want of a Bishop," and in 1597 he requested two bishops for England. However, the institution of the archpriest in 1598, which Persons proposed when the bishops were not forthcoming, was later regarded as his way of avoiding a bishop (P. Hughes, *Rome*, pp. 183, 287-300).
2475-76 it had not power...your throat] Codner had been in some kind of trouble in 1628. A letter from one Anne Good says that Dom David, "beinge in my house 14 weeks, many disputations [were] held by him and most vehemently against your [the bishop's] Jurisdiction....he being grieved...forsook my house from whence he went to Mrs Smithe one of his converting which since is turned, she being demanded the reason of her recanting answer'd in my hearing that his lewdenes did so must detest hir that she will not be a [C]hatholik for all the world" (AAW, A, 22: 76). This is accompanied by a letter from Henry Good alleging the licentious behavior of Dom David with Martha Birde, sister-in-law of Mrs. Smithe (ibid.). Both letters are dated July 1, 1628, and addressed to "most reverend Sir," presumably the bishop. There are also letters from January-February 1627/8, indicating that Viscount Montague had forbidden Dom David his house because he had been violent against the bishop of Chalcedon and repeating the infuriated letter that Dom David had written to Montague in protest (AAW, A, 22: 11). Lunn suggests that these attacks on Codner were stimulated by the bishop's supporters, who "in October 1627...were heartened into taking the initiative....They turned their attention to the most vulnerable of the monks, the Cassinese, and Codner's reputation suffered a beating from which it did not really recover" (Lunn, "Benedictine Opposition," p. 10).
2483-84 he was conveyed/ Invisibly out of the world] This may refer to some unnamed enemy (the dog) or, more sinisterly, to the 2d Viscount Montague, who died October 23, 1629.
2768-72 two or three decrees...new sodalities] Smith asked for the suspension of the sodality of the Immaculate Conception in 1626, apparently because this famous Jesuit sodality had divided the laity into sodality and non-sodality Catholics. "The fathers were stated to oblige their sodalists to confess only to Jesuits" (P. Hughes, *Rome*, p. 339). It seems that the sodality was ordered suspended, but the order was not obeyed. A letter from the Propaganda Archives reports "vi siano in questi tempi sospese le Confraternità, perchè suscitano più tosto fattioni, che seruino alla pietà, e s'è fatto bene a dar ordine al Generale per detta sospensione, perchè li Regolari non l'obediscono, sfugendo con varii pretesti la sua authorità" (P.R.O.G, Series 6, p.

102, transcripts from Archivio Propaganda Fide, *Lettere 1628*). There is also a letter from the bishop on July 11, 1629, complaining that the Jesuits refused to suspend their sodality, though the Congregation of Propaganda had ordered them to (AAW, B, 2: 327).

2779-81 A public breve...ordinaries] Propaganda's decree of June 5, 1627, ordered the bishop to inspect the letters of appointment and faculties of all missionaries. In December of the same year, the Holy Office, to whom the question was transferred, temporized: it told Smith not to insist on approbation, but nevertheless ordered regulars to ask approbation for baptism, extreme unction, and matrimony, the parochial sacraments (P. Hughes, *Rome*, p. 355). Southcot's diary reflects the confusion. In 1628 he has two entries: "The Bishop of Chalcedon published a decree the 7 of February for approving all the Regulars in England"; "The Bishop of Chalcedon made another proposition to the Regulars by order from superiors touching the three parochial sacraments, with offer to leave them free from asking approbation, in March, but the Regulars refused that motion as much as approbation itself" (C.R.S., 1:104). In a letter from Bishop Smith to Propaganda he says he has heard that the question has been transferred from them to the Holy Office and he continues, "I do persuade myself that you are not inhibited from defending your two decrees; in one of which your Eminences bid me take cognizance of the faculties of missionaries, sent or to be sent into England; and in the other you desire the Jesuits to suspend their sodality of the Conception of the Blessed Virgin until God shall grant better days to the English" (translated in Thomas Hughes, *History of the Society of Jesus in North America* [Cleveland, 1907-17], 1: 215). None of these decrees seems to have been enacted directly by the pope, as stated in 1. 2770.

2792 pretend] Claim.

2911-15 the clamors moved...from ourselves] The allegation that Ghibellines, i.e., regulars, were responsible for arousing the Privy Council to proclaim Smith a traitor was made by the bishop's party. According to an account the bishop sent to Rome by his agent, the regulars were "worried until somehow it had been brought about that the king would take action against the bishop....Therefore a certain nobleman...a most factious partisan of the Jesuits, drew up a...declaration...professing himself to speak for the whole Catholic body, that the Catholics...were not willing to allow the present bishop of Chalcedon to exercise his episcopal jurisdiction upon them. This petition was presented to the council...two days later...the secretary produced nine probates of wills—forged—which were said to have been granted by the bishop of Chalcedon....And so it was achieved that a proclamation was issued against the bishop" (P. Hughes, *Rome*, pp. 371-73). Hughes expresses skepticism at this "most extraordinary story" (p. 373), but Bossy accepts it and says the nobleman was probably Brudenell (*English Catholic Community*, pp. 58-59). Cf. Introduction.

2982 spiritual exercise] The Spiritual Exercises of Loyola were an important element in the religious life of Jesuits and their penitents.

2998 The state takes notice of him] The two proclamations against Smith of December 11, 1628, and March 24, 1629 (C.R.S., 1: 105).

3070-71 The Ghibellines were sent/ (Theabeliza reigning)] The Jesuits were first sent to England in 1580, during the reign of Queen Elizabeth.

3072-5 The charitable Guelfs...warmed them] "Both Campion and Persons in their letters to Rome sing the praises of the secular clergy and are deeply grateful for the welcome afforded by their fellow priests" (Bernard Basset, *The English Jesuits* [London, 1967], p. 48).

3107-11 Procuring from the pope...long resisted] It is usually said that the Jesuits, particularly Persons, requested an archpriest when appeals for a bishop failed. An early eyewitness account is John Bennett's *Narrative* of 1621 (C.R.S., 22: 132-46). T. G. Law in *The Archpriest Controversy* (Camden Society, London, 1896; 1898) and P. Hughes follow Bennett, with Hughes specifying that no secular priests were consulted by the Roman officials (*Rome*, p. 294). However L. Hicks, S.J., cites evidence that the idea came from the Holy See (C.R.S., 41: 127, n. 36). In either case the archpriest was long resisted by the Appellant faction among the secular clergy.

3130-1 And came to be their masters...colleges] In particular, the Jesuits ruled the English College in Rome, though it trained secular priests.

3138 The scholars resting innocent and free] The manuscript breaks off here. Probably what followed was an account of troubles in the English College, told from the point of view of a student who wished to become a secular priest. The material may have been removed for consideration by the college Jesuits. For an account of the possible connection between these college difficulties and an alleged author of *Hierarchomachia*, see Introduction, section 4.
3139 *Sapertonus*. Then we are free] The synod is now in progress. The manuscript broke off in Act 5, scene iii; it picks up in Act 5, scene iv. Sapertonus seems to be answering a question like, "What will happen if we succeed in driving out the bishop?" Present are Candle and Erudius, aside; the three women; the Jesuits Bolnutus and Onoplutus; the Benedictines Spirius, Sapertonus, and Davus; the Dominicans Nicodimus and Pamoppus; the lay gentlemen Polinodus, Rudelbinus, and Corbus; and Bitomattus and Aggeus.
3178-3214 Then with what forehead....depends] Various letters attest that Brudenell was not naturally predisposed against a bishop but was drawn into the controversy by friends; cf. note to l. 750.
3180-81 to speak...prelate of the church] Brudenell was one of the authors of "The 3 Laye Gentlemens Letter to My Lord Bishop."
3257-64 The Trentine council...state] The argument ran that if the decrees of the Council of Trent were not published in parish churches in England, the bishop could not insist on approving the regulars.
3292-94 The laity to resist him...no friend to Caesar] Cf. note to ll. 2911-15; in the nobility's statement to the Privy Council they refused "to admit Smith's exterior jurisdiction as contrary to their allegiance" (Bossy, *The English Catholic Community*, p. 58).
3372 naturally] A natural was an idiot.
3395 Amias] Amice.
3419 Themisus] Smith.
3458-60 I am a prey...command] Preston lived in the Clink prison, protected by the government and the archbishop of Canterbury for writing in favor of the Oath of Allegiance under the alias of Roger Widdrington. Shortly after the writing of *Hierarchomachia* an incident occurred that verifies its general accuracy: Preston "was probably so accustomed to walking about town as he pleased that he had become careless about carrying his safe-conducts with him. In August 1634...he was arrested by the pursuivants, Newton and Dale, and subjected to search and other indignities....Preston managed to bribe his way out with a gift of twenty shillings to Newton" (Webb, "Thomas Preston," p. 250). In *Hierarchomachia* Sapertonus pays nothing.
3529-30 Justice Guyon,/ Filpott, and Telfon] Justice Young, Richard Topcliffe, and Felton. These three persecutors of Catholics all came from an earlier period. A Justice Young committed Leonard Hyde to Wisbeach prison in the 1580s; Mr. Young, possibly a different person, examined Robert Southwell in 1592 (Foley, *Records*. 7: 387-88; 1: 353). Father Gerard called Topcliffe "the cruelest tyrant of all England"; Robert Southwell was one of his victims (idem, 1: 323 and passim). A letter of Father Anthony Rivers written January 13, 1601, says, "My Lord Chief Justice concurreth with all his industry to further Felton in his finding out the livings and goods of the recusants" (idem, 1: 8). The account of searching for priestholes was particularly apposite after the discovery of the Jesuit College at Clerkenwell in March 1628 (idem, 1: 98-141).
3601. Dunkirkers.] Dunkirk was a noted center for pirates.
3657. You Spirius] A letter of April 4, 1628, from J. Brightwood [?] to Thomas Blacklo at Rome, which is primarily about the Chalcedon controversy, includes the comment, "of Mr. Price's apprehension by Cross, supposes he heard long ago" (Calendar of State Papers, Domestic, C, 41).
3667-71 The gallows...came with ease] True. See for representative lists Tierney's *Church History*, 4: 179-80, "A List of Catholics Executed for Religion During the Reign of James I," the last date of which is 1618, or Foley's list of "Martyrs of the English Province S.J.," which includes only one between 1608 and 1642 (Records, 7; lxiii-lxiv). According to Philip Hughes there were 189 martyrs in Elizabeth's reign, and a combined total of 52 for the

reigns of James I, Charles I, and the Commonwealth (pp. 240-41, n. 3).

3688-91 no lawyer's fee...A huge estate] Jurist Sir Edward Coke (1552-1634) grew rich in many ways. He served as Elizabeth's attorney general and as chief justice of the Common Pleas and as chief justice of the King's Bench under James I. He was strongly anti-Papist, and prosecuted, among others, the Gunpowder Plotters and Father Garnet.

3748 the Mount] St. Michael's Mount, off Cornwall.

3760-61 the time...have died] In 1604 Thomas Pound protested against Serjeant Phelips, who "had condemned a man to death simply for 'entertaining a Jesuit'" (Samuel R. Gardiner, *History of England from the Accession of James I to the Outbreak of the Civil War 1603-1642* [London, 1887], 1: 223).

3835-38 Dii quibus....mersus] Candle quotes lines 264-67 of Book 6 of *The Aeneid*, translated: "Ye gods, who hold the domain of spirits! ye voiceless shades! Thou, Chaos, and thou, Phlegethon, ye broad, silent tracts of night! Suffer me to tell what I have heard; suffer me of your grace to unfold secrets buried in the depths and darkness of the earth!" (*Virgil, with an English Translation* by H. Rushton Fairclough, Revised Edition [London, 1960]; 1: 525). The lines point both to Candle's secret and to *Hierarchomachia*'s concealed meaning.

3879-80 the papal law/ Condemned the Ghibellines] Lucianus must say this before the appearance of the brief *Britannia* (May 9, 1631), which rebuked the bishop.

SELECTED BIBLIOGRAPHY

Albion, Gordon. *Charles I and the Court of Rome*. London, 1935.

Allison, A. F. "John Gerard and the Gunpowder Plot." *Recusant History* 5 (1959): 43-63.

———. "Richard Smith, Richelieu and the French Marriage. The political context of Smith's appointment as bishop for England in 1624." *Recusant History* 7 (1964): 148-211.

Anstruther, Godfrey, O.P. *A Hundred Homeless Years: English Dominicans 1558-1658*. London, 1958.

———. *The Seminary Priests*. Vol. 1, Ware, 1969; Vol. 2, Great Wakering, 1975.

Basset, Bernard, S.J. *The English Jesuits from Campion to Martindale*. London, 1967.

Beales, A. C. F. *Education under Penalty: English Catholic Education from the Reformation to the Fall of James II 1547-1689*. London, 1963.

[Birch, Thomas.] *The Court and Times of Charles the First*; *illustrated by Authentic and Confidential Letters . . . including Memoirs of the Mission in England of the Capuchin Friars*. 2 vols. London, 1848.

Bossy, John. "The Character of Elizabethan Catholicism." In *Crisis in Europe 1560-1660*, edited by Trevor Aston. New York. 1965.

———. *The English Catholic Community 1570-1850*. London, 1975.

———. "Henry IV, the Appellants and the Jesuits." *Recusant History* 8 (1965): 80-122.

Dodd, Charles. *Church History of England*, edited by M. A. Tierney. 5 vols. London, 1839-43.

Feil, John P. "Sir Tobie Matthew and His *Collection of Letters*." Ph.D. diss., University of Chicago, 1962.

Foley, Henry. *Records of the English Province of the Society of Jesus*. 7 vols. London, 1877-83.

Gardiner, Samuel R. *History of England from the Accession of James I to the Outbreak of the Civil War 1603-1642*. 10 vols. London, 1884-91.

Guilday, Peter. *The English Catholic Refugees on the Continent 1558-1795*. London, 1914.

Havran, Martin J. *The Catholics in Caroline England.* Stanford, California, 1962.

Hughes, Philip. *Rome and the Counter-Reformation in England.* London, 1942.

Hughes, Thomas, S.J. *The History of the Society of Jesus in North America Colonial and Federal.* 4 vols. Cleveland, Ohio, 1907-17.

Huxley, Gervas. *Endymion Porter.* London, 1959.

Kelly, Wilfrid, ed. *Liber Ruber Venerabilis Collegii Anglorum de Urbe Annales Collegii. Pars Prima. Nomina Alumnorum I. A.D. 1579-1630.* Catholic Record Society, vol. 37. London, 1940.

Kenney, Anthony, ed. *Responsa Scholarum of the English College, Rome.* Part I: 1598-1621. Catholic Record Society, vol. 54. London, 1962. Part II: 1622-1685. Catholic Record Society, vol. 55, London, 1963.

The Lady Falkland: Her Life from a manuscript in the Imperial Archives at Lille. London, 1861.

Law, Thomas Graves. *The Archpriest Controversy. Documents relating to the Dissensions of the Roman Catholic Clergy 1597-1602.* 2 vols. London: Camden Society, 1896, 1898.

———. *A Historical Sketch of the Conflicts between Jesuits and Seculars in the Reign of Queen Elizabeth.* London, 1889.

Lunn, Maurus, O.S.B. "Benedictine Opposition to Bishop Richard Smith (1625-1629)." *Recusant History* 11 (1971): 1-20.

Mathew, David. *Catholicism in England 1535-1935.* London, 1936.

Murdock, Kenneth B. *The Sun at Noon.* New York, 1939.

Murtagh, Cyril. "Hierarchomachia or the Anti-Bishop." *The Venerabile* 17 (1955): 164-68.

Nichols, John G., ed. *The Discovery of the Jesuits' College at Clerkenwell in March 1627-8.* London: Camden Society, 1852.

Pastor, Ludwig von. *The History of the Popes.* Translated by Dom Ernest Graf, O.S.B. Vol. 29. London, 1938.

Revill, Philippa, and Steer, Francis W. "George Gage I and George Gage II." *Bulletin of the Institute of Historical Research* 31 (1958): 141-58.

Southcote, John. "The Notebook of John Southcote, D.D." Catholic Record Society, vol. 1. London, 1905. Pp. 97-116.

Stanfield, Canon Raymund, ed. "The Archpriest Controversy." Catholic Record Society, vol. 22. London, 1921. Pp. 132-86.

Webb, W. K. L., S.J. "Thomas Preston O.S.B., alias Roger Widdrington (1567-1640)." *Biographical Studies* 2 (1954): 216-68.

Williams, Michael E. *The Venerable English College Rome: A History 1579–1979.* London, 1979.